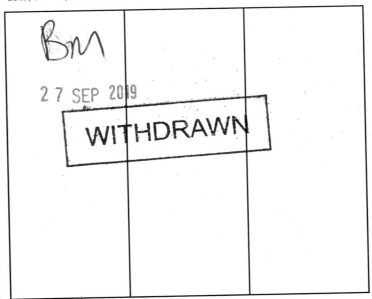

RUN TO THE SOUND OF THE GUNS

OSPREY
PUBLISHING

RUN TO THE SOUND OF THE GUNS

"The riveting true story of a Ranger taking the fight to the enemies of our country. The courage exhibited by Moore and his Rangers is extraordinary and all Americans have reason to feel pride in these men. They serve each other, their Regiment, the Army and the United States. I highly recommend Run to the Sound of the Guns. The unrivaled and fantastic story of an American Ranger."

Michael A. Kelso, Command Sergeant Major (Ret.), Rhodesian Commando and U.S. Army Ranger, Army Ranger Hall of Fame

"*Run to the Sound of the Guns* is a riveting account of the journey of a Ranger from a private to a platoon sergeant in the 75th Ranger Regiment. This book captures the heart, soul and mindset of what it's like to deploy as a Ranger in a Ranger battalion. Each chapter of this book will keep you on the edge of your seat. If I was still serving I would make this mandatory reading for my Rangers."

Howard "Mad Max" Mullen, Master Sergeant (Ret.), 2013 Army Ranger Hall of Fame and 2013 Distinguished Member of the Ranger Training Brigade

"'Ranger' always likes to read about Rangers, and this book does not disappoint. Nick provides the reader a first-person narrative of 2nd Ranger Battalion's part in the Regiment's breakout of the Abrams Charter and its transformation into the robust and agile force it is today. If you are student, fan, or veteran of the Ranger world; read this book."

Mark T. Lisi, Colonel (Ret.), was a founding member of the 2nd Ranger Battalion and served as a private through to sergeant in B Company between May 1975 and November 1977.

"Nick Moore tells the story of a band of American sons who willingly make it their choice to run to the sound of guns. Though my experience in combat with the Rangers is dated, Nick brought me back to the days where young men dreamed of battle and, when they got their chance, they delivered. Ugly, brutal, and straightforward, Nick Moore's story is worth your time."

Matt Eversmann, First Sergeant (Ret.), U.S. Army Ranger, author of THE BATTLE OF MOGADISHU

"Nicholas Moore chronicles the development of the Ranger Regiment as a leader in the Global War on Terrorism from the perspective of the few who carry the burden of the fight. Our nation has little knowledge of the brave men and women who have kept the wolf at bay, and *Run to the Sound of the Guns* gives us a glimpse of the unsung leadership and sacrifice of the modern U.S. Army Ranger."

Karl Monger, U.S. Army Ranger, Founder and Executive Officer, GallantFew

"This is the searing account of Nicholas Moore's decade-plus service as a Ranger. The first line of the prologue sets the temper for this relentless, adrenalin-charged memoir of action in Afghanistan and Iraq. The firefights are close-up and personal: you can literally smell the cordite, the blood, the fear."

Chris Cocks, Rhodesian Light Infantry,
author of the classic war memoir FIREFORCE

"In this day and age, few of us can begin to comprehend the determination and sacrifice of the modern warrior. Nicholas Moore's harrowing account of his service as an Army Ranger in Afghanistan and Iraq is the real deal, crackling with action and drama as it tells an unforgettable story with breathtaking urgency and real-life intimacy. Every American should read this book."

Noam Dromi, Writer and Executive Producer,
GHOST RECON WILDLANDS: WAR WITHIN THE CARTEL

"Nicholas Moore has written a terrific contemporary military memoir which is the perfect mix of action, reflection and inspiration. His lean, efficient prose leads us from intensive training to combat missions in Afghanistan and Iraq. This telling starkly outlines the myriad challenges that confront the 21st century warrior and reassures us that America can still produce soldiers equal to the task."

D.B. Sweeney, Actor and Producer

"We the living Rangers will never forget our fallen comrades. They and the ideals for which they fought will remain ever-present among us. For we fully understand the extent of their heroic sacrifices. We will carry their spirit with us into all walks of life; into all corners of America. Our hearts join together in sorrow for their loss; but also our hearts swell with pride to have fought alongside such valiant men. They will never be considered dead, for they live with us in spirit."

Colonel William Orlando Darby

NICHOLAS MOORE

& MIR BAHMANYAR

RUN TO THE SOUND OF THE GUNS

THE TRUE STORY OF AN AMERICAN RANGER AT WAR IN AFGHANISTAN AND IRAQ

Bloomsbury Publishing Plc
PO Box 883, Oxford, OX1 9PL, UK
1385 Broadway, 5th Floor, New York, NY 10018, USA
E-mail: info@ospreypublishing.com
www.ospreypublishing.com

OSPREY is a trademark of Osprey Publishing Ltd

First published in Great Britain in 2018

ISBN: HB 978 1 4728 2706 7; eBook 978 1 4728 2707 4; ePDF 978 1 4728 2705 0; XML 978 1 4728 2708 1

18 19 20 21 22   10 9 8 7 6 5 4 3 2 1

Maps by Bounford.com
Index by Zoe Ross
Originated by PDQ Digital Media Solutions, Bungay, UK
Printed and bound in Great Britain by CPI (Group) UK Ltd, Croydon CR0 4YY

Front cover: An MH-6 Little Bird piloted by members of the 160th SOAR maneuvers overhead during an International Special Operations Forces capacities exercise, May 25, 2016. (Luke Sharrett/Bloomberg via Getty Images); A U.S. Army Ranger, 2nd Battalion, 75th Ranger Regiment, during Task Force training on Fort Hunter Liggett, California, January 30, 2014. (U.S. Army photo by Specialist Steven Hitchcock/Released)

Osprey Publishing supports the Woodland Trust, the UK's leading woodland conservation charity. Between 2014 and 2018 our donations are being spent on their Centenary Woods project in the UK.

To find out more about our authors and books visit **www.ospreypublishing.com**. Here you will find extracts, author interviews, details of forthcoming events and the option to sign up for our newsletter.

CONTENTS

FOREWORDS

This is a riveting foxhole-level view of more than a decade of modern war. Ranger Nick Moore fought across Afghanistan and Iraq in some of the most difficult operations, while at the same time rising from private to platoon sergeant, and offers a candid, but mature, account of his experiences that is as entertaining as it is informative.

I was involved, directly and indirectly, with the 75th Ranger Regiment during many of these years as I commanded counterterrorism forces in both Iraq and Afghanistan, before ultimately commanding all U.S. and ISAF forces in Afghanistan. At my level of command there is always a certain perspective, and it has been fascinating to look back on so many well-known events and engagements, and to re-visit places such as Ramadi, Mosul, and others that bring back so many memories. Only this time the point of view is that of the Ranger on the ground involved in a constantly changing battlefield environment against a range of different threats.

Indeed, perhaps the most interesting element of this account is how the Rangers have evolved in the years since 9/11, from a Special Operations support force to a stand-alone Special Operations strike force on a level with all the other units that operate in this field. This evolution is captured brilliantly and, although I was immensely proud of the Rangers when I commanded them in 1999, it is awe inspiring to see what they have now become.

General (Ret.) Stanley A. McChrystal, US Army
May 2018

War has been described as long periods of boredom punctuated by short periods of frenzied excitement and terror. *Run to the Sound of the Guns* not only captures the essence of war as experienced by a 14-year veteran of the 75th Ranger Regiment, but it details those experiences in a way that any reader can appreciate and understand.

Nicholas Moore takes us through the training, daily life and combat experiences of an Army Ranger. We can feel the grind of the assessment program and preparation required to become and remain a member of the 75th Ranger Regiment. We see the meticulous preparations necessary to deploy to war in a unit that specializes in short- or no-notice exercises and combat operations, and truly get a feel for those long periods of boredom as well as the frenzied excitement once contact with an armed enemy is made.

We also come to appreciate the meticulous planning and execution required to conduct squad and platoon level high-risk tactical operations in the 75th Ranger Regiment. No other unit in the military places the trust in junior leaders that is placed in the team, squad and platoon level leaders of the Rangers, and especially the seasoned and highly experienced non-commissioned officers like Nicholas Moore. The skills, knowledge and attributes learned and performed in training and in combat by Ranger NCOs is unmatched, and *Run to the Sound of the Guns* helps the reader see that clearly.

Finally, we feel the pain of loss as comrades are wounded and killed, as well as the frustration Nicholas felt while dealing with his own serious wounds and rehabilitation.

I highly recommend *Run to the Sounds of the Guns* for anyone who wants to know what life is like at the tip of the spear that is the individual Rangers and squads and platoons of the 75th Ranger Regiment.

Command Sergeant Major (Ret.) Jeff Mellinger, US Army
Distinguished Member of the 75th Ranger Regiment

ACKNOWLEDGMENTS

To my wife Cheryl, thank you for your steadfastness, your enduring love, and your friendship over the past 15 years, and thank you for your support during my most trying times. None of this would be possible without you, your unending patience with me, and your steadfast love, you are the best 90 percent of who I am. To our children, Justin, Ian, Jessica, Mark, Christie, Jeffrey, Josiah, Samuel, and Eliana. Thank you for your love and support during my time in the Army, and for always being willing to help your mother during my absence. Thank you for letting me be a part of this loveable, crazy family.

To my parents Kevin and Debbie, thank you for raising me right, and instilling in me the values I hold dear. Thank you for the support for every endeavor I chose to do.

To my Ranger buddy and brother Neil, thanks for riding the roller coaster of combat with me.

I would additionally like to thank my friend and Ranger Tim Abell for listening to my stories while chasing white-tailed deer and introducing me to Mir. Both of you are true great friends.

To our agent Alec Shane at Writers House, thanks for all you have done to get us this far, and to the folks at Osprey Publishing, Marcus Cowper, Kate Moore, Gemma Gardner, and the countless others, thank you for making this what it is.

Thank you to Colonel (Ret.) Mike Kershaw, for assisting us in getting this to other Ranger officers, General (Ret.) Stan McCrystal,

Command Sergeant Major (Ret.) Jeff Mellinger, and for everyone's honest opinions of the written text.

Lastly, to Mir Bahmanyar, for taking the countless hours to write this out, believing there was a great story to tell and prodding this along when it seemed to stall. Patience is not always a Ranger virtue, but you have it when it counts.

I dedicate this book to the Rangers of the past, present, and future. It is written to honor our fallen "Airborne Rangers in the Sky" – to pay homage to your valor and dedication to the mission at hand, and the mission of the future.

The decision to write this book was to honor your achievements and to inspire the future generations of U.S. Army Rangers, and to tell just a piece of our story.

It was an honor to have stood among you and count you all as some of the greatest warriors on the planet. To see the transformation of the Ranger Regiment from the days before September 11, 2001 to a stand-alone fighting unit that can rival any Special Ops unit on any given night.

It takes a special kind of American to strap it on night after night, to load onto the backs of helicopters, to take a flight into the unknown, and calmly step into the dark, to face the unknown threat that lays before you.

Rangers Lead the Way!

Nicholas Moore

Run to the Sound of the Guns is a memoir that represents the views of one Ranger who grew up at the 2nd Ranger Battalion, 75th Ranger Regiment, during the Global War on Terrorism. Nicholas was born in Kansas and spent fourteen years in the Ranger Regiment. He participated in Special Operations from 2002 to 2013 and conducted over 1000 missions, including some very well-known ones. Every effort has been made to describe events from his perspective as accurately as possible. We also did not include "salty" language, because it would not contribute much to the book. Rangers use strong language – often. Although centered around Nicholas, this book is about the Rangers who served and are still serving today, who made and are making American military history. It is dedicated to them.

The odyssey began in 2015 and I want to thank my very good friend Ranger Tim Abell from C/2/75 (1970s), an excellent but underappreciated actor in Hollywood, for having introduced Ranger Nicholas Moore from B/C/HHC/2/75 (2000s) to me. For a short time I too served in B/2/75 (1980s). I guess it proves that the Second Ranger Battalion is the closest-knit band of brothers of the 75th Ranger Regiment – or maybe it does not – but we do know that 2nd Batt is the best of all battalions! Tim, Nicholas and I have different opinions on many issues and we disagree on a lot. But we talk to one another. We have a great country and it is up to us to protect and preserve our institutions and freedoms. "Onward we stagger" is what Darby's Rangers used to say and so do we…

I want to thank Marcus Cowper, at Osprey Publishing, for commissioning a very important memoir about the most significant transition in the history of the 75th Ranger Regiment. No unit in modern history has transformed itself more rapidly and brilliantly than the Regiment. Thanks are also due to the great people at Bloomsbury and Osprey – Kate Moore, Gemma Gardner and Christian Waters.

A big thank you to Alec Shane, our super-agent at the great literary agency Writers House. Alec is awesome. He is, in the world of literary agents, the equivalent of a Ranger. I don't hold it against him that he is friends with a Navy SEAL – we can't all be perfect.

We are grateful to General (Ret.) Stan McChrystal and Command Sergeant Major (Ret.) Jeff Mellinger for their kind words about the book and their introductions to the memoir. RLTW!

A very special thanks to Ranger Colonel (Ret.) Mike Kershaw, whom I first met at B/2/75 when I was a Tabless machine-gun carrying specialist and he a first lieutenant. Mike was the first person to read the manuscript once the Pentagon cleared it after an eight-month-long review. The book is better because of his thoughtful and detailed suggestions. Any and all errors remain Nicholas's and mine.

Lastly and most importantly, I thank Nicholas for his trust in sharing his personal memories.

Nicholas, I have a feeling you're not in Kansas anymore!

Rangers Lead the Way!

Mir Bahmanyar

IMAGES AND MAPS

LIST OF IMAGES

Me with members of 2nd and 3rd Squads and the platoon headquarters element who recovered Luttrell.

Vehicle PMCS time in Mosul, as we prepare for the day's missions.

A platoon photo in front of the SOF memorial at Bagram airfield, July 2005.

Standing on the flight line in Mosul (2006).

Fast-rope training in Mosul.

Perimeter security on the narrow city streets of Mosul.

Me and Nick during a site exploitation.

Me and Mitch on the same objective.

A quick squad photo while waiting for the QRF.

A "costume contest" in Ramadi, October 2006.

The battalion standing in formation: from left to right, companies A–E and HHC.

Our 2009–10 platoon photo, taken on the Range.

First Platoon, Bravo Company during the CAPEX 2011 at Fort Bragg, North Carolina.

CAPEX 2011. Pulling security and preparing to move to breach.

Plate section two

CAPEX 2011. Sergeant Holtz gives sectors of fire to his rifleman.

CAPEX 2011. Captain Jake leads his element during the fast-rope demonstration.

CAPEX 2011. I run to the Last Cover and Concealment.

CAPEX 2011. I lead my element during the ground infil.

First Platoon after the final demonstration during CAPEX 2011.

Rangers conduct fast-rope training from an MH-47.

Rangers preparing to conduct parachute training.

A Ranger leader moonlight silhouette.

Rangers on target conducting external site exploitation.

An MH-47 flares, preparing to land.

A CH-47 and two Black Hawks refuelling at Kandahar airfield.

Internal site exploitation. Rangers look for weapons and information.

A sniper pulling security from a rooftop position.

A Ranger walking to exfil during the early part of the morning.

Passing information during site exploitation.

The manifest for Extortion 1-7, removed from the pocket of USN Chief Robert Reeves.

The wound vac placed in my right leg to drain the fluid swelling.

Ranger Memorial Ceremony 2012, picture with the Cerros family.

Rangers exfil the target during live-fire training.

Department of the Army official photo for master sergeant promotion packet.

Meeting my daughter for the first time post deployment 2012.

A welcome-home kiss from my wife on return from my last deployment.

LIST OF MAPS

MAJOR DEPLOYMENT AREAS IN AFGHANISTAN

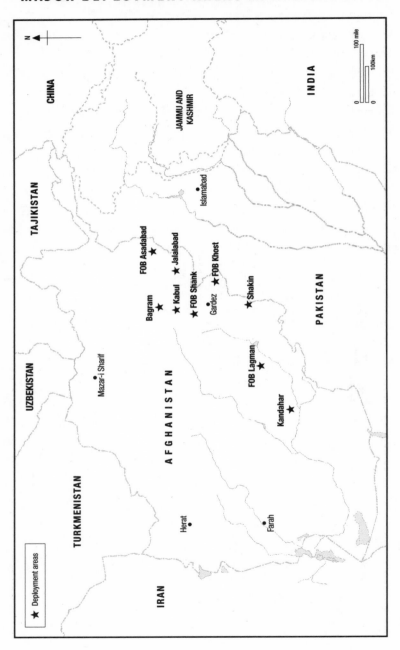

MAJOR DEPLOYMENT AREAS IN IRAQ

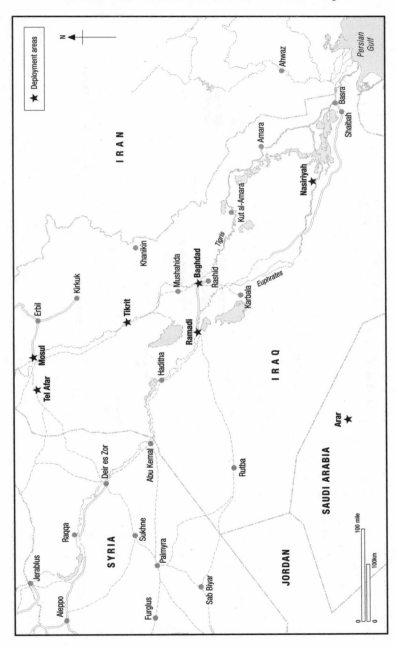

PROLOGUE

The three-round burst fired from an AK inside the compound slams hard into me – punches me back, spins me around, thumps me off balance like a marionette manipulated by invisible strings. My helmet's night vision device is knocked out, its comforting green hue extinguished. I shouldn't have stretched my leg across the gate opening the way I just did. My bell is rung and everything moves in slow motion.

Beside me, Shawn unloads his M4 through the gateway, hammering doors and windows of the target building – brass flips slowly and lazily through the moonlit night while bullets scream angrily downrange toward the compound. Close-quarters battle all around. I hear my guys running to the sound of the guns.

My leg feels like it's been hit with a sledgehammer. My head is a mess. *My wife is gonna kill me.*

Training kicks in: *apply a tourniquet.* I fumble for it in my calf pocket, slide it over my right leg as high as possible, and crank down hard. It hurts like hell; I grit my teeth and I am angry. I don't know if seconds or minutes have passed but small-arms fire continues to batter the alley and the compound. I think Doc Brent is around. *Is he working on me?* Garret seems nearby, Cerros crouched by my feet.

I make out Shawn's muffled warning of "grenade." I know there isn't a whole heck of a lot I can do but roll away from it to my left – hope that the explosion will hit my butt, hope for the best. The alleyway erupts; shrapnel promises more pain and death. Moans puncture the night, moans from my guys, my assault squad, my brothers…

PART ONE

PRIVATE FIRST CLASS AND SPECIALIST

CHAPTER ONE

A LONG TIME AGO IN A WORLD FAR, FAR AWAY, 2001

U.S. ARMY RANGER SCHOOL, CAMP DARBY, FORT BENNING, GEORGIA

My twin brother Neil and I had enlisted at the age of 17 in the summer of 1998 for four years through the Army Delayed Entry Program and eventually reported for duty at Fort Benning, Georgia one week after graduating from high school in June of 1999. After 16 weeks of basic and advanced infantry training, we graduated from the three-week-long Airborne School and the Ranger Indoctrination Program (RIP). RIP was a three-week selection course designed to teach rudimentary Ranger skills and weed out the weak, with half the class usually failing. In 2010 it was changed to an eight-week-long program called RASP, the Ranger Assessment and Selection Program. My brother and I were assigned to the 2nd Battalion, 75th Ranger Regiment out of Fort Lewis, Washington. We both served in Bravo Company – he, in 3rd Platoon and I, in 1st. At 2nd Battalion we were trained to a high standard, the Ranger Standard, in skills required for our jobs. Within two years we separately attended Ranger School.

The U.S. Army Ranger School at Fort Benning, Georgia, is the Army's premier combat leadership program taught through small unit tactics and perfected by Rangers. Although the school's name starts with Ranger, it is by no means limited to us. The program is open to all combat arms in the regular army, usually seasoned personnel made up of sergeants and above as well as junior officers such as lieutenants and captains. Sometimes they even let in sailors, the SEALs and the Marines of the U.S. Navy, though very few of them volunteer for it. The 75th Ranger Regiment, however, sends its junior enlisted personnel instead. These are young privates and specialists with just a year or two of service. That should tell you about the high standards expected of all Rangers. Rangers from the battalions attending the course are commonly called Battboys. The school is in fact operated by the Army Training and Doctrine Command and is not part of the 75th Ranger Regiment, although the cadre is made up of former members of the Ranger Regiment. Ranger School has three phases where small unit leadership skills are taught over two months in various environments such as mountains and jungles. At one point it had four phases but this was changed to three in the 1990s. Phase 1 is the Darby phase at Fort Benning, Phase 2 is called Mountains at Camp Frank D. Merrill near Dahlonega, Georgia, and the Swamp phase is at Auxiliary Field 7, Eglin Air Force Base, Florida.

A successful graduate must pass a number of patrols during each phase in a leadership role, be that running a small fire team or controlling a platoon of around 40 students. The successful graduate is then "Ranger" qualified and authorized to wear the black and gold colored Ranger Tab. But the true mark of a Ranger is the 75th

Ranger Regiment's distinctive black, white, and red unit scroll, which is based on the patch originally worn by Colonel Darby's elite World War II Rangers. The saying is that "the Scroll is a way of life and the Tab a school." Only members of the Regiment carry the title "Army Ranger." In the military hierarchy the 75th Ranger Regiment is the best light infantry unit. Over the past decade, the mission of the regiment has transitioned to those previously only executed by other Special Operation Forces units.

The Ranger Regiment decided a long time ago that its Battboys needed an additional month of pre-Ranger School training to increase their chances of graduation. So, Rangers get to spend three months, instead of two, in the mud with the bugs and with very little sleep or food. As Battboys our constant companions at school are the *Ranger Handbook*, with the inscription "Not for the weak or fainthearted," the "Ranger Creed," which is a code of conduct for Rangers, and the "Standing Orders, Rogers' Rangers" based on Major Robert Rogers' original 28 rules of ranging found in his *Journals of Major Robert Rogers* written in 1759 during the French and Indian War. And, of course, copious amounts of Copenhagen chew – traditionally a Ranger's best friend. But not so fast – I was in the first class which banned tobacco products!

• • •

September 11, 2001 started just like any other day. Our class got ready for land navigation during the Darby Phase of Ranger School. We were tired from a combination of extreme physical exertion and a lack of sleep and this phase sucked. It included taking a physical fitness test to the Ranger Standard, which is more exacting than the regular army standard, along with an obstacle course and rudimentary small unit skills. Who can forget the red Georgian clay, the chiggers, the bug juice, the long nights and days, the seemingly never-ending push-ups? Little did we realize the value of all our training for our future deployments. But on this day we had just completed an 8-km run and waited for the Ranger instructors to come out of their sheds to begin the class. And it took a while. I looked around and thought about the different ways we Battboys wore our patrol caps (PCs) – a "Ranger roll" or "Ranger crush." The chosen style was accomplished by crushing or rolling the sides of the cap into your hands, removing the rigid flat top in the process. It was frowned upon and in violation of Ranger Standard Operating Procedure, but the PC-roll was part of Ranger tradition no matter how often higher command tried to crush our spirits with endless regulations. What we got in trouble for the most though was the way in which we wore them. Battboys from 1st Battalion wore theirs slightly above parallel to the marching surface, at 2nd Battalion we pushed the bill just up above the hair line, and the poor unfortunate souls closest to the Regimental Headquarters, the 3rd Battboys, wore their patrol caps in accordance with the Army standard. While waiting for the cadre I thought about Copenhagen and how much I missed it. What were the odds that I would be in the first class in which it was banned?

At long last the Ranger instructors emerged and asked the class if any of us had family in New York City. "Why?" we asked. "Because someone crashed airplanes into the World Trade Center and we have just gone to war." Our class had a good laugh at the cruelty of the instructors for playing up to our worst fears that when the country goes to war, our own Ranger battalions deploy for combat operations, while we are stuck in Ranger School. It sounded so far-fetched, no one actually believed it.

The cadre returned to their shed while we waited and waited on the gravel formation area. Anxiety grew as we tried to digest this mean-spirited joke. Forty-five long minutes later they re-emerged and asked if any of us had family at the Pentagon. One Battboy from 3rd Battalion raised his hand and said his father was stationed there. They motioned him into the shed where he made a call. To this Ranger's luck, his dad had been out of the office when the plane had crashed into the Pentagon. Meanwhile, everyone else outside continued to question the sanity or cruelty of the Ranger instructors. We were interrupted when the instructors came back yet again, but this time they pushed a TV out of their shed. They commanded a handful of us to take a look. I suppose they knew we did not believe them. The few took a look and returned to us, explaining what they had seen.

"Holy crap," they said. "This is real."

You can imagine the electric charge that went through the ranks. Everyone's heart sank; it was that emotional gut punch no one liked. We had no idea that the attack had centered on the World Trade Center, nor did we know that buildings collapsed a short while thereafter. In fact, I never saw any actual footage of the attack until a year later.

But war gave us meaning and purpose. Nobody wanted to recycle and stay any longer than we had to. All the Battboys banded together and we did everything we could to pass each patrol and each phase together. Inter-regimental rivalries were cast aside. It was "one for all, and all for one." We received a letter written by the then colonel of the 75th Ranger Regiment addressed to the Training Brigade. It stipulated that any Ranger who purposely failed the school in order to rejoin his battalion for war would be relieved for failing to meet the Ranger Standard and sent packing to a regular army unit – a horrible punishment for us elite Rangers. The letter was rather funny – we did not need threats to motivate us.

As long as a Battboy gave his all, we did everything to help him. There was one, however, who did not, for weeks on end, and so we dropped him. Our rationale was simple: if he was a major problem here, who would want to go into combat with him? Other non-Battboys were also peered out. Peering is a vote within your squad to get rid of the weakest, or least liked, member of the group. There is a whole culture surrounding the peering system, such as officers versus enlisted, enlisted versus enlisted, Battboys versus everybody else. And nobody liked being in a class disproportionately heavy with officers who always peered the enlisted men. It may not always be fair, but to this day it is an integral part of the program.

We waited for the final grades in Mountain Phase at Camp Frank D. Merrill, near Dahlonega, Georgia, to see who would be moving on to the next phase, when the Ranger instructors assembled everyone. They made us watch CNN's coverage of the 3rd Ranger Battalion's combat parachute jump behind enemy lines to secure Objective *Rhino*, around Kandahar, Afghanistan, as part of Operation *Enduring Freedom*. The mission was conducted during the night of October 19 and 20, 2001. Almost on cue, all of us from the 1st and 2nd Battalions laughed at the crestfallen Battboys from the 3rd.

"Why are you laughing?" was the common complaint. "We missed everything. This is horrible news."

The answer was simple. "Our batts haven't deployed yet, so we haven't missed a thing," we taunted. We knew our battalions were going to war next. Yes!

The interesting thing about 9/11's impact on Ranger School was to see the amount of drive expended to have students pass the patrols and pass the phases. Our Ranger instructors knew better than we did what was going on and pushed hard to move us forward into the next phase to graduate. Whereas in previous classes you might get two patrols or more, now we passed one patrol in a leadership position and got no more – in effect passing the phase. This saved graded positions for those who had previously failed and needed to pass a leadership position to advance to the next phase. Even if you did well in your patrol position, you still wanted to help fellow students because we all wanted to get back to our battalions. We helped weaker students as much as possible and I can write honestly that Battboys pushed the train forward, especially during assaults where most of the weight fell on us. We carried the load to make others as successful as possible and often we took over more senior leadership positions such as platoon sergeant or platoon leader during the graded patrols. Successful patrols meant few, if any, students had to recycle. There was always a lot of pressure on us to make things run smoothly, not just for ourselves but for everyone, including those from the 10th Mountain Division and the 82nd and 101st Airborne Divisions, amongst others who had sent their soldiers to Ranger School.

At long last we graduated in November of 2001 and the class had only lost half a dozen soldiers who were held back and recycled to the incoming class. The normal attrition rate was 50 percent. I lost about 25–30 pounds during Ranger School – I only started with 155. But the excitement and high spirits of graduation, of finally pinning the precious Ranger Tab on our shoulders, were unquestionably doubled, because not only did we graduate but we had a purpose – war.

CHAPTER TWO

OPERATION *ENDURE THIS*

Afghanistan, 2002

After returning to Fort Lewis from Ranger School, we took a week of recovery because the school is that tough – it grinds you and your equipment down. I traded in my unserviceable uniforms, got new ones issued, and had them all resewn with new patches including the Ranger Tab. I unpacked my belongings, which had been in a locker in my room during my absence, and then repacked everything to the prescribed Battalion Standard of what to pack where and how – everything was tied down with 550 parachute cord so you didn't lose any of your equipment while patrolling at night. I reintegrated into my squad and platoon. War was on the horizon, or so we thought...

But our exuberance was bitterly crushed. We did not know the details of the combat parachute assault conducted by the 3rd Ranger Battalion right after 9/11 – there were, at this point in time, no secure computer networks outside of those at battalion staff and so most of our information came filtered down from our chain of command, which was not much more than what the news put out. We had a window of when we expected to deploy and we were pumped since 3rd Battalion was still on invasion deployment and we were ready to relieve them. But then we were told that 1st Battalion was going next instead of us. Nobody expected the war to still be ongoing by the time 1st Battalion returned. It was a huge disappointment not to be next in line. Previous Ranger combat operations in Grenada (Operation *Urgent Fury*, 1983) and Panama (Operation *Just Cause*, 1989) had only lasted about six weeks. We were missing out on war. Or so we thought. It sucked.

In typical Ranger fashion we put one foot in front of the other and went back to our bread and butter training of battalion-sized rehearsals and airfield seizures. This type of training is called a fixed-wing (aircraft) bi-lateral (Bi-Lats) exercise. This is always a battalion event to train staff since the actual execution for the average Ranger is fairly straightforward – you jump in, you clear the airfield of all emplaced obstacles, you assemble with your platoon, and then you execute your platoon's tasking (mission) of the company's overall objective. The real training objectives for this are at the battalion staff level to sharpen coordination between units, tracking battlefield progress, and various other staff activities.

We further conducted company-sized training at Gray Army Airfield, near Fort Lewis, and finally traveled to Fort Knox, Kentucky, for a massive live-fire event for a rotary-wing (helicopter) Bi-Lats exercise with all the bells and whistles, including helicopter insertions and clearance of targets. We spent about a month doing that, culminating in an excellent company live-fire which was our final exam. In fact, this was a chance to practice the deployment load-out sequence in preparation for a Ranger battalion to move anywhere in the world within 18 hours, from the alert process, to getting all personnel assembled and accounted for, all the way to getting us deployed. Once we were at Fort Knox we also conducted our standard small-arms range training and used a new and different MOUT (Military Operations in Urban Terrain, usually pronounced "mount") site, which was great because you do learn the tricks and layouts of buildings on your home station sites. Fort Knox's site is unique because it was contracted out and built by companies that build and design movie sets. This MOUT site featured ambient sounds and noises, moving cars, and explosions. The time there was carved into three one-week blocks. There was one week for ranges, shooting known distance, Close-Quarters Battle (CQB) drills, and qualification ranges for our weapons. The second week was dedicated to MOUT training. The third week was a company live-fire exercise which included working with and utilizing the helicopters in our mission. In typical Ranger fashion, the actual live-fire was broken into two separate 24-hour periods. The first one was the blank-fire day, consisting of a day blank-fire and a night blank-fire progression through our target. The second one was live-fire, again conducted during both the day and night. Our company, Bravo, was rated the best of the entire battalion.

After successful completion of these three intense weeks we traveled back to Fort Lewis and cleaned up our equipment, refitted, and then took our annual two-week block leave. Happily, upon our return from leave, we found out that our battalion was, at long last, going to war! We packed our gear for overseas combat deployment to Afghanistan to mount Special Operations missions in support of *Enduring Freedom*. Special Operations Forces (SOF) deployments lasted 90 days; later they would expand to 120 days. We left U.S. soil a month later, with the battalion deploying over the end of March and the beginning of April

2002. Bravo Company's platoons were split between Bagram and Kandahar. My platoon was stationed at Kandahar.

By now I was a specialist (E-4) in 1st Platoon, Bravo Company; my job was that of SAW gunner (Squad Automatic Weapon), operating an M249 light machine gun that fired a 5.56mm round and shot up to 800 rounds per minute. On mobility patrols in our HUMVEEs (High Mobility Multipurpose Wheeled Vehicles), my responsibility was to man the mounted MK19 automatic grenade launcher that fired 40mm-sized grenades. It packed a punch. The regiment had switched from RSOVs (Ranger Special Operations Vehicles based on the Land Rover Defender) to HUMVEEs in the winter of 2001 based on experience on the ground in Afghanistan. During 1st Battalion, 75th Ranger Regiment's earlier deployment in fall 2001, the RSOV was still in use. Picture in your mind a Land Rover, chop the top off, add a roll bar with turret ring, and that was an RSOV. Due to the light nature of the vehicle, and its original intended purpose of being employed during an airfield seizure, racing out of the back of aircraft to various locations, it soon became clear that it could not handle the necessary amount of equipment, ammunition or personnel now required. There were a number of resulting mechanical issues; in particular, the clutches did not hold up well to the excessive weight. The regiment deemed that the HUMVEE would be a better platform for three reasons. First, it could handle the equipment and personnel weight of approximately 9,000–11,000 pounds when fully loaded; second, it had an automatic transmission which aided drivers who might not have been great at driving stick shift, in comparison to the RSOV's five-speed manual transmission; and finally, the HUMVEE is a wider based vehicle. The latter meant that during contact the vehicle would not "rock" during the firing of the .50cal heavy machine gun or the MK19 automatic grenade launcher. By comparison, the RSOV had a lighter suspension and a narrower wheel base that would rock when its weapons were fired from a vehicle-mounted position. To deal with this issue, one drill we had when using the RSOV was to engage the target and dismount the personnel, who then established a base of fire, in turn allowing for the dismount of the big gun which was then placed on its tripod.

• • •

Looking back on my first deployment in late spring 2002 I realize that there was no centralized command and control in place. The 10th Mountain Division's area of operations was in the north, while the 101st Airborne Division operated in the south and SOF including us Rangers tried to fit in wherever we were required. There was a total lack of communication within the country in terms of shared targeting intelligence.

Our primary mission seemed to be to expand the Special Operations infrastructure and footprint in Afghanistan. But the first couple weeks in Afghanistan were a massive disappointment – nothing was going on. The highlight of the day was PMCS'ing (Preventative Maintenance Check and Services) our vehicles. Then it was into the movie tent to watch the same movies over and over again, with an intermittent guard shift thrown in. The only real shock to the system was the weather. It was quite something coming from the cool climate of Washington State to the heat and dust of landlocked Afghanistan. But basically, we did nothing. At long last, after a couple of weeks, we received a tasking for a squad-sized element to assist a U.S. Army Special Forces Operational Detachment Alpha (ODA), the Green Berets, who were expanding their footprint in a firebase on the eastern border of Afghanistan. This could be an exciting mission since it got us out to actually do something and experience more than just the Forward Operating Base (FOB) life of doing absolutely nothing.

As we staged for our mission in mid-April, we high-fived 3rd Platoon at Bagram who had just finished their tasking at Roberts

Ridge, the scene of the first casualties suffered by Special Operations, including those from the 1st Ranger Battalion. On March 3–4 2002, during the first large-scale American offensive, called Operation *Anaconda*, Navy SEAL team Petty Officer First Class Neil C. Roberts had fallen out of an under-fire Chinook helicopter at the mountain range of Takur Ghar during infil (infiltration). A SEAL team reinserted, but in the ensuing firefight, outgunned, they were forced to abandon a presumed dead Air Force combat controller, Technical Sergeant John A. Chapman. Chapman in fact died alone in a desperate firefight. He was awarded the Medal of Honor in 2018. A Ranger Quick Reaction Force (QRF) was sent erroneously to the same location instead of being off-set, and was shot down almost immediately, taking five casualties, including two members of the air crew. The survivors hung on until another dismounted Ranger QRF joined them.

My brother was a sniper with 3rd Platoon, detailed to protect the area of the shot-down helicopter after the battle, while it was being evaluated by a maintenance group to see if it could fly again. The men suffered through the freezing weather high up in the mountains of Takur Ghar while attempting to recover the Chinook. The conclusion was that it could not operate again and the mission called for a high-altitude and heavy-lift capable helicopter to salvage the Chinook. The U.S. did not have any heavy-lift capable ones in their inventory at the time. In the end 3rd Platoon was there for two weeks waiting for the diplomatic paperwork that allowed an MIL MI-4 Russian helicopter to sling-load the medium-sized Chinook helicopter back to its base.

Speaking of Russians, a month or so after my first mission out in the east I bumped into a private from 3rd Platoon, Bravo Company, who had immigrated to the U.S. from Russia. He was in his mid-to-late 30s and was actually part of the Russian war machine that had been stationed in Afghanistan toward the end of their decade-long occupation. He became our tour guide at

Bagram, where we temporarily waited for helicopters for a mission, and provided intelligence about the airfield and his previous experiences. What are the chances of a Russian army guy joining the U.S. Army and being stationed here again during wartime? That's Afghanistan for you.

In any event, our squad-sized element left Kandahar to tie in and operate alongside the ODA after they had initially set up a firebase at the village of Surobi. Our squad was basically our platoon's forward element to ensure there was enough space for approximately 40 Rangers to operate out of. We flew in on a British CH-47 and saw the terrain change from Bagram, going east into the mountains, but we also overflew the large flat areas around the village of Surobi. This was one of my favorite flights during my time in Afghanistan, flying nap-of-the-earth, a low-altitude flight to avoid detection. It was absolutely beautiful and cool. It was also always a great time for us, especially when someone on board got airsick. Ah, Ranger humor.

At Surobi we tied in with the U.S. Army Special Forces ODA detachment and were given a place to stay. We had no communications with our platoon and we basically were nine Rangers enjoying our time away from our "mom" and so we tried to have some fun. The ODA asked us to join them on impromptu patrol in their two pick-up trucks, cruising the surrounding countryside. I can tell you that riding in the back of a Toyota pick-up with combat gear and weapons was always a cramped, uncomfortable experience, especially when there were four guys in the mini truck bed. The thing about the U.S. Army Special Forces Green Berets is that we did not like them. There was and is a reason for that. Rangers are hard-charging alpha males, wired tightly with a tough, dress-right-dress mindset – hardcore warriors. The Green Berets operate completely differently – they are inherently more lackadaisical in their structure and work in a different environment – one with a hands-off approach to most things and the constant need to chat with the locals, who may very well want to kill you or tried to kill you the day before. You know, hearts and minds kind of stuff. They looked and acted unprofessionally in my mind. How is this even the army? Needless to say we had a few personality conflicts. On the other hand, the SEALs we operated with over the years always thought they were the best, they were not I promise you, and wanted to fight. That suited the Ranger mentality far better. Over my military career from private first class to platoon sergeant, I never cared for the hands-off approach.

We came back to Surobi after our uneventful patrol and cleaned our gear and weapons. The MRE (Meal, Ready to Eat) was still as horrible as ever and the Afghan chow made of flat bread, goat meat, and rice was just as bad. MREs were never my first choice; I preferred not to eat them, even if it meant going 24 or more hours without a meal – good thing I always had plenty of energy bars.

We had set up an infrastructure for about nine days, when, with one hour's notice, our company commander arrived who was less than impressed by our appearance. The ODA had asked us to blend in more and not to shave – unheard of in the Ranger Regiment, where the weekly high and tight haircut, almost like a Mohawk haircut, and a daily clean shave were the law of the land. Eventually the regiment relaxed its grooming standards as the nature of our missions changed.

Our commanding officer stayed a day and initiated the next phase. We prepped for a couple of days to move to a new firebase at Shkin, Paktika Province, about 6 "klicks" (kilometers) from the Pakistani border with an elevation near 8,000 feet. The commanding officer did not like our current location at Surobi, and higher command wanted a new firebase closer to the border, nearer the ratlines funneling in men and equipment from Pakistan. The reason for the move was two-fold then. Higher command wanted the Combat Outpost (COP) closer to the border – Surobi was too far away, whereas Shkin put us within eyesight of the border. And, secondly, the current location was too small to house a full Ranger platoon, all of our vehicles, and our logistical needs to conduct modern-day combat operations. We packed up all assets into a fairly large convoy of non-military trucks made up of the ODA's Toyotas and very colorful "jingle" trucks. It took us most of the day to cover the 76 klicks to Shkin, which to this day remains an active firebase, eventually renamed Firebase Lilley. We originally called it Camelot – a fun poke at the British liaison officer stationed back at the Joint Operations Center (JOC) in Bagram. It was eventually renamed after Special Forces Master Sergeant Arthur L. Lilley, who was killed in a firefight there in 2007. During late April and early May 2002, we helped establish the initial footprint of the firebase. We expected the rest of our platoon to arrive in a few short days with all the trucks, our six GMVs (Gun-Mounted Vehicles), and a plethora of gear and equipment for a full-sized Ranger platoon. Meanwhile, we relied on the aerial Combat Delivery System (CDS) – a system that dropped supplies to us by aircraft, including fuel and all necessities for establishing a brand-new firebase.

Camelot, the firebase at Shkin, was about 6 or 7 klicks to Pakistan's border, ideally suited for our battalion's 120mm mortars. The weapons were operated by our heavy mortar platoon. In the early days, Shkin was manned by an ODA, 1st Platoon, and the Ranger heavy mortar section. A few Rangers from the signal communication platoon came around to establish secure and reliable communications. Shkin eventually became known as the "most evilest place on earth" due to the nearly constant fighting around it. Yet every time I was there it was the most boring place, without an enemy in sight.

Rangers were and are expert at patrols. We conducted three-day patrols from the firebase, with two days back at Shkin to recover and refit, just to see what was out there. A typical Ranger patrol meant we drove near dark to a specified drop-off point and conducted a few dismounted patrols from there toward our base, each time setting up hide sites. We kept small footprints and made sure the largest hide sites held no more than 15 men. We spent long hours observing the empty vastness of the countryside, slept during the day beneath the burning sun and then, at night, moved out again. After three nights we coordinated a nighttime exfil (exfiltration) using trucks. These kinds of patrols were straight out of the book of old-school Rangering techniques. Looking back, those were the good days, when patrolling meant no body armor, just chest racks, weapons, and rucksacks. The good Ranger life.

We did conduct one raid, which I missed because I was on guard duty at the FOB when the mission came down. Normally we had privates on guard and all Tabs (Ranger School graduates) and above would be relieved to go on the missions. The platoon leader and platoon sergeant this time decided everyone needed exposure to missions and those on guard would stay, and not be rotated off. The firefight itself lasted less than ten seconds, and the only man shooting was our platoon leader. Nothing really happened during that fight. In fact, nothing much happened in Afghanistan at that time. We stayed for about three weeks and rotated back to Bagram after we were relieved in place by 2nd Platoon out of Kandahar.

A couple of weeks later orders came down to set up another firebase at Asadabad in the Kunar Province. This time 3rd Platoon was supposed to fly straight to Asadabad in CH-47s, while 1st was supposed to be flown to Jalalabad and then drive to Asadabad. C-130s were to fly the HUMVEEs for 1st Platoon down to Jalalabad in a total of three lifts, with each lift transporting two HUMVEEs. Our plan was to take the six gun-trucks, our HUMVEEs, fly to the airfield in Jalalabad, offload them, and drive about 80km to the new firebase. This was a solo Ranger operation. Originally it only comprised 1st Platoon and so we were responsible for all the equipment needed, including the heavy mortars. We did have a small problem. A miscommunication with 3rd Platoon's helicopters led to them being dropped at Jalalabad instead of going straight to Asadabad. Since 3rd Platoon ended up in Jalalabad we had to hold for 24 hours before starting our drive so they had enough time to get the helicopters back to take them to their correct location at Asadabad. The language of choice became Russian because our 3rd Platoon's platoon leader, Jason, spoke it, having previously served with the Green Berets, before attending the Officer Candidate School and then joining the 75th Ranger Regiment. We were able to communicate with the locals, the remnants of the Northern Alliance who "owned" the airfield, by speaking Russian.

A point of note: the location of firebases in Afghanistan was essentially based on distances and proximities to the highways and how far units could maneuver and drive, based on the fuel consumption of their vehicles, basically traveling from fuel point to fuel point. Nobody wanted to get stuck in hostile territories because they ran out of fuel to get to the next firebase. We managed to successfully establish the American footprint in the area with the new firebase at Asadabad.

By now we had been in-country for two months and by late May and early June the temperature definitely got hotter, but at least we were not at Bagram or Kandahar because nobody liked to be near the command headquarters, the so-called "flagpole." Being by the flagpole was always miserable because the high number of staff officers and senior non-commissioned officers had nothing better to do than to micromanage the platoons. It was always best to keep busy, avoiding interference from higher command, and keep to ourselves.

But all good things must come to an end and so we returned to Bagram in early June. After three weeks, we realized that absolutely nothing was going on in terms of combat operations in Afghanistan. In typical Ranger mode we spent a lot of time southeast of Bagram airfield on ranges shooting and doing Ranger stuff – the good life. After a while we figured out that patrolling was better than sitting around all night in hot Bagram crawling with senior officers. But still nothing happened.

We wrapped up our first combat deployment to Afghanistan after 90 days. Everyone had gone in with high expectations. We anticipated nothing but firefights. Instead, we concluded our tour with nothing remotely close to even just one. It was a huge letdown for everyone. The reality was that the enemy had decided to lay low after the first couple of months into Operation *Enduring Freedom* to evaluate and feel out the U.S. as much as we were figuring them out. The enemy had learnt well from their war with the Soviets but now faced a far better equipped and trained military. We all thought the war in Afghanistan was over, and I thought this was to be my only time here because what could possibly make the war last longer than 12–18 months? Who knew?! Looking back, I was a pretty ignorant 21-year-old, but then again what did a lowly E-4 know about all of that? The culture shock though had been huge. What Afghans consider an acceptable quality of life is diametrically opposed to our standards in the west and particularly the U.S. of A. Normal to us means technology, cars, and paved roads, as opposed to dirt huts, deserts, and mountain living without any visible and lasting infrastructure. It truly seemed like a country lost in time – at least the areas we operated in.

• • •

Back home at Fort Lewis we unpacked the pallets and took care of our equipment. We readied ourselves to go on our two-week block leave. But when, within a six-week period, four wives were murdered by their overseas-returning SOF husbands at Fort Bragg, North Carolina, everything changed. Two of the men also committed suicide. One of the possible causes was reported to have been the use of an anti-malarial drug called Lariam. Routinely given to soldiers deploying overseas, the drug can, supposedly, cause neurological issues. Perhaps there were other stress-related reasons. At battalion, though, our leave was hung up until everyone had been talked to about our well-being, ensuring that no one would kill someone or themselves. Once that was done, we were free to go and enjoy our time off.

My brother and I went home to see our family and friends. It was the last time I hung out with my high school friends. We also went fishing and enjoyed the time spent with our family. I was a 21-year-old Ranger specialist from 1st Platoon, Bravo Company, 2nd Ranger Battalion, on block leave with no idea of what I was doing but it wasn't going to be what my friends were doing, who, for the most part, acted like they were still in high school.

Upon my return, I re-enlisted in Bravo Company for an additional three years. I wanted to serve a bit longer and considered leaving the military after I had completed a full eight years, which would fulfil the requirement for the Inactive Ready Reserve. Back at Lewis, we continued our training cycles, while some Ranger School qualified personnel were sent to various schools including Pathfinder, Jump Master, SCUBA, and various leadership type courses.

* * *

As soon as Iraq was mentioned in the news we knew something was going to happen, just not when. Around Christmas of 2002 we felt confident that Saddam Hussein was not going to cooperate or accept President Bush's demands. We did not know the decision to go to war in Iraq had already been reached earlier in 2002 by the Bush administration. We all wanted to do this – have a piece of the fun in Iraq – especially since our first combat deployment to Afghanistan had, in our opinion, been a bust. Iraq promised the excitement of squaring off with a country that had a real army – an army that would fight, or so we thought.

As always, we conducted our standard training and rehearsals – airfield seizures, company and platoon live-fires – but this time more tailored to the new real-world scenarios we were facing, away from the training rooted in the 1980s through 2000 of battling drug cartels in Panama and South America. Ranger training missions have always been based on real-world target scenarios, but with Afghanistan and now Iraq, our training was focused on fighting these types of wars. We casually joked that we were not sure if we had mentally beaten the FARC (Revolutionary Armed Forces of Colombia), Colombia's guerrilla movement, or we simply had decided we did not want to play with them anymore. But it was definitely time to move on. The shift could not have been more dramatic. It was new for us to train in open terrain, maintaining longer distances in formations. Rather than the typical 3–5 meters between each Ranger employed in heavily wooded forests, we were now spread out to almost double that, which meant that a platoon's range had increased from approximately 300–500 meters to roughly 1,600 meters.

Our big training rehearsal for the battalion was at Fort Bliss, Texas, out in the middle of nowhere, where we conducted live-fire missions. This was the first time we conducted both fixed-wing and rotary in one training deployment.

We also executed airfield seizures on a large airfield at Roswell, New Mexico, in November 2002, in possible anticipation of assaulting the Baghdad International Airport. This was part of our annual exercise that lasted one month. The running joke was that certain hangars were off limits. Young Ranger privates always asked if the large hangars contained alien spacecraft and it was one of the dumbest questions! The answer was always, "No, we did not find any alien spacecraft. And no, there ain't no aliens in there." The first thing on our tasking list at Roswell was the battalion-sized airfield seizure, but it was more like how many Rangers could we damage early on! We were to jump, land, and assemble as fast as possible, then attack our objectives. I liked jumping, even more so after I became jump master qualified, working the aircraft or the Drop Zone (DZ). As we prepared to jump, I thought of what it would be like to combat jump into Baghdad at night with an actual enemy on the DZ, a thousand other Rangers running around on the airfield, and then always the link up… to assault. My mind drifted to things

I had read about the jump into Panama and the unexpected things Rangers had encountered on their DZs. I also thought about the size of the force required to clear an entire civilian airport terminal. I remember after we eventually got to Baghdad how awestruck I was about the size of the airport. It would have been one hell of a night had we jumped. Back in New Mexico, we experienced a shocking, eye-opening moment with the Air Force. There was a lack of communication or expectation between the Air Force planners' training objectives and ours. The Air Force's intention was to simulate taking ground fire, and with that came a zero reduction in speed to the 130 knots we required for a normal mass tactical parachute exit. Their intention was to keep the aircraft moving fast across the drop zone and to make the airplane a difficult target for enemy ground fire. But the maximum speed our parachutes could handle was 160 knots. The difference between what we got versus what we had expected was extreme. What we got were the normal ten-minute warnings to conduct our own parachute commands from "get ready, all personnel stand-up, hook-up, check equipment, sound-off for equipment check." But instead of feeling the plane decrease in speed at the three-minute warning, which is normally when the door is supposed to be opened and handed over to the jump masters, the plane continued at speed, until the one-minute time command was given, at which time the doors were opened. The Air Force load masters must check the door before it can be handed to the Army, which ate up the last 60 seconds before the green light. So, the doors opened and the green light came on simultaneously. Needless to say, the door still had to be checked by the jump master, and the first 60 seconds of green light were wasted with the door check, before jumpers could begin to exit.

Why is this important? The order in which the jumpers are loaded is based on time, the relative distance on the ground, and the location of each company's objectives on the ground, all based entirely on the green light coming on. This was a "mass tactical" exit, meaning jumpers were exiting both jump doors at the same time, separated by half-second intervals between the doors, and one second per jumper exiting out the same door. I know it sounds like rocket science, but it's not. The half-second interval is in fact created by human reaction time between the jump masters telling their respective doors to "go." The one-second interval is created between the jumpers by extending their arm onto the parachute pack of the man in front of him and holding this spacing until exiting the aircraft. That one-second interval translates to ground distance of 60 meters' space per jumper, but since it was a mass exit, the next closest jumper is off-set at about 30 meters, and the man you followed is 60 meters to your front. So allocating enough time and reducing speed accordingly were key for a successful mass tactical jump. But at the three-minute warning the airplanes did not slow down as they normally did, preventing us from doing what we needed to do. At the one-minute warning the doors opened, the Air Force crew conducted their safety checks and then passed control of the doors to our jump masters – but at the same time as the green lights came on, indicating a "go." Our jump masters did not have the time to check the doors whatsoever. We, on the other hand, barely had enough time to walk forward with all of our attached gear to exit the aircraft. Traveling at a higher speed also meant that your parachute opened in two seconds instead of four, and everything below your belly button was rammed up your throat. Luckily, we only sent about 30–40 Rangers to the hospital that night! An entire platoon out of the battalion was injured with ankle and femur sprains, breaks, and concussions. At 160 knots the parachute oscillates back and forth like a pendulum, resulting in hard, uncontrolled landings. I survived with three dislocated toes on my right foot. What was I going to do? Ranger on is all you can do and of course I did. Rangers Lead the Way!

My roommate Josh, the platoon leader's radio telephone operator, had been knocked out and had no memory of hitting the ground.

But Josh had managed to mostly pack up his parachute and get his radio into operation before sitting down on his rucksack, staring off into the black of night. One of the team leaders from our platoon had come across Josh sitting on his gear and asked him if he was okay. The reply was a disturbing "Where am I?" Josh was policed up and brought to the platoon assembly area, where he "came to." No one thought it wasn't a good idea for him to be the radio telephone operator, even though he was clearly concussed. Josh had no recollection of anything at that point, but he still got the radio into operation when he regained consciousness and made a radio check to the company commander's radio telephone operator. He had no idea how he did it. Josh was sat on his ruck, next to his packed 'chute, staring off into the distance when the platoon leader showed up and took away his radio. Josh had, in fact, conducted a radio check at a point in the mission when radio silence was required.

First Platoon's responsibility for the mission, after the parachute assault, was to exfil the precious cargo, in this instance a safe intended to represent some kind of bio weapon, which meant we were to be the first ones out on a C-130. In November 2002, it was cold in New Mexico so none of us wanted to dilly-dally around for long. But nobody told us that part of the exercise was a simulated crash of our aircraft caused by small-arms fire with a follow-on Downed Aircraft Recovery (DAR). This is a fundamental pilot task. DAR is a simple list of preplanned checkpoints which are briefed by the crew to their command but not passed on to the passengers unless and until it crashes. For example, if it is a cargo transport like a C-130 or C-17 that crashes, the crew is responsible for briefing the personnel being transported as to location and movement away from the crashed aircraft either to a new location or other checkpoints. That is, if everyone is able to walk away from the crash. In training everyone is, of course, fine. DAR is only for operations which put the aircraft behind enemy lines. Anyone who attends SERE School (Survival, Evasion, Resistance, and Escape) understands this concept. A DAR is also what launches the Combat Search and Rescue operation (CSAR).

We should have realized that another training objective was getting thrown in because what's fair about a platoon only spending a short time in the actual training exercise? Our aircraft "crashed" and our short-lived fantasy of an easy ending to our mission came to a brutal conclusion. We now had to drag the precious cargo, the 100-pound safe, in our Skedco litter carrier for 30 klicks. Our entire platoon of about 40 guys dragged it overland while maintaining proper patrolling formation as the rest of the battalion finished their mission. We patrolled farther than we intended because we repeatedly took cover behind the dunes whenever headlights approached, assuming them to be enemy patrols. Unfortunately for us, the continuous headlights were in fact from the 5-ton trucks the battalion used trying to locate us. Who knew?! We hid out of sight for so long that the entire battalion had completed their mission and was back in camp. You forget about the fun little extras that got thrown in your way or at you when you were a young Ranger. "This sucks!" was a common refrain that night. When you walk long distances through the desert and see lights on the horizon, and that's all you ever see, nothing ever seems to get closer because there is nothing else to look at except for the rolling dunes. It felt like we were making no progress but we stuck at it.

But the exercise was still not finished with us. We refitted and did it all over again just 24 hours later. This time the Air Force listened to our after-action reports and our second jump followed standard operating procedures. Everything went well but we did not exfil immediately this time because of a fog so thick it threatened to ground all aircraft. The battalion commander decided to "flush," which meant sending all aircraft off the objective and keeping simply the massive transport C-5 aircraft on the ground. We sat around for forever until the fog finally lifted.

This was not our only preparation for combat in Iraq. Other training exercises included rotary-wing Bi-Lats with the 160th

Special Operations Aviation Regiment (SOAR). We coordinated and worked with them on air assaults and conducted live-fire assaults onto objectives at the platoon and company level. We also ironed out and worked through a lot of mobility training. The entire battalion down to the fire team level figured out new Tactics, Techniques, and Procedures (TTPs), Standard Operating Procedures (SOPs) and all the joys that mobility platforms brought. A lot of growing pains were involved. It sucked big time driving at night using Night Optical Devices (NODs) because it was difficult and not everybody was good at adapting to it. For B Company, mobility training was a new thing. In the 1970s and '80s each Ranger company had had a mobility platoon, but during the '90s mobility was consolidated to one company, which was Alpha, so they had all the vehicle knowledge unless your company had a squad leader or platoon sergeant who had spent time in A Company. At 1st Platoon, luckily, we had both!

Part of mobility training included launching attacks on ground-based targets with our HUMVEE ground assault force driving around the desert of western Texas. In typical Ranger fashion all training pitted companies against one another to be the best of the best. We were lucky this time, because B Company was the last company to finish the live-fire training exercise of the year and we managed to get a lot of after action report comments from Alpha and Charlie Companies. It was cheating of a kind, but we knew a lot of people in the other companies and they helped us when it was our turn. Rangers did not mind sharing their experiences with others, especially with the new war approaching. Bravo Company finished best in the battalion.

We redeployed to Fort Lewis and went on block leave.

CHAPTER
THREE

FIRST BLOOD

Iraq, 2003

After leave we conducted more home station training through January and February of 2003. Our training was specifically tailored toward worldwide threats. We knew that on the diplomatic front the situation with Iraq was clearly deteriorating and we heard through the grapevine that the 3rd Infantry Division out of Fort Stewart, Georgia was, like us, waiting on the word to go to war.

It was also time for 2nd Battalion to rotate back into Afghanistan, and with that commitment Charlie Company was sent in January of 2003. The general consensus seemingly from the command groups was that major combat operations were shutting down in Afghanistan and SOF were significantly reduced because theoretically there was no longer a role for them in the theater of operation. In essence, and much to Charlie Company's chagrin, they were sent to pack up all of the Special Operations' equipment in-country, to close the camp, break down the tents, and pack up and inventory all remaining equipment. They also suffered the indignity of staying in-country twice as long – six months instead of three – since the regiment was on stand-by for the invasion of Iraq and was not going to rotate another Ranger company into Afghanistan to replace Charlie.

As it turned out, we deployed into Iraq during the very first night of the air campaign. We had in fact been scheduled to arrive 24 hours earlier, but unfortunately there had been a 24-hour maintenance delay of our aircraft at McChord Air Force Base in Washington state. Going into Iraq was different to our experience traveling to Afghanistan. We flew from Washington state to Germany and from there to Saudi Arabia. In Germany we had to dig out our protective masks and have them accessible by our seats because of Iraq's past use of chemical weapons. The center section of our aircraft was jam packed with pallets of all of our gear and equipment for the anticipated full-scale invasion. Our mobility platform was sent forward earlier, but we only had enough for one platoon per company of six-gun trucks and one cargo vehicle used by the medics. In Afghanistan we drove out of the FOB, and the vehicles returned with a skeleton crew; the platoons then conducted dismounted patrols. In Iraq this was totally different. Our staging area for the invasion was Saudi Arabia, the same place Special Operations launched from during *Desert Storm* in 1990. American military forces were not supposed to be in Saudi Arabia at all because a U.S. troop presence there, the cradle of Islam, was one of the key reasons Osama Bin Laden, a religious fanatic, had declared war on the U.S.A. and Saudi Arabia. As such, everything that was launched from the kingdom was done at night, which was when we operated anyway, but nonetheless we all hoped not to be seen on departure into Iraq.

• • •

The first night the air campaign started we were still unloading our C-17 aircraft. A fighter pilot made an emergency landing because his plane had been badly damaged by Iraqi ground fire. This was our first glimpse into the realities of war and that people would actually shoot back at us. It was finally a time to get tested, such is the ignorance of youth.

Ranger briefings were disseminated by the platoon sergeant to the squad leaders, down to the team leaders and then to the privates. There still were no computer networks at this point. We all expected to be part of the ground campaign. Ultimately, we did all participate. Within the first week we conducted clearance patrols. We drove forward to confirm or deny Iraqi forces in certain locations along the border crossing points and the small military outposts that littered the frontier. Our first such patrol lasted two days. The first mission remains memorable, not only because I was an MK19 gunner in our Ground Assault Force (GAF), but on this particular night the battery cap on my night vision had come disconnected and popped out, rendering it useless. I hoped the battery cap was still in the vehicle so I didn't tell anyone because there wasn't anything that could be done; nobody likes losing equipment or getting the attention of the team leader and up. I spent the remainder of the night with my face planted in my thermal scope. Once the sun rose I discovered my battery cap next to my gunner's platform.

Meanwhile, 3rd Platoon was forced to abort a mission due to a severe sandstorm. They were completely stalled until sun-up and were then finally able to return despite the continuing storm. In our genius wisdom of trying to be cool, we had asked the mechanics to remove the HUMVEEs' windshields and now Rangers in Iraq drove against 80–90mph winds with baseball-sized rocks flying directly at the drivers. Third Platoon tried to cover their eyes with MRE boxes but it did little. Everything was tied down in the vehicles and onto them which was an experience in itself, 550 nylon parachute cord lines tied everything to everybody, everywhere. They couldn't see anything and everything was covered in dirt. Still trying to be smart and ingenious they then used garbage bags to cover their machine guns but in no way did that work. Sand was everywhere and in everything. The storm lasted for a full five days.

Another mission for 2nd Battalion was to conduct ground operations while 1st and 3rd Ranger Battalions executed combat parachute assaults into H1 and H2, airfields in western Iraq. After 1st and 3rd Battalions secured their objectives we were tasked with linking up with them using a vehicle convoy. Our job was escort security, so my platoon, 1st Platoon, Bravo Company, linked up with the two battalions to bring them back. We were to escort the refueling trucks and to lead the large convoy back. Our rolling convoy was 1.5km or so long and we never trained to move an element that size. It was tough to move it forward. The primary difficulty was that it was not Rangers driving the fuel trucks and attached vehicles. Instead they were being driven by support personnel who had no experience driving using night vision and zero experience driving in tactical situations. It was painfully slow because we had to allow everyone to catch up. Our first sergeant briefed us to increase 10mph at a time. Once it was assumed everyone was at the same speed, another increase was announced over the radio. We allowed about five to six minutes per turn but it took a while to get it all going. It was a never-ending night. A six-vehicle convoy moves quickly but not this operation. It took us all night and into the next morning to effect the link-up.

Despite the slow progress we still hoped for a gunfight. We heard about the 3rd Infantry Division fighting but we saw and encountered nothing out west except a few remnants. I take it back, we did see 12-foot-tall murals of Saddam during this op and we took the opportunity for target practice using our .50cal machine guns and MK19 automatic grenade launchers we had mounted on top of the gun trucks.

● ● ●

We had spent 10–14 days so far conducting mounted cross border operations. The whole war lasted approximately 23 days, and all we heard about was the speed with which 3rd Infantry Division and the Marines swept across Iraq and the contacts they had. During this time, B Company, 3rd Ranger Battalion seized the Haditha Dam after a hard-fought battle. All I could think was a sarcastic, *Awesome, we are not having any.*

Our convoy struggled back. We had gone for 24 hours without any sleep. Almost immediately our company commander came out of the briefing tent. An American hostage was held in the town of An Nasiriyah, situated 360km south of Baghdad on the banks of the Euphrates River, and the Marines were unable to effect a crossing. We were told by our commanding officer that everyone was going to the hostage rescue. By "everyone" from the 2nd Ranger Battalion I mean Alpha and Bravo companies because Charlie was, of course, still deployed to Afghanistan on an extended tour. We had just a few hours to refit and to clean up all the crap stuck in our gear and equipment. We "pushed forward" and ended up sitting at the airfield of Nasiriyah while rescue plans were being put together by the regiment and battalion staff. In the meantime, our temporary home was an aircraft bunker.

The feeling everyone had was of excitement – not, of course, that an American had been taken prisoner of war, but that this would be a POW rescue, and we might actually get into a fight, a real mission, and if nothing else, it would be a proud, defining moment of our military careers. Everybody from the regiment got a piece of the marching order. It was a lot of fun being reunited with the regiment, which had been spread out with its operational commitments in Iraq. We bumped into guys we knew as privates in RIP or from Ranger School. We also reunited with a few former 2nd Battboys who had reenlisted and were stationed in Georgia with 1st Battalion. But there was only a small amount of time to exchange information about the impending mission and everyone's respective piece of the pie of the coming POW rescue operation.

We had been briefed that an American maintenance convoy had taken a wrong turning and had been ambushed. Under heavy fire there had been a number of fatalities, but there was one confirmed survivor currently being held in the local hospital at An Nasiriyah. There wasn't a huge amount of intel but this didn't matter to us. The basic op called for Special Forces to clear the hospital while we held the ground with blocking positions to prevent potential enemy reinforcements and to provide additional muscle in the event of a firefight. Most importantly, we were to secure the exfil areas. Our particular mission was to secure the western exfil route in case of ground fire during the initial infil. The Marines were bogged down at the bridge where the Iraqis had put up stiff resistance. Some of us did think about what would happen if we could not provide enough firepower and if sufficient aircraft could not be brought in with support fire missions. What was the alternate exfil route? Well, let me tell you, seemingly the alternate exfil plan was for us to drop our body armor at the riverbank and swim across to safety. "You do know nine Marines drowned trying to cross that very river," we said. It turned out to be four Marines who had drowned when their tank rolled off a bridge into the canal, but we did not know this at the time. Needless to say, it was not a comforting thought.

But despite the obvious risks, this was far better than driving through empty deserts. We had trained for this exact kind of mission. We packed up everything and went in kind of heavy because Marine

Corps intel informed us that up to 5,000 Republican Guards and *Fedajeen* fighters were in the city. Those were the same guys who had given the Marines a hard time and we were going in front of that so naturally we carried a lot more ammo for all of our weapons. To even get near to the hospital might require a fight. Perhaps this was going be like Somalia – a long night in a city with a big gunfight. Of course, it could also mean nothing at all would happen. We simply had no idea. On our end we packed more claymores for our blocking positions. Traditionally, as a SAW gunner I took a load of 600 rounds but for the mission I brought 1,000-plus rounds of 5.56mm ammunition. Whatever was to happen, we were ready.

We were not only briefed about the large number of Iraqi soldiers but also to be watchful for civilians with combat boots on since civilians wore sandals. If we spotted boots on a civilian we were to assume they were hostiles who may fight as part of the fighting populace or perhaps they were defectors – in either case they were enemy soldiers.

We helo'd in but not on CH-47 Chinooks with which we had trained but on Marine Corps CH-46s because they were already there. It was a learning experience to operate from these much smaller configured helicopters. Everyone had to duck to fit into the bird as the airframe was that short. We flew across the river and exited the craft. My helmet hit the door as I got out, forcing me to look back where a tall Ranger, with wall breaching material strapped to his back, forgot to duck and performed a back flip off the ramp. Too funny. The breaching charge he carried had gotten tangled in the headset communication cables that were in the helo for crew communication. So in his hurry to not get left behind, he unshouldered the charge from his back and left it on the helicopter. This did not make his team leader or squad leader happy, as it was missing vital explosive equipment. The Marines' 46s took off and cycled in the rest of the platoon, two squads at a time. I was nervously excited like the rest of the platoon. We turned left from the infil area. Crap – literally. We were headed across a drainage field for raw sewage. We had thought it was dry when we landed, but wearing our heavy MOPP (Mission Oriented Protective Posture) suits, body armor, and extra munitions we soon found ourselves sinking. Aaron from 3rd Platoon sank in a sinkhole up to his chest in this stuff. Funny. As the night progressed we saw ourselves underneath the streetlights – we all were covered in crap. You can imagine the cussing.

We hit the road, turned left, right, and then another left, and ran three long city blocks too far north of where we were supposed to go. We were smashing our way into the house when our squad leader shouted at us that we were too far north. The squad leader was more tightly wound than a German Shepherd, and in his excitement, he had taken us to the wrong spot. Instead of taking a tactical pause after the 46s flushed, to orient our location and to identify our proper blocking position, our squad leader just took off running to what he simply assumed was the proper location. This was based on the actual Helicopter Landing Zone (HLZ), where the CH-46s were supposed to have landed. But, of course, they had been forced to shift their landing due to debris found on the original HLZ on their approach. The remaining two squads tried to figure out where they actually were by using lasers. First and 2nd Squads of our platoon had infiled first, being in the first cycle of the helicopters, and we took off running based on the "original" HLZ locations, not on what we saw on the ground. Third Squad and the Platoon Headquarters element cycled in second and took the tactical pause to ID the actual HLZ location to the planned blocking position. That's how they discovered us being at the wrong location.

We moved back the required distance and took over the houses down the street by breaching and blocking off the surrounding area. One fire team was in the courtyard, while the other breached the building. I thought I had found the perfect spot behind some large fuel barrels in a carport. What a great spot for a SAW gunner to put his SAW down and not have to hold it the entire time – well, that was my theory at least. That was a lesson I never forgot, and I never let it be repeated by anyone else because, of course, fuel drums can ignite and explode in combat. Dummy.

The sector I covered was the left side of the house and I was watching lasers and tactical lights on the first floor. I noticed bed sheets or *dishdashas* on a laundry line directly in front of me. Suddenly two shots rang out, accompanied by muzzle flashes, from behind those very sheets. *Oh, it's probably nothing, just the guys clearing*, I thought. *Was that a muzzle flash from a window? Did that come from the inside or are our guys using a shotgun to breach stuff?* It took a second for me to register as another round struck nearby. Once that shot rang out it was like a lightbulb went off in my head. *Wait a minute, that's coming at me! Holy crap, someone is actually shooting at me!* It was a surreal moment but then I raked the area. The platoon only had about eight radios in total and those were with the leaders. So, they had no idea what was going on. I heard Jason, my team leader, yell, "What the hell you shooting at?" Jason came to the corner, peered around, and then a fourth round went off just then and there.

"Someone's shooting at me."

"No shit."

We returned fire and moved forward where we found traces of blood on the ground, on the wall and more on top of the wall. We had been on the ground for about an hour by now.

The house was secured but we had no interpreters to make ourselves understood to the occupants. So, hand and arm signals accompanied our English as we tried to make ourselves understood. One of our main frustrations during the early part of the war was the sheer inability to communicate effectively.

I repositioned from the side of the house to the front door of the courtyard so I could see down the street. In the near distance I saw the hospital and Rangers from 1st Battalion digging with their hands along the side walls of a compound. First Battalion had driven around the outskirts of the city, the east side, and had come in from the north, driving south. This was done to hopefully bypass any road blocks that had been emplaced to stop coalition forces. The Battboys rotated digging and occasionally I saw a few of them throw up as they unearthed decomposing bodies. By this stage we knew that the Iraqi source in the area had told U.S. forces that Private First Class Jessica Lynch was the only one alive and the rest of those killed during the ambush had been buried in shallow graves. Recovery was left to 1st Ranger Battalion and it was a pretty bad scene. Nobody can possibly understand or imagine the horrific reality of decomposing corpses.

The Special Forces team had assaulted the hospital exactly as we had landed. But by the time we had returned from our miscue they were already on their way out. Now it was time for us to exfil after accounting for the dead and all the Rangers in the operation. The Special Forces team spent no more than 10–15 minutes on the ground.

We collapsed our security positions and exfiled two platoons with the same Marine helicopters that had cycled us in earlier. Our total time on the ground was about three hours. We flew to the airfield at Nasiriyah and then back to Saudi Arabia.

We had a tremendous sense of pride upon our return. We had participated in the successful return of an American POW and recovered the remains of the fallen convoy members. It was, in fact, the first successful rescue of a serving member of U.S. forces in approximately four decades.

●●●

In Saudi Arabia plans were made to seize Baghdad Airport, then still officially known as Saddam International Airport. The warning order that an operation was to begin was pitched. M1950 weapons cases to securely hold our weapons during the parachute assault had been passed out, and initial assignments had been issued. The problem was that no matter how much the Air Force pounded the anti-aircraft locations, the threat was not sufficiently mitigated to risk a combat parachute assault. Based on the unacceptable potential loss of life and equipment, the operation was cancelled and the armored 3rd Infantry Division eventually rolled across the airport and secured it.

The airport, now renamed Baghdad International Airport, became our new staging point. We had a massive load list of all our equipment to move from Saudi Arabia to our new location, which meant we had to have everything repacked and loaded, for the entire regiment, minus the guys still on duty in Afghanistan. During combat operations there is mission essential equipment, and non-essential, but for sustained operations the requirements are virtually endless – everything from bullets and beans, to vehicles, tents, air conditioning units, tables and chairs. Imagine all the items in your place of work, then think about what is absolutely needed to conduct business. That equipment always gets moved first; the "comfort" stuff comes later, as it is required. For us, it was our fighting gear, our rucksacks, with standard packing list. Our vehicles would come second, as aircraft availability allowed, followed by all of our sustaining infrastructure.

We were transported in CH-47 Chinooks. We crammed 40–45 Rangers into each helicopter. We got "painted," lit up by an enemy anti-aircraft weapons system, about six minutes out from landing. All of a sudden the helicopter spewed chaff countermeasures into the air as we all went weightless. The helo dove to a few hundred feet above ground level. *What the crap?* was all I could think as the helicopter rapidly lost altitude. It was not uncommon for static electricity to sometimes set off the chaff but usually it would only be one or two flares of the pod. This time all of it blew and the helicopter lost altitude. This was clearly more than just static electricity.

We and our gear were all over the place – good thing we had secured ourselves to the bird. But we landed safely and found out that ground surface-to-air missiles had locked on to us. All I could think was, *Thanks, it would have been nice to have gotten a warning shout.*

We had landed on the military side of the airfield at night and our new home was one large military aircraft hangar that was opposite the passenger terminal. We spent two full months here, along with 1st Battalion and elements from 160th SOAR.

The first day or two we did not do much other than try to figure out the logistics about when our vehicles would show up and how. We also tried to coordinate light armored rides from 3rd Infantry Division into the city since it was still being fought for, and we were trying to figure out how we were going to get into this fight. "Would it involve clearing every house or what?" some of us pondered. We needed to work out exactly how to clear zones through Baghdad including door-to-door clearances. But for us junior enlisted Rangers not much happened. We finally received one tasking that went something along the lines of, "If you have nothing to do, you have a few hours as squads to snatch vehicles. That would be helpful for the battalion." In no time at all we stole a fleet of civilian vehicles, which were used to run back and forth, and were subsequently used by staff officers after our own mobility platform showed up.

We also made sure to examine a Joint Direct Attack Munition (JDAM), a 2,000-pounder. It had hit the runways and we were taken aback by the damage one created. We figured that several JDAMs must have in fact hit since the crater was 6 feet deep and half the width of the runway. It took the engineers several weeks to acquire all the materials and equipment needed to repair the damage.

● ● ●

Everybody was still excited in Baghdad. We knew we would get into the fight by hook or by crook. None of us wanted the fight to be over. Within a few days of being in Baghdad we started to run "confirm or denial" missions in downtown, including the university campus, where some of the most wanted members of Saddam's government, identified by the identification deck of cards issued to all coalition forces, may have been hiding. These missions were split so that everybody got a piece of the pie and was happy.

Vehicle platforms were something we had not used before. Four Bradley fighting vehicles from 3rd Infantry Division came over and ran dry rehearsals with us. We tried to figure out how many Rangers and gear we could stow in each Bradley. The crews briefed us on the speed of the vehicle, the 25mm cannon, and other key parts during the overall familiarization process. Designed to fit seven soldiers in the back, we came up with the brilliant idea to cram in 13 Rangers like sardines in a tin. It was a mess but we made it work.

The majority of the last week of April was spent in Bradleys and it was the worst ride in my life – tracked vehicles suck. It was during this time I bumped into someone from basic training who told us stories about their awesome gunfights rolling through cities and deserts. All great stories.

"What did you guys do?" he asked.

"Well we drove through the desert, did the Lynch rescue."

"Oh man, how many people did you get?"

"Maybe two," I deadpanned.

"Really?" He seemed to think surely you are not telling me everything. After all we had conducted high-speed special operations and secured all of western Iraq. Yet we had had no real contact.

"Yeah." So much for that.

We spent our time continuing confirm or deny missions in known target buildings. We also gathered intel and anything we thought useful for our intelligence folks. So much material was gathered that we had to resort to using large garbage bags.

The guys from 3rd Battalion eventually rolled back into the fold in the second week of April from Haditha and talked about their gunfight at the dam. At least they had got some fun.

We hung out since we were out of places to go to in the city. Fast, actionable intel didn't really exist at this stage. The communications network was simply not there; every intel had to be passed from radio to radio which took time and was decentralized between various divisions in the area of operations. Whatever computer networks did exist did not communicate directly with Special Operations and this led to a significant time delay.

Finally, a new tasking saw us traveling 30–50 klicks out of town to a bunker complex supposedly storing Weapons of Mass Destruction (WMD). We were babysitting several bio-chemical type guys in our newly arrived gun vehicles. Trace material was detected and it was glorified as, "Hey, we found something." But in reality it was only trace material. "Wow this is awesome; it's 115 degrees out in the sun with no shade and we are roasting. When do we get to go back?" was all we asked. We did not know. We had to wait for different equipment to arrive so we were stuck, and, in typical Ranger fashion, when bored we came up with some stupid ideas. We got the Skedcos out and tobogganed down the dirt around the massive bunker complexes we were guarding. The heat got to us as we had not prepared for a long stay and had only about a quarter of the water we needed. Lying under the vehicles did not help either; it simply stopped sunburn. A young and very bored specialist named Marcus had the idea to run naked from blocking position to blocking position. A team leader had dared him. He did it and the unexpected sight of a specialist running naked in the desert did make us laugh. In fact, whenever some of us are together again we still have a laugh about it. There is an expression in the Army: when all else fails, "naked is always funny." At long last this less than wonderful task was assigned to 3rd Platoon who relieved us in place. I think they stayed one more day before even the chem boys' interest negated and they too came back.

A raid took place on the evening of June 11, 2003, at a location about a two-hour flight to the west. Assets employed by our intelligence had discovered a massing of Military-Aged Males (MAMs) centered near a small but typical village at a wadi. Here, twice daily, they held formations on top of the bank. It was thought that these fighters would shortly launch an organized counterattack against coalition forces. The mission tasking was to disrupt this attempt with a pre-emptive strike.

The area of operation was under the control of the 101st Airborne Division, the Screaming Eagles, out of Fort Campbell, Kentucky, and together with higher command they discussed the specifics of the mission and how quickly the attack could be launched. The 101st required a week of preparatory work, including gathering additional intelligence and writing out orders for tasking purposes. It was decided by higher command to go around the table to see who else could execute the mission faster since time was of the essence. The Ranger element present confidently stated that they could launch the raid within 24 hours, basically that very same evening. Without a doubt a few choice words must have been said during that meeting but the objective was passed onto us. After all, this is what we did for a living – nighttime raids. This was our bread and butter and we did not require a lot of planning or rehearsals. We only needed to refine it to the particular requirements for the raid objective. From what we understood, the objective featured some tents and trucks, and perhaps technicals with mounted machine guns. There were no hard buildings. The tents seemed important. After a short planning process and using map imagery, we laid out the objective outside of our hangar using MRE boxes and engineer tape. During the operations order we were told that everybody on this objective was a hostile target and to engage everyone. Estimates of the forces we were to eliminate ranged from 80 to 150 fighters. There was a lot of potential for some serious firefights.

Objective *Reindeer* was a sunken wadi about 15 meters long, 10 meters deep, and was adjacent to a large streambed with steep rocky sides. Two smaller wadis channeled into *Reindeer*. We knew the washed-out creek was big enough for trucks. Objective *Reindeer* was further divided into three smaller objectives. My squad from 1st Platoon was assigned left flank security at Objective *Rudolph*, while 2nd and 3rd Squads were tasked with the main effort at Objective *Dasher*. Second Platoon handled right flank security and blocking any fleeing survivors at Objective *Comet*.

Third Platoon, however, had an even shorter planning cycle as they had to drive to the objective to provide far-side security to the west, along with the 81mm and 120mm mortar platoon. They were also the Forward, Arming, and Refueling Point (FARP) security for our helicopter support. Third Platoon received a warning order, which basically gives notice of an impending op, and almost immediately the operation order. They discussed their plan while driving to the objective. It was a demonstration of our flexibility and competence with which we were able to virtually instantly launch the mission.

We conducted our rehearsals well and set pre-assault fires as per Ranger SOP. Forward observers and the fire support section coordinated for pre-assault fire from fixed-wing aircraft. We had an AC-130 gunship in support as well. This raid saw the first use of a JDAM in airburst mode rather than of impact detonation. In total six were dropped.

I remember feeling excited and anxious as we loaded onto the MH-47s, rethinking the plan through my head. We had a two-hour flight ahead of us with a fueling stop at the FARP close to our objective. One of the aircraft had a "hard break" – some form of mechanical failure with the helicopter – making it unable to fly safely. It is not uncommon, but it is always a buzz kill. This break didn't happen until the pilots went to restart the helicopters after refueling. As a result, 2nd Platoon had to leave one squad behind. That sucked for them. When we offloaded at the refueling stop, we made our privates back-brief to make sure they understood the mission and the actions to be taken once we touched down. We re-embarked and headed to Objective *Reindeer*.

We approached our target area in the night. Each of us was on one knee inside the Chinook, snap-linked into anchor points, waiting for the commands and for the wheels to touch down, freeing us from its metal bowl. Adrenaline coursed within me as I recalled my piece of the pie as well as my squad's in the overall scheme of things. We all wanted to be tested. Would I personally have it? A ten-minute warning tore me away from my thoughts and I refocused. We were getting it on, the pre-assault fires were completed, and the Little Birds from the 160th SOAR made their gun runs, pouring lead into the enemy.

Our wheels touched down; I unsnapped my link. I never unsnapped early. I always waited until the wheels touched down and then unsnapped my link. Doing otherwise can cause problems should your aircraft maneuver at the very last minute to avoid gunfire or if it took a hit and recoiled as we had seen happen at Takur Ghar in Afghanistan in 2002.

Everybody offloaded as quickly and calmly as possible. Coming off the ramp, the basics rang through my head. *Did I unsnap?* Check. *Charge the weapon?* Check. At this time we never flew with a round in the chamber so there couldn't be an accidental discharge in the helicopter causing an issue with the aircraft. When I hit the ground, the objective could have fooled me into believing this was just another company live-fire training exercise at home. This was testament to our realistic training. But the smell wasn't what I expected: it smelled like freshly plowed dirt, because the JDAMs had thrown up so much earth. I know the smell well since I grew up next to wheat fields. There was also the smell of explosives – most explosives have a kind of sweet smell. I cleared the brown-out caused by the helo. I took a knee and looked around to get my bearing to identify my team leader. Then I moved toward the objective. I saw 2nd Squad rush south into the wadi. My adrenaline started pumping heavily and I tried to be as calm and composed as possible. We moved toward our sectors as we had rehearsed. The battle erupted into a two-way firefight.

The Little Birds of the 160th littered the nighttime sky, dodging incoming Rocket-Propelled Grenade (RPG) rounds and getting back on track. Brass and explosions painted a canvas illuminating the otherwise dark night. *Now this is for real*, I thought. I hooked left from the helicopter and sprinted a couple hundred meters to the left end of the company to my blocking position. Second and 3rd Squads pushed straight into the mouth of the enemy position. Everything was going to hell.

●●●

Fifteen of us got to our blocking position and we set up just back of the wadi lip. We took a knee. We set the snipers to the far left, the machine gun to the far right, and our two fire teams sandwiched in between. Our set-up stretched between 75 and 100 meters. Once set, we moved in closer to get plunging fire into the objective with our M240 machine gun.

A truck or two, if not more, were on fire. A fast and furious firefight centered around the mouth of the wadi within its tall walls. We were in the fight for less than a minute when the radio announced our first casualty at the mouth of the wadi – the very location the enemy used for their vehicles to enter at Objective *Dasher*. We did not need to listen to the radio because everyone heard my friend Sergeant Matt Watters, a team leader of 2nd Squad, scream a profanity-laced tirade at the top of his lungs. He had got hit just as he yelled "RPG" and engaged the enemy gunner. Sergeant Watters took the impact of an RPG round that amputated his left leg below the knee and then exploded behind him against the wadi wall, showering him with shrapnel. What I remember still vividly was that he shouted out, "That son of a bitch shot my shifting leg off."

Funny guy. Matt, a motocross enthusiast and a true Ranger, engaged the enemy with the remainder of his magazine of ammunition, while shouting, "12 o'clock! 30 meters! Kill that motherfucker!" To this day he doesn't actually remember doing it, but when his weapon was cleared, unloaded, for medical transport, the guys found the magazine empty. Matt's rifle should have been inoperable due to the amount of shrapnel damage it had taken, but it still fired! Other Rangers ran to the sound of the guns and engaged the enemy at close quarters.

At the bottom of the wadi was an abundance of 6- to 8-foot-tall elephant grass that was ideal for the enemy to hide in. We suspected that the enemy held positions here, and instead of blocking up high, everybody pushed toward the wadi and moved forward. There was a curved space big enough to squeeze in and hide. In fact, there were enemy in the cracks in the wadi wall, in recesses the size of small linen closets. Two or three guys hid there as Rangers crushed into the wadi toward their hiding spot. We engaged them from above, nearly straight down. Blaine, a rifleman E-4, and I took care of business and killed two to three fighters. We then shot at suspected enemy locations in the tall elephant grass. If the "shadows" in our night vision from the grass shifted, then we engaged them as "likely" enemy positions.

The gunfight raged while Ryan, the first sergeant's radio telephone operator, helped the platoon medics carry Matt's Skedco litter out of the wadi back toward ground we owned. The battle was intense and close and Ryan's shoulder strap buckle to his ruck was shot off. But they got Matt out.

We killed off the insurgents in numbers. The fight waned as 3rd Platoon pushed their vehicles in and the gunfight finally ended.

A rough count of enemy ammunition was conducted and pictures were taken during the Sensitive Site Exploitation (SSE). We then prepped for exfil. The cache inside the tents contained enough ammunition to arm an infantry battalion and could have done a lot of damage. Inside were 6-foot-high stacks of AK ammo boxes and a range of small arms, including RPGs and mines. During the invasion Iraqi soldiers abandoned their posts and either aided or were simply not around to prevent the stealing of war materiel, much of which would end up in the hands of insurgents. During planning, the decision was made not to hit the tents with air strikes because we wanted to find out exactly what was in those tents.

I had lost my ear plugs during the flight in, so my ears were ringing from the whine of the CH-47. During the initial five minutes of the mission, the gunfire was deafening, as though I had Earpro hearing protection, which was great. But when my hearing came back, shooting wasn't as much fun. After the target was cleared and secured I remembered I had a spare pair safety-pinned in my medical pouch. I put them in for the exfil.

The entire operation from infil to exfil lasted three hours – the typical length of a peace-time company live fire. There were no high fives, fist bumps or any genuine celebration as everyone was thinking about Matt.

We returned to our base. The sun came up as we landed, and we had a quick huddle with our company commander who told us what a great job we had done on a very solid objective and so forth. We were all tired and worried about Matt. I saw the back of the pants of a Ranger private covered in red and knew he hadn't been shot. I quietly told him to change his pants – it was Matt's blood. Our helo had been the medevac (medical evacuation) aircraft, and in the time it took to get Matt from the battlefield to the surgeons, and return for our exfil, there hadn't been time to wash out the back of the 47.

We cleaned up, rearmed, and grabbed something to eat. We were in the midst of this when we heard about 3rd Platoon's gunfight and a downed Apache helicopter. We went to our tent and readied ourselves to be on stand-by as a quick reaction force.

Third Platoon had stayed behind and handed over the battlespace to the original owners, the 101st Screaming Eagles. They provided a rough estimate of the number of enemy fighters killed that night. An enemy counterattack was launched that morning during the Bomb Damage Assessment (BDA) around 9am local time. The BDA was still in progress, trying to conduct a rough count. Bodies were moved into countable piles to avoid double-counting, and the objective was cleared again to ensure there were no survivors who could pose a potential threat.

Meanwhile, Apache gunships cycled in and were orbiting in the skies above the objective while Black Hawks transported in elements from the 101st. Apaches were engaged by gunfire from the wadi and one was hit and fell straight down from the sky. Within one minute 3rd Platoon's Rangers ran out of the wadi and mounted their vehicles to engage the threat. One Ranger later recalled how the six-gun trucks and mortar trucks, about ten vehicles in total, looked like the "Baja 1000" as they raced to the crest of the rise and ran straight into a technical with a mounted Dishka heavy machine gun. They were immediately engaged by approximately 14–18 enemy fighters. The gunfight lasted several hours. In this time the Rangers took two casualties. During the fight, one of the Ranger machine-gun crews, the gunner and his assistant gunner, barreled through to get to the Apache and its pinned pilots. The helicopter was on fire. Fortunately, the learning capacity of Rangers is tremendous and they quickly read the instructions on the cockpit on how to open it. They then undid the seatbelts and successfully extricated the pilots before the ordnance of the Apache exploded. The machine-gunner then laid down as much volume of fire as possible from an M240, while the assistant gunner ran the pilots back to the rest of platoon. The suppressive fire from the platoon allowed for the safe return of the gunner to the platoon line. The distance across the open ground to the Apache was 80–100 meters, and without hesitation the Rangers exposed themselves to harm in order to save the lives of their comrades.

The battle at Objective *Reindeer* resulted in 70 killed and was our first legitimate fight for Bravo Company. It was a typical Ranger smash-and-destroy-everything mission. In total, 2,000 RPGs, 50 RPK machine guns, 87 SA-7 surface-to-air missiles, and a huge stockpile of ammunition were captured. The operation's success was a testament to the many hours we had spent on the Bi-lats training we had conducted with the 160th SOAR.

The machine-gunner who had rescued the Apache pilots was recommended for the Silver Star. Two Purple Hearts and a handful of Bronze Stars with Valor Devices were also eventually awarded as well. Matt made a full recovery, minus a leg, and was discharged from the Army. He is now a police officer.

●●●

After the raid we conducted ground convoys to assist SOF in Tikrit. Other missions included hunting for members of the 52 Card Deck. By the middle of June things wound down, big FOBs were put together, a new Post Exchange (PX) was a novelty, and the infrastructure improved.

We were in Tikrit, having driven up from Baghdad, and it was fun seeing something different. The FOB was next to the river, and after one mission we didn't want to go back to Baghdad until dark because we preferred night driving as that was when we normally operated and it was considerably cooler. Someone suggested we go swimming since it was hotter than hell outside. Looking back on it now and knowing the filth of the Euphrates River, I can see this was not such a good idea. But as a 21-year-old Ranger it was a great decision as ignorance is bliss. There was a pump stand at the river which reached pretty far into the water from which around 30 of us jumped off. A great time was had in that nasty river. Soldiers from the 4th Infantry Division in Tikrit stared at us, as in, "How come you get to do that?" But they eventually jumped in too. We had some fun. It turned into a beach party, just without the beach.

But all good things must come to an end and we rotated back home by the end of June 2003 and turned in our equipment. We had a week-long recovery process, then our traditional two-week block leave.

PART TWO

SERGEANT – TEAM LEADER

CHAPTER FOUR

NOW IS THE WINTER OF OUR DISCONTENT

The Winter Surge in Afghanistan, 2003

I went before the sergeant (E-5) promotion board upon our return from Iraq. Having been selected for promotion, I said farewell to Bravo Company and moved across the Quad to Charlie Company in July of 2003. Charlie Company, as you may recall, had got stuck with an extended six-month deployment in Afghanistan, repacking the logistics of SOF once the focus shifted to Iraq. Although Charlie Company did conduct some ground assault force patrols in Afghanistan, it did not come as a surprise that there was a mass exodus from the company, which was only at 90 percent strength in any event. Many of the Rangers felt they had been screwed over by being left out of the Iraq invasion. The company of about 120 lost roughly 30–40 Rangers. I stayed with Charlie Company's 3rd Platoon for the next five years.

Around this time we started changing our training models from company-focused events to more platoon-level events because that is how we would be operating for the foreseeable future. Gone were the huge company live-fire exercises, although battalion-level events remained, but evaluations were now based on platoon live-fires and platoon MOUT raids in training. Sprinkled in were weeks of flat-range work, shoot-houses, proficiency jumps, driver training, and fire team and squad live-fires. This is sometimes called the "wash, rinse, repeat" training cycle, as each is basically a repeat of the cycle before. Ranger battalions are always influxing new privates, and training focused on the basics, teaching everyone shooting positions and how to use barricades. Barricade shooting teaches Rangers how to shoot around and under things found in combat situations – for example, how to properly utilize a car for cover and to shoot around it, and even under it. It can also be applied to buildings and shooting through holes in a wall or, as snipers call it, a loop hole. This can be referred to as the "crawl, walk, run" approach – you've got to learn to crawl before you can run. Team leaders and squad leaders are always refreshing and teaching the proper basics and integrating new Rangers into how business is done – essentially what is and isn't acceptable, especially during downtime in deployments. On forward ranges leaders got to teach more advanced skills to new personnel.

With the U.S. still heavily committed to both Afghanistan and Iraq, everyone knew that another deployment was on the cards at some point in the future. But none of us knew that we would be deployed again so quickly, this time as part of the much wider strategic surge initiative in Afghanistan. The request was to hit the mountains of Afghanistan and clear some of the areas previously untouched by Operation *Anaconda* – the March 2002 offensive. The intention was to establish a clear American presence and to confirm or deny the presence of al Qaeda and Taliban forces. We were to expand the American footprint and demonstrate our resolve by getting out there, mingling, and chasing down any threats or possible threats. General Stanley McChrystal had promised to commit Special Operations troops high up into the northeastern part of Kunar Province amongst others. It seemed hard to convince other units to put troops in those areas and to hole up for the winter. But, hey, that's why they had Rangers! We lead the way!

So, for the first time during the Global War on Terrorism (GWOT), the regiment deployed outside of its normal rotation cycle. Usually one battalion is in recovery, the other is deployed for 90 days – although later in the war this was increased to 120 days – and the third battalion is in preparation and training for approximately six months. Therefore, a battalion's cycle was usually three to four months deployed and about six months of training with some holidays and leave thrown in. A surge meant someone was going to have to deploy outside of the established pattern.

But the mass exodus yielded consequences for our company pre-deployment. The rifle squads, normally made up of two teams of four plus a squad leader, were reduced to five-man squads. A common squad now had one squad leader, two team leaders, and one rifleman each, yet we shipped equipment for an entire squad. All mission essential equipment was packed and we did not think about spreading out the loads. This was probably one of the worst examples of what I call "common sense fail" or a violation of the "principles of patrolling." Not every squad needed every single item, such as breaching tools for assaulting objectives, and we should have tailored it to the size of the actual force. To give you an idea of the weight we eventually carried up and down the mountains during this deployment, here is a rough breakdown. The helmet alone weighed about 5–6 pounds, the chest rack depended on the weapons system but mine was about 2 pounds' worth of cloth, holding eight magazines at 1 ½ pounds each and 12 high-explosive (HE) M203 grenade rounds at approximately 1 pound each. My M4 carbine with magazine came in at 7 ½, the M203 grenade weapon system itself weighed 3 and, finally, the "bleeder kit," the medical pouch, added another 3–4 pounds. Our rucks weighed in at a meaty 90-plus pounds and then there was the load-bearing equipment. We basically humped about 130–140 pounds. Fort Lewis is located 200 feet above sea level and if you compare that to the 8,000–13,000 feet we traversed in Afghanistan you definitely felt the altitude change. Unsurprisingly, a few Rangers suffered from altitude sickness.

When Charlie Company had previously deployed to Afghanistan, the war was, in theory, winding down and therefore their role was effectively to shut down the counterterrorism command. There seemed to be no further need for this task force in Afghanistan. But this deployment would start the unpacking process and the re-expansion of the counterterrorism footprint throughout the country.

We arrived in late October of 2003 and almost immediately launched company-sized elements up into the valleys and draws not too far outside of Asadabad, the capital city of the Kunar Province. The infil was fairly long and conducted by trucks driven and maintained by the 1st Ranger Battalion. We drove the majority of the day up the valley as far as they could go, where we then dismounted and walked. Our patrol turned into two, three-week-long tours reminiscent of Mountain Phase at Ranger School. It was, in a word, brutal.

Early in our deployment our battalion suffered its first killed in action (KIA) since Panama, and the first during the GWOT – Sergeant Jay Blessing, who was the battalion's arms room non-commissioned officer. He and Gary, a civilian contractor, were in Afghanistan en route to Alpha Company to repair a couple of machine guns when they hit an improvised explosive device (IED). The front of the vehicle was destroyed from the front bumper to the B-post behind the driver where the front door latches. Jay was killed instantly. We heard the news over the battalion command net. Some had served with Jay and it left us all with a bad feeling. What a horrible way to start this thing. Gary suffered a lot of serious injuries to his body. He became deaf in both ears. Before the explosion he was a cranky old man, and now he became even crankier. Who could blame him? His arms were badly injured, as was his left side, but he remained whole and survived the explosion, and to the best of my knowledge he is still the battalion armorer.

During our patrol we located a valley fork wide enough to allow for aerial resupplies or to be used as an HLZ. We only packed and carried our basic packing list and were resupplied every couple of days. The fork had a compound we rented and secured from the local forces and it became the hub. Charlie Company was on the left finger of the valley. The right finger was patrolled by another company. The hub was the central point for command and control and located at the bottom of the valley where we spent the night and pulled security.

Afghanistan gets very dark to the point where you can barely see anything without night vision. One of the advantages to Afghanistan was that there were no standard building codes to anything – well, actually it was not an advantage whatsoever and you will see why. We had one door which led into the compound, though there was a second door as well. Early into our operation, a young private, Monty, did not pay attention and took the wrong door to exit the building. There were no lights and he was not wearing a headlamp. And, like in a cartoon, he stepped out into the pitch-black nothingness of an 8-foot fall. He plunged into sharp, jagged rocks and was busted up pretty good. He only wore his fighting equipment without his body armor or even his Kevlar helmet. He had no protection whatsoever. We needed to "Nine-line" medevac him because of his facial injuries, which could have impacted his breathing. Essentially Nine-lining requires basic information on the injured person, and as such a standard operating procedure was followed. Nine-lining him, using nine points of information, sounds simple, but it involved a detailed checklist that looked like this:

1. Location
2. Call Sign
3. # of patients by type
A. URGENT (1HR); B. PRIORITY (4HR); C. ROUTINE (24HR)
4. Special Equipment
A. NONE; B. HOIST/WINCH; C. EXTRACTION; D. VENTILATOR
5. # of patients by type
L. LITTER; A. AMBULATORY; E. ESCORT (women/children)
6. Security at HLZ
N. NO ENEMY; B. COALITION CIVILIAN; C. NON-COALITION SECURITY FORCE;
X. ARMED ESCORT REQUIRED
7. HLZ Marking Method
A. PANELS; B. PYRO; C. SMOKE; D. NONE; E. OTHER
8. Nationality/Status
A. COALITION FORCES B. COALITION CIVILIAN C. NON-COALITION SECURITY
FORCE D. NON-COALITION CIVILIAN
9. Nuclear-Biological-Chemical (NBC) THREAT

Then the MIST report followed the Nine-liner:

M: MECHANISM OF INJURY
I: INJURY
S: SYMPTOMS/VITAL SIGNS (AIRWAY, BREATHING RATE, PULSE RATE, UN/CONSCIOUS)
T: TREATMENT GIVEN

We were already short of guys. *What an awesome way to start the operation*, I thought sarcastically. It was one of those avoidable/unavoidable things. We had briefed everyone about the door situation prior to the guard shifts starting, but we just didn't think to tape a red chemlight to the inside of the door. It was kind of like an "oops," an oversight, when we should have marked the door that led to nowhere.

We made ourselves mobile to fight at high altitude. We stopped wearing body armor because IEDs were still not a huge threat. And given the altitudes we planned to walk at, body armor made it almost impossible to react quickly. We just carried our Load Carrying Equipment (LCE) and chest rigs underneath our rucks.

The next morning saw the awful, slow walk up the valley – a long hike in the treacherous mountains in winter. It was really bad. We took the same normal trails the Afghans had been using for centuries because those trails were the only way to get up the valleys. We patrolled 5–7 klicks a day and then kept on walking for six long weeks. The first valley was the Kantiwa River Valley, Nuristan Province, and the second valley was the Pesch River Valley in the Kunar Province. The higher we climbed the colder it got and sometimes we patrolled in snow. It was miserable. Just imagine any mountain range in the United States, put on 130 pounds of gear, and struggle up and down the ridges, crossing gorges and riverbeds filled with massive boulders while maintaining some semblance of a combat patrol. Some of the cliffs we encountered were staggering by their sheer drop-offs. The elevations were rugged and required intestinal fortitude to climb up and down for weeks on end.

Below the snow line we rented compounds from the locals and set them up as secure staging areas for the weeks to come. They provided shelter and we stayed there for a couple of days at a time. From here our company conducted squad-sized patrols up and down the mountains and valleys. We demonstrated an American presence deeper and farther than anybody else had. We talked to locals who didn't even know that Americans were in Afghanistan. They thought we were Russians. It was amazing to realize how tribal and decentralized Afghanistan is to the point that many villagers we encountered still thought this. They were happy to hear we were here to get rid of the Taliban because most couldn't stand them.

We had no interpreters with us, something that would change drastically over the years. It was hard to get civilian contractors to walk 10,000-foot mountain ranges in the bitterly cold winter months of October and November. We could have used, and needed, dedicated interpreters, but most commanders did not even think that Rangers would be in there long enough.

● ● ●

It was probably our fourth or fifth day patrolling. We had rented a guest house from a local about halfway up the Kantiwa River Valley to use as our base of operation. First Platoon patrolled the ridge to the north, when they called in a compromise by an enemy which prompted us to react quickly in support of them and, wouldn't you know it, it was our "down" day. We ran up the ridge; going from 9,000 feet to around 12,000 was a bear wearing all our gear. We were "smoked" when we got there, and it turned out to be a false alarm. Once we reached them we saw 1st Platoon calmly pull security while their platoon leader and platoon sergeant drank tea with the village elders. Man, were we pissed!

The mountainous terrain ultimately forced us into using pack mules to move supplies. The animals were not controlled by us; we "rented" the services of the mules or donkeys from the locals who walked them for us as we patrolled. It wasn't too bad operating with them except for the couple of times the pack animals decided they simply did not want to move, although this did give us longer rest periods. It was just like Merrill's Marauders, who, during World War II, used mules while conducting their long-range patrols in the China–Burma–India theater. At least we thought so.

Charlie Company was tasked with clearing the bottom half of the Kantiwa River Valley, while Bravo Company cleared the top half of the valley. Weeks later we finally met in the middle. We received word that we were to exfil this valley soon to refit and to get clean. Up until this point we had only brushed our teeth and shaved.

Another less than wonderful patrol happened during our last week in the second valley, the Pesch River Valley in the Kunar Province. Our platoon was tasked with a day patrol to the map reference "87 grid line," to see what or who was there. This patrol was miserable because we had been patrolling for six long weeks at this point and everyone was tired and sore, beaten down by the arduous terrain we had been operating in. And that's an understatement! But we patrolled anyway because that's what Rangers do. What made it worse was that halfway to our target location we lost the trail and hopped boulders along the river bottom. This hopping was tough on our joints bearing all the weight. We ended at about the "85 grid line" and decided to climb up terraced fields for several hundred feet to the nearby village. By the time we made it there everyone was "smoked," and I mean smoked to the point where our machine-gun teams were basically ineffective if we had to fight. Those Rangers carried a heavier load than most. We decided to pull out the binoculars and glassed up the valley to our intended target but there was nothing except for mountains, rocks, and the river. We rested while the platoon leader and platoon sergeant drank tea with the village elders to ask them about possible Taliban and al Qaeda presence. Drinking hot tea always helped in cold weather. We patrolled back to our positions using the trails this time and returned just in time for "stand-to," when we had to get ready to face any potential threat. This is usually done at dawn – just the thing you didn't want to do after hard weeks of body-breaking patrolling. We cleaned our gear and resumed our security positions for guard duty.

• • •

We had only just arrived back at Bagram when intel sent us out again without so much as a hello. A High-Value Target (HVT) or Time-Sensitive Target (TST) had been located and we were tasked with a quick turn-around, rapidly cleaning our weapons and grabbing a basic load of chow and water. There was no changing of socks, since our deployment bags had been pushed forward to another staging area where a helicopter had a mechanical failure and executed a hard landing. For six weeks I wore the same top and bottom and four pairs of socks. All I could think about was how I ought to try to wash them with a bar of soap I had. Eight hours later we loaded CH-47s for an early morning infil. We inserted into an area of fields at 10,000 feet, on the low side of the target village. This made our movement to our blocking position an uphill one. Usually it is a plus to gain elevation, but with our overweight rucks it was a very familiar pain. We climbed terraced fields and jumped over irrigation ditches and the creeks that were spread throughout the valley.

A SEAL team came along for this TST mission. They didn't want to "hike" down the ridge from the big village, across the valley floor, and back up the other side to hit a follow-on house. So instead they called for a Huey helicopter – it was white by the way – to fly them across, so they could be lazy, and not be out of breath from the hike. Because, you know, lifting weights and exercising beach muscles has nothing to do with cardio training for altitude. We just stood there dumbstruck as they did it. We couldn't figure out why! They wasted a few hours waiting for the aircraft when they could have Sunday strolled over there and been fine. Everything, and I mean everything, for them was about the "cool" factor maxed at level 10.

We did not find the HVT. We cleared the village, spread out our force – one platoon patrolled up one valley, another platoon the other side of the valley, and another platoon went straight down. The locals wanted to know why Americans were there instead of Russians – again! But the village did prove to be a good hub for us. The initial objective area had nicely terraced fields where one could land two to three helicopters at a time so it was a good place to hold on to and secure. We even considered using it as an exfil point. We pushed up the valley for about one klick while all platoons remained in sight of one another in case of a fight. We basically staged a large oversized company patrol base there. From this patrol base we rotated and launched platoons and squads into day patrols, conducting combat patrols as dictated by command.

Our interactions with the locals were good. For the majority of the villagers this was the first time they had learnt that the country was no longer occupied by Soviet forces. The villagers had little concept of time and we indicated that no Soviet Russians had been in their country for "10 snows." They thanked us for chasing away the enemy, which made us laugh, and, to be fair, we did communicate that the Russians had left on their own. We told them our purpose was to liberate them from the Taliban and al Qaeda. The villagers told us they had not seen any in a while and had previously chased them away when they sought shelter during the last winter. Today they probably hold a very different opinion of us than they did back then.

●　●　●

At this point everyone was absolutely and utterly beaten down after the weeks of constant patrolling in the mountains. The weather was freezing and we humped all over the area. Thanksgiving Day arrived and I could not take it anymore. Jay, another team leader, and I decided that after weeks without a shower it was time to wash socks, armpits, and everything else. We walked to a creek near the village just outside of the compound. It was the coldest water I have ever been in but the feeling of finally getting clean was nearly overwhelming. I even put on my last clean T-shirt that I had been saving, and together with the wash it was a mental victory – I thought to myself, *I am not a complete scumbag.* Jay also took the plunge and enjoyed the icy water as much as I did, despite it being so freaking cold. What a great moment. And if you are curious about bathroom use – well we did it where the locals did – in the woods.

We were told that we could put small elements together and hike down to company headquarters by the HLZ for Thanksgiving – mind you, it was a 2km round trip. Half of us decided not to go but I wanted a hot meal and a chance to hang out a bit. I had great friends in my 3rd Platoon but there were only so many conversations you could have with the same people before you want to see what's going on with the other platoons. It was quite a sight to see Black Hawks choppering in Mermite containers with all the Thanksgiving Day fixings. The sun started to go down and we swapped stories with different platoons and squads. We enjoyed ourselves throughout the afternoon and evening and eventually we climbed back up to our own squads.

We conducted one more combat patrol and then exfiled to Bagram where we repacked, left our remaining ammunition with the depot, and redeployed home. Over the six weeks most had lost a lot of weight. I had easily dropped 20 pounds. Nobody enjoyed the MREs, and coupled with the continuous excursion, it was a small wonder we hadn't dropped more.

This six-week surge was by far the most memorable experience of my military career to this point, not because of any significant contact or enemy encounters, but because of the constant pain and the suffering registering differently in the brain. For those of us who stayed for years to come, it became the basis of what "suck" would be defined as, and a point to explain to young Rangers that it can always be worse. It was not remembered as a bad time but a good time in the sense of real, hardcore Rangering. But this experience was the breaking point for a few Rangers who decided this wasn't what they wanted to do. For me, I won't lie, it was miserable, but in typical Ranger mentality it was "just another day at the office."

Back at Fort Lewis we had a few days off before starting a new training cycle. The end of 2003 going into 2004 was a time of transition for the regiment in terms of operational capabilities along with technological advances. Our SOPs changed and morphed into new ones. Our basic Ranger SOPs worked in generic ways very well and by now we created new SOPs, more detailed and tailored to particular scenarios. We spent time figuring out the best way to conduct certain missions and looked throughout the battalion to see how other companies or platoons operated. In war, conditions change, the enemy adapts, so the Ranger battalions needed to change as well. We never got stuck in a rut and always understood that a plan was just a plan and a fight was the fight. A great plan never survived the first contact, and after contact, you had to fight the fight, not the plan. The enemy always got a say! The changes came so fast and developed so quickly we did not even have time to write them down! Loading, dismount drills, load lists were all tailored to the current threat. Basically, there were no real SOPs but essentially only TTPs. The SOPs were better developed once we moved into the Strykers. Our changes only started to begin; soon enough we would be conducting top missions along with other Special Forces.

CHAPTER FIVE

SPRINGTIME FOR HUSSEIN AND IRAQ

The Spring Surge, 2004

After our redeployment home from the surge in Afghanistan, which only lasted approximately two months, we would deploy in yet another surge but this time into Iraq. We conducted more training stateside, as per our battalion standard. This was Charlie Company's first trip to Iraq, with the exception of a handful of Rangers who had previous deployment experience in the theater of war such as me. Thanks to the increasing IED threat we were no longer able to drive older-style soft-skin open-air jeeps or RSOVs, instead we were in armored HUMVEEs

– which sucked! The early up-armored HUMVEEs, the M1114s, did not have air conditioning, and let's face it, in triple-digit temperatures with no windows down, it really sucked. We converted the vehicles from the basic HUMVEE turtle shells of 2003–2004 into new open-air steel boxes, to get more guys into the fight quickly with fewer vehicles. We used 1-inch-thick milled steel that was not hardened, or shrapnel-proof, but it did offer some minor protection. It was the best steel we could get in Iraq but it hardly sufficed.

Third Platoon did not do much, whereas other platoons, spread throughout the country's FOBs, did a whole lot more. We were in Baghdad and the signs were there for the ferocious combat to come. It was not the Wild West yet, but the early stages of "cranking-up" routinely flared. The organization of the enemy wasn't quite fully developed but it didn't take long to get to that point. IEDs became prevalent. The IEDs in use ranged from small pop-can sizes to larger concrete blocks, which were usually hidden in the middle of the road. We played a deadly game of cat and mouse with the IEDs. Could we spot them and what were they? A dangerous, lethal, frustrating game. We began to understand the threat but in our eyes the gunfight was still considered the biggest risk.

My platoon had a few new Ranger privates and so most of our squads were six to seven strong instead of the previous five. The priority in personnel was always to reinforce the weapons squad because machine guns were the deadliest small arms in combat. Weapons squad was brought up to strength to provide firepower for our vehicle-mounted guns and also for our dismounted patrols.

In April or May of 2004, we experienced a blue-on-blue incident when we were tasked with an escort convoy for Army Special Forces. This was about a week after Pat Tillman of A Company, 2nd Ranger Battalion was killed by friendly fire in Afghanistan on April 22, 2004. As I sit here recalling that night of the blue-on-blue in Iraq I shake my head at the misfortunes of war, where you can do everything right but still get hit hard in your gut. Everything is coming back to me now about that catastrophic moment. Even to this day, this is a low point in my Ranger history. I constantly play devil's advocate in my mind – the "what ifs," and "if I had only…"

We set off from Baghdad International Airport and it was hot. We drove with the lights out, traveling basically from a black hole toward a sporadically lit town. It almost felt like we drove into sunset because of the various lights dotting the night landscape. The illuminations created a spot or halo effect in our night vision. We had some issues as we drove down the highway but we did our best not to be affected by them.

I drove the lead vehicle. Staff Sergeant Dave McDowell, who was the weapons squad leader and as such the vehicle commander, was beside me. Dave would be killed in action four years later during a firefight in Afghanistan. We had a pretty good understanding of the heavily patrolled highway. Our mobility SOP had also changed. We no longer drove in single file with 100-meter spacing in between the vehicles. Instead, our convoy was staggered like we used to conduct our old road march formations. We were off-set, staggered on the left and right side of the freeway, thereby making us less vulnerable in case we triggered an IED, or drove into an unseen hole, or were ambushed. A staggered formation also allowed for better reactions to a threat. It also kept the dust down and increased visibility for the trailing vehicles.

My vehicle was on the left side of the road and we were about halfway between Baghdad Airport and our objective. We were to link up with Army Special Forces in Baghdad, and to finalize the plan before departing to the objective area. There were U.S. Abrams tanks immediately to our left and I asked Dave if we should change sides or adjust. He was the senior non-commissioned officer in our vehicle and he said no. What we simply did not see was the Abrams tank traversing its barrel to look at something. The halo-type spots interfered randomly with my night vision. I did not make the movement out and neither did Dave or Ricky, the turret gunner, until the barrel was right above our vehicle. I slammed hard on the brake while yelling at our gunner, who did not make out anything because of the ballistic shield in front of his mounted MK19 automatic grenade launcher. Our truck went right underneath the barrel and it struck the ballistic blade above uncompromisingly. Metal on metal, sparks everywhere. The heavy barrel had knocked the MK19 off its pintle and it dragged the whole thing across the back of our truck at 60mph. It was ugly.

The barrel had struck the shield, smashing into Ricky as it went up and over our vehicle. The transference of weight and power tossed equipment throughout our HUMVEE. Our platoon medic, Doc, was in the back of the truck and he was hit in the head by the MK19. Ricky was stuck in the turret, laid out and bent over backwards. His knees had buckled and we immediately knew he was unconscious. There was no muscle tension at all – nothing. Fortunately, we heard him groan, so at least we knew he was still alive.

I had slammed on the brakes and pulled over to the right shoulder of the highway; we were about 400 meters from the impact area. Dave and I jumped onto the top of the hood of the truck, trying to figure out how to get Ricky out of the turret. In the meantime, Doc regained consciousness.

There was quite a bit of confusion throughout our convoy because nobody had seen the tank. Everybody thought we had taken an RPG round to the turret considering all the sparks from the impact. The tank crew ran over as well as did a number of Rangers ready to assist.

It took a little while, but we finally managed to get Ricky out of the turret and we carefully placed him on the side of the road to provide Doc the necessary space to attend him. The medevac was called in as Doc did his job. The platoon sergeant worked hard to get a Black Hawk to fly Ricky back to base. The medevac took forever and I thought it might have been faster to have driven him back to the airport.

We did not know Ricky's status or what the actual damage was. Did he have a broken back? I mean, a heavy-duty 120mm metal barrel had crushed into him. Doc took off Ricky's chest plate armor and the plates were soft and pliable at this point. Clearly, he had taken a massive hit to his upper body. Our platoon medic checked for broken ribs. Ricky's face swelled up quickly. He drifted in and out of consciousness and was moaning a fair bit. He was clearly in a ton of pain and fought off Doc a little bit. There was major trauma to his body and face. Doc did tremendous work as he dealt with Rick's semi-resistance and intubated him to maintain his airway. Then Doc checked to make sure there was no unusual bruising of the chest cavity. Ricky's face was a mess; almost all of his teeth were gone and it looked totally broken. Doc shot him up with a light dose of morphine to reduce the pain and calm him down. He maintained Ricky until the medevac finally arrived. He was flown straight away to the hospital in the Green Zone for emergency surgery.

Back at the scene we located two pieces of the three or four parts of the MK19. The barrel was in three pieces, and the receiver was bent like a banana. We never did find the ballistic strike shield. After we policed the area and cleaned up we drove into the Green Zone. Here we traded our damaged truck with 1st Battalion, 75th Ranger Regiment, who, along with Army Special Forces, were at the SOF base located within the zone. We briefly discussed the need to continue the mission to keep our heads in the game and, in typical Ranger fashion, the mission to provide a blocking force for Army Special Forces took priority. We did a rapid intel update with them. Our platoon sergeant gave a quick talk to the boys – that accidents and injuries happen, but that the mission continued. The boys refocused and we rolled out into town to conduct the tasking. As per our brief, we isolated the block with our six HUMVEEs and Army Special Forces assaulted their target. At this point in the operation there really wasn't a lot that ever happened in the blocking positions, so after about 15 minutes on target, we usually went up and down the block smashing out the lights that affected our night vision. The Iraqis love 4-foot florescent lights. The mission proved uneventful.

Upon our return to the SOF base we checked in on Ricky at the hospital. His face had 13 broken pieces, including six separate pieces of his jaw. One eye socket was broken and detached. They set and wired his jaw shut. His entire body had swollen to such a degree he resembled the Michelin Man. The surgeons had medically induced a coma and he would stay in this state for three weeks. Four or five days after the accident and once he was stable, with no undiagnosed internal injuries, he was flown to Landstuhl, Germany. We went back to visit him before he was transported to Germany, and the trip from our base at Baghdad Airport to the Green Zone almost required an entire operations order. Everybody was down in the dumps as Ricky was always the life of the party and made everyone laugh, especially during difficult situations. He was and is well liked. Ricky hails from New England and currently still has some memory issues but otherwise is alright. At the time of the incident he held the rank of a corporal. On his return to the U.S. he stayed at Walter Reed Medical Center in Washington for a long time. By the time he returned to the battalion he basically came to clear out of the Army. In contrast, the Abrams' barrel barely had a scratch of paint. We know this because we had to find the tank and its crew, take pictures, and conduct interviews for the post-accident investigation.

• • •

Overall, however, it was an uneventful surge for Charlie Company. We spent 45 days in Iraq, and other than the blue-on-blue incident not much happened. We supported Army Special Forces by providing escort convoys and blocking positions. Our platoon sergeant knew a lot of guys in Army Special Forces. There was a stigma attached to leaving the Ranger Regiment to join Army Special Forces. Some people at the battalion felt that those Rangers had abandoned our unit. But I never shared those sentiments. The company commander and the first sergeant pushed back or accepted the fact that some Rangers wanted to leave. Often the discussions centered around whether or not the individual had properly finished his commitment to the regiment, or whether or not there was an interest in pushing the Ranger into leadership roles as squad leader or platoon sergeant. The older, long-serving Rangers who had been in the regiment for decades took it a lot harder when someone left the fold. The operations in Mogadishu, Somalia, in 1993 had exposed some difficulties in the working relationship between the Ranger Regiment and Army Special Forces. Afterwards both sides developed closer ties because the overriding need was to work jointly and execute tasks smoothly and efficiently. No matter if the Rangers actually executed joint missions; the key change lay in the fact that planning and operations involved all the counterterrorism elements.

As I mentioned already, starting in 2002 through 2004 there was a huge reworking and rewriting of the SOPs of the Ranger Regiment as well as TTPs. Training-wise this translated into far fewer patrols in wooded terrain and a greater focus on the urban environment and the threats encountered in such a setting. In addition, there was also a greater focus on mobility patrols, and vehicle SOPs and TTPs. We figured out that we did not clear buildings as well as we should so the learning curve for the Rangers was big. It was great fun to be on the edge of this and to see what other companies did and thought, to see what worked best, and we based our rewrite of the SOPs on these hard-won experiences. But as fast as new SOPs emerged, things changed on the battlefield. We had to change and adapt even more quickly, to be fluid as well to adapt to the changes on the ground. During this time retention was good. There was an upswing, in fact, riding the rising tide of enlistment. It was a growing phase for the regiment and there was no mass exodus.

There were also some very interesting changes happening within the counterterrorism community. The relationships within the various units which fell under the umbrella of counterterrorism started to evolve well. Trust greatly improved and one of the unforeseen consequences of the Rangers joining the counterterrorism command meant that they really knew what we were capable of, and, as such, they argued for greater inclusion and responsibilities for the Ranger Regiment. The departing Rangers helped form and cement the new relationship.

A perfect example for this newfound inter-unit relationship was found in our platoon leader, who had been an Army Special Forces operator during the early stages of the GWOT. Throughout his career he participated in conversations on both sides of the coin. Old reputations dictated that Army Special Forces was used like a surgeon's knife, whereas bringing in a bunch of young "Hooahs," as seen in Somalia in 1993, was like bringing in a bush hog who leaves behind a swath of damage. In its own right it was good to have that reputation, but as the wars progressed the Ranger Regiment proved its ability to be surgical as and when required. But we could just as easily flip the switch back and destroy everything. This was a nice development for us, because now we were looked upon as a multi-faceted, capable unit. Of course, it could be argued that we were not quite as surgical as Army Special Forces because we traditionally operated in platoons of 40 Rangers and Army Special Forces used a far smaller, more surgical, element.

Of course, there always was a difference in how particular squadrons inside those other elements treated us. Sometimes the squadrons were predominately former Rangers and a lot of trust and acceptance was given and returned. There was a sense of comfort seeing and working with former friends. Other Army Special Forces squadrons pushed back. Sometimes it was the annoying kid-brother treatment. We also worked with SEAL teams. A lot of the relationships depended on the FOB, who was around, and whether or not our company commander wanted to work with the SEALs. Certainly, we might not have looked as "pretty" as Army Special Forces but we were just as effective. Our biggest problem, if there was one, was the turnover rate and age. In general, our Rangers were between 19 and 24 years old with limited experiences in life and in the military. So, some of the Army Special Forces raised big question marks about us. But there was always a team

After finishing up training it is customary to take platoon pictures; this one was taken on the beach at Camp Rilea, Oregon, circa 2000. (Nicholas Moore)

Ranger School Graduation Class 11-01 (I am on the third row, sixth from the right). (U.S. Department of Defense photo)

Platoon Leadership 2010–2011 with the 1st Platoon, Bravo Company battle flag. Front row (left to right): Mike, David. Back row: Me, Nick "Nasty," Brandon, Jake. (Brandon McClure)

Pulling security during the Iraq invasion. This photo was taken while waiting for the link-up of other Ranger elements involved in the jump on H1 (desert landing strip). Later this day would begin our slow crawl back to friendly lines, and ultimately a follow-on to rescue Private First Class Jessica Lynch. (Nicholas Moore)

First Platoon picture taken at one of Saddam Hussein's many palaces in Baghdad, Iraq. This palace had been claimed as a Command Headquarters for members of the 1st Armored Division, who are not seen in this photo, as they had found the boat house and were enjoying a little water skiing. (Nicholas Moore)

Battalion photo taken prior to redeployment home. After shuttling the Battalion to the Crossed Sabers military parade field in Bagdad, we took Company and Battalion (minus) pictures. I am sitting on the Bradley fighting vehicle on the right side of the picture. (Nicholas Moore)

Rangers "consolidate the force" on day one of the winter strike, before moving by Hilux pick-up into the Kantiwa River Valley. Sergeant Jay Blessing would be killed the next morning. (Casey Davis)

Moving by Hilux pick-up up into the Kantiwa River Valley. The road network to get to our starting point was too narrow for HUMVEEs. (Casey Davis)

In typical Afghanistan mountain village construction, villages are terraced onto the mountainside. While waiting to cross a one-vehicle bridge, Casey snaps a quick picture. (Casey Davis)

The convoy stops short of the next picture location, and leadership sorts out sleeping arrangements. It's a great opportunity to stretch after a cramped day-long ride. (Casey Davis)

Getting ready to sleep for the night. This photo was taken from the guard post on the second day of the winter strike. The next day, we would start patrolling in the mountains, up into the snow of the Kantiwa River Valley. (Casey Davis)

Chris (platoon sergeant, 3rd Platoon) and Casey (squad leader, 1st Squad) converse about blowing up the small mortar cache we found. (Casey Davis)

Afghanistan rush hour. Casey decides to try and pet the livestock as Afghan herders move the goats down the trail we are walking up. (Casey Davis)

Slow and steady is the pace for patrolling in the Kantiwa River Valley, as fast isn't possible with 90–120-pound rucks. (Casey Davis)

Afghans hired to pack mules (or donkeys in this case) work out the logistical loads for the donkeys. Rangers in the foreground enjoy the time out from under the rucks and equipment. (Casey Davis)

A short halt during movement to take off "snivel gear" (cold weather gear). Overheating from too much cold weather clothing is always a concern. (Casey Davis)

Casey sucking wind after our mad dash up the mountain to reinforce 1st Platoon (on our "down day") after they called up a compromise, only for us to watch them drinking tea as we gasp for breath. (Casey Davis)

SEALs hate to walk. Instead of walking across the valley, SEALs waited for a helo to ferry them to target. (Nicholas Moore)

Rangers watching the SEALs' helo insertion. This was our first morning in the Pesch River Valley. (Casey Davis)

Me (front left) with members of 2nd and 3rd Squads and the platoon headquarters element who recovered Marcus Luttrell. This picture was taken once word was given we would be relieved in place. We wait for darkness to move to the exfil location.
(Nicholas Moore)

Vehicle PMCS time in Mosul, as we prepare for the day's missions to come. After PMCS is complete, there's always time to reminisce and talk about things from times past and what plans everyone has for after the deployment.
(Jason Conde)

A platoon photo in front of the SOF memorial at Bagram airfield, July 2005. This was taken after the recovery of Turbine 33 and Marcus Luttrell. Platoon baseball hats have always been popular, usually for personal wear. They are never authorized for uniforms, unless for platoon pictures. (Nicholas Moore)

Standing on the flight line in Mosul (2006), waiting on the Black Hawks to arrive before some "in-country" Fast Rope Insertion Extraction System (FRIES) rehearsals. I am wearing the soft armor carrier and sporting our platoon patch. (Casey Davis)

Fast-rope training in Mosul. Rangers work on their speed while clearing the aircraft. (Casey Davis)

Perimeter security on the narrow city streets of Mosul. Some streets would only allow us a foot of clearance on each side. (Casey Davis)

Me (left) and Nick, photo op during site exploitation on a daytime operation. (Casey Davis)

Me (left) and Mitch (not Catfish), photo op on the same objective as in the previous photo in Mosul. (Casey Davis)

Waiting on QRF allows the opportunity for a quick squad photo. From left to right: Front row: David, Casey, Me. Second row: Ryan, Mitch, Nick, Josh, Erich, Anousa. Back row: Unknown, Cesar. (Casey Davis)

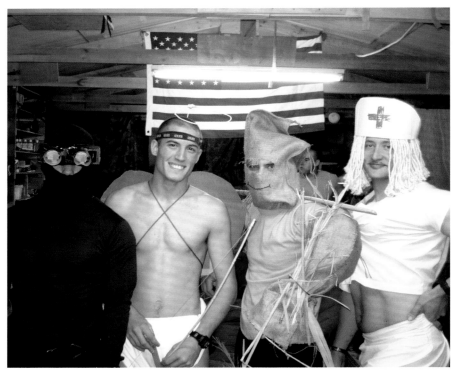

October 2006 in Ramadi would spark a "costume contest" for the privates, judged by the platoon leader and platoon sergeant. The winner would get a month off from typical details assigned to them. These are 3rd Squad's entries. From left to right: Splinter cell, cherub angel, scarecrow, and Nick the Nurse, who would be the victor! (Casey Davis)

The battalion standing in formation: from left to right, companies A–E and HHC. This photo was taken in summer of 2009, before the demolition of the original battalion headquarters building. (Nicholas Moore)

Our 2009–10 platoon photo, taken on the Range (FOB Salerno) during
my first deployment as platoon sergeant. I am eighth from the left. Everyone loves the
"Band of Brothers"-style photo (Nicholas Moore)

The next seven photos show 1st Platoon, Bravo Company during the CAPEX 2011 at Fort
Bragg, North Carolina. This event lasted a week, with only one hour of mandatory exhibition a
day. The rest of the time was spent on the ranges, preparing for the upcoming deployment.
(U.S. Army photo by Sergeant First Class Michael R. Noggle/CC BY 2.0)

CAPEX 2011. Pulling security and preparing to move to breach, Rangers show how business is done. (U.S. Army Photo by Trish Harris-Brownlee/CC BY 2.0)

leader and squad leader right there to ensure there were no young Ranger "issues."

During the early part of the GWOT our equipment started to change as well, in part because of the IED threat. There were small things; for example, if you were not an 84mm recoilless rifle or Carl Gustav gunner you did not receive ear plugs unless you got your own. Body armor remained the same, but the ballistic plates themselves were updated. But real changes to the equipment occurred after 2004, when our load-bearing carriers were updated. Before this, we had been allowed to purchase some LCE gear from civilian vendors. Off-the-shelf, tactical load-bearing equipment, such as chest racks, was far better than the official LCE of old as well as the Modular Lightweight Load Carrying Equipment (MOLLE) system offered by the Army.

The battalion had previously tested some MOLLE systems in early 2000 and it was universally disliked. Nonetheless, the MOLLE was issued and deviated from our previously standardized LCE. The MOLLE was badly designed; the pouches were particularly bad and Rangers simply did not want to use the system, preferring shoulder and chest rigs which were easy to put on and take off. Speed was essential in combat, especially when changing magazines. It was also easier to cross-load, or trade equipment when the situation arose, which usually happened when guys were required to be gunners on vehicles. The MOLLE had to be taken off like a jacket. During the early days Rangers patched it together to be more functional, but, in reality, the changes we made were only band aids to a far larger problem. New equipment slowly reached the regiment's inventory and because of that we were authorized to wear our older-style issued LCE or were allowed to purchase some from civilian vendors. My civilian-bought version lasted nearly five years. A modular system allowed us to tailor pouches and loads to our unique weapons systems. For example, instead of wearing a 203 grenade vest, we could use a belt which held the 203 rounds and kit up as a standard rifleman carrying the belt over the shoulder. Basically, you looked and dressed like riflemen except for the ammo belt of 203 rounds. It was much easier to individually tailor your gear to your actual job within the squad. I only wore the old Kevlar-styled "Fritz" helmet for about six months. This was replaced by the Advanced Combat Helmet, which, in turn, was eventually replaced by the Modular Integrated Communications Helmet (MICH) in 2012.

During the opening stages of the GWOT we were still light, because our lineage and heritage was based on being the best light infantry unit in the world. To that end, our vehicles had to be mobile and light, but our open-air gun trucks became heavier. But at the same time the armored HUMVEEs were not heavy enough for the types of combat missions we were increasingly executing. Our vehicle platform changed in the mid-2000s to include Mine-Resistant Ambush Protected vehicles (MRAPs) and Strykers. A lot of time was spent learning how to operate the heavy vehicles. Previously a driving course lasted a week, but now Rangers no longer conducted in-house driving courses; instead, we had to attend an actual on-post school for a month. This ate into the training cycle, and frankly, it became a bit too much, but you did learn the ins and outs of the vehicles including their limitations.

●●●

In Afghanistan we suffered a lack of great missions due to a poor understanding about how the enemy operated. Everything became more fluid, and passing intel down to the units was not as quick as the fast-changing battlefield conditions. Early on, the information technology bubble that was available was not as good as it is today. As years went on and the wars progressed, we were able to track patterns and networks – where did this guy operate and how? That is how we ultimately developed tier-targeting of individuals.

But morale was good at Charlie Company because during our first deployment to Iraq we got to see and do some things. Our short surge of 45 days allowed us to step in and fill gaps while other elements stood down and relocated. The quality of our senior leaders was usually very good. Of course, there was always one bad battalion commander, but for one bad one you did get a number of great ones.

Back at Fort Lewis, where I had started as a private first class and was now a 23-year-old sergeant, questions were being asked about my possible future career in the Ranger Battalion. "What are your plans? Are you going to stay Ranger or get out or what? Or are you joining Army Special Forces?" I had no intention to go to Army Special Forces Selection. My thinking was simply if Rangering stopped being fun, then I would either get out of the Army or perhaps consider joining other SOF units. But it was always great, always fun, and I enjoyed the job at hand, such as training privates and seeing them grow. When I was a platoon sergeant it was immensely gratifying to see them rise from privates to team leaders and squad leaders. They developed into first-rate Ranger leaders who were capable, confident, competent, and intelligent, unafraid to question the validity of a mission, to challenge procedures with better ones, and to never forget that a target has to be worth the risk to his men.

We dove back into our training cycle of platoon live-fires, TST missions, and generally putting the platoon in pressure-cooker situations to find out how many missions we could plan and execute in a 24-hour period. This was always fun because we were pretty much guaranteed at least four missions, but like anything Ranger, it became a competition. Some platoons really clicked, planning and executing upwards of six graded training missions in 24 hours. We required a quick operational mindset that we started to roll on and it became easy to figure out. We were always under the watchful eyes of the battalion staff, observing the platoons clear buildings amongst a myriad of other missions.

Eventually we deployed in July to Mosul, Iraq, and our first deployment set up our successes when we revisited the city in 2006 and 2008.

CHAPTER SIX

FAST AND FURIOUS

Mosul Part One, Iraq, 2004

We always trained for every deployment, but in general terms we could not train for any particular city. Overall we rehearsed as we normally did but with the addition of a few specific tasks, such as mobility platforms. The HUMVEE was still the platform of choice in Afghanistan, and we still used it in Iraq as well, but the Stryker was the main vehicle in Iraq, with all the abilities and limitations it brought along.

We traveled to Iraq from Fort Lewis through Germany. Germany was always fun because we got to catch up with the other battalions deploying back home and we managed to find the time to chat with guys we had not seen in years. Flying from Germany to Iraq took about four to six hours, in contrast to a flight to Afghanistan, which lasted a full eight hours. We traveled directly into Mosul.

This first deployment to Mosul was not that eventful but it did set up and help all our deployments to this town in northern Iraq. Our HUMVEEs were still our platform and pretty much drove on any parts of the street and the city. By doing this we figured out what roads supported what kind of vehicles during different weather conditions. On this deployment Charlie Company split between Ramadi and Baghdad for 1st and 2nd Platoon and Mosul for 3rd Platoon.

On September 21, 2004, Charlie Company saw its first KIA, Private First Class Nathan E. Stahl, after an IED exploded near his vehicle in Ramadi. The IED threat continued to grow over the years.

Our three-month deployment into Mosul had us located at the northern end of the town. Mosul at the time had two FOBs, Diamondback at the Airhead, an airfield, and Camp Liberty. After our deployment, Camp Liberty was eventually shut down to consolidate forces. Two days after our departure from Camp Liberty it was hit hard by mortars. Mortars were a big threat in Mosul and in Iraq in general. You could almost set your clock to it – virtually every time we would sit down to eat chow we heard the mortars. Their crews were not that good, but they were slowly starting to dial the rounds in. Breakfast, lunch, and dinner were always accompanied by mortar rounds. The rule was that you were supposed to duck under the table if rounds were impacting outside. But honestly, what's a plastic table going to do? We just sat there and continued to eat, while laughing at the Big Army units diving under a plastic table. We almost always got a "talking to" by a first sergeant or command sergeant major, to which we politely asked the clarifying question, "Is this table going to stop anything?"

We conducted primary maintenance on our vehicles, machine guns, and automatic grenade launchers during the mornings. We cleaned out the trucks, rotated water on and off them, and since there were concerns about potential fuel explosions we did not carry any fuel cans. Instead we fueled up every day at the depot. A new targeting system came into place while we were here and we worked hard to understand and grasp it as it was implemented. We worked through the hiccups of targeting based on signals intelligence, but this type of targeting was to pay major dividends in the years to come.

Early during our tasking in Mosul we were attached to Army Special Forces. Our jobs usually involved lots of blocking positions while they executed their part of the mission. As our platoon sergeant knew a number of the Army Special Forces operators and because they eventually noticed that we were pretty good at our jobs, we were asked to execute similar missions as they had. From then on, we stopped providing street-corner blocking positions and began clearing buildings. We moved off the streets and stomped in doors and executed the missions in a way similar if not identical to that of Army Special Forces. Signals targeting was new and our ability to use it was not yet as refined as it ultimately became. In the beginning we cleared three, four, or even five target buildings before hitting the correct one. Our missions were usually conducted at night, although some missions did run day and night. There was no real IED threat in Mosul itself at the time, so there was freedom of movement throughout the city any time of the day. It was almost always what we call a "semi-permissive" environment. For the first time the regular army Strykers operated in-country and we all capitalized on the space they created, wreaking havoc in the city. They owned the city and were pulling bad guys off as fast as we were – they accomplished this through their sheer firepower.

Time-permitting, we conducted weekly runs to the small military convenience store, the Post Exchange that was located at FOB Diamondback – again, the lack of IEDs allowed us the freedom to drive anywhere. We always went through a checklist before doing a PX run; for example, are we currently tracking a target? Is he a legacy target? Do we have dead time of say two to three hours, and if so then could we take the short trip to the PX to make a supply run? The drive there was always an early morning trip and then we were forced to wait for it to open. Occasionally it worked out that we hit the PX post-operation, since the detention facility was not far from it.

Although we used the mobility platform for most of our tasks or operations, we did occasionally conduct helicopter assault missions because at times this was the faster insertion method. It was a lot more fun in Iraq to fly in Black Hawks with feet hanging out the doors. It was exhilarating actually. The Black Hawks transported 12–15 heavily armed and equipped Rangers. Sometimes you got stuck with the platoon leader and his antenna farm, or the platoon sergeant and the medic. For us this meant one full rifle squad and a machine-gun team. Our platoon was almost full of its complement of men, although there were always Rangers who were off attending schools and a few who were getting ready to leave the Army.

We did not know this at the time but the War on Terror was still in its infancy, and by now private military contracting firms were pulling hard to get our guys and other SOF away from the Army. To accomplish this, ironically, they offered lucrative amounts of tax payers' money. A reasonably experienced man, intent on making money his priority, could make one million dollars over a two-year period. Naturally, the downside was that a well-trained soldier ended his career prematurely for money's sake and placed a strain on recruitment for the military. We did lose a few Rangers, mostly squad leaders not lower enlisted men, to these recruitment drives. When I bumped into them later they did say that contracting was great regarding money and health benefits, but in a gunfight there was no support whatsoever. For contractors there were no gunships or attack helicopters, never mind any armored vehicles. And this was before four contractors were killed in Fallujah in 2004. Being in the military certainly had its advantages when in combat. The contractors' experiences opened the eyes to some of the Rangers who were considering joining a private military contractor. The contractors' only chance to survive deadly combat was to scrape by until the Army maybe sent in a ground element to save them. This was always a long, drawn-out process since the contractors don't answer to the Army and do not brief their missions. So, knowing where they were, or what they were doing, proved difficult at best, especially when they were already in a fight and asking for help.

As mentioned previously, we started our deployments by providing extra muscle to Army Special Forces. We provided security and blocking positions, while the others executed their surgical strikes. But after we earned their confidence and respect we ended up running side-by-side missions. We hit other buildings down the street or next door to them. This made sense, as intermingling the two units was not the best way forward because each had different SOPs, different ways to execute the precise mission. Rangers handled the very same missions but not quite to the level of the performance of Army Special Forces at this time. This wasn't due to a lack of experience, but a difference in SOPs, and the speed with which they cleared the target. They were fluid like water, while we were more methodical. This would change quickly over the coming deployments. But this was the beginning and within a few short years we became an exceptional unit, sneaking into buildings or executing missions with the violence of action when required.

We operated with SEAL teams and Army Special Forces squadrons and for the most part it was great to operate alongside them, to see their TTPs, pick up a few tricks, and hopefully not pick up any of their bad habits. Other times, not so much. You could tell a lot based on how they briefed their missions and how they conducted themselves in the FOBs. There was a level of professionalism one expected from the higher-tiered SOF elements, whether Army Special Forces or other teams, but some SEALs believed in their self-created Hollywood legacy. This was more of a SEAL team issue and much less so with Army Special Forces since a lot of their operators were former Rangers who understood our skill level. As we cycled up as the war continued our new Rangers were trained harder than anybody else Army Special Forces ran with. On the few days we had no missions we would be training, from range time to dry rehearsals, all to ensure a high level of proficiency for every Ranger. Our new privates were going to get it right and we repeated drills constantly because repetition creates perfection. Occasionally an operator joined us at the range, not to teach us, but just to shoot. However, it usually turned into an impromptu shooting class with new drills or techniques. It was always a huge learning curve, but since the basics were mastered, it didn't take long to implement anything gleaned from them. We kept at it and, worst case, we moved some not so great Rangers to the trucks to avoid them becoming a tactical problem. It was never really an issue for us. We asked ourselves, could we operate without him? Is he better suited in the arms room? Often these Rangers proved to be exceptional in their new tasks. Others may simply have needed time to mature and would later return to the rifle squads. These in-house moves subsequently yielded some very good Rangers.

This deployment was also great in that we finally had about 90–95 percent of a company's manning roster. During my time we had maybe one to two deployments, with a larger contingent of something more like 13-man squads instead of the prescribed ten, including the squad leader, which was great. In 2008–2009 the Army began to downsize but in 2005 a lot of new Rangers came into the regiment. Whereas incorporating one or two new privates was easy, trying to bring up three to four new Rangers was quite a task. As a team leader or squad leader you had to keep an eye on them to see what level they were at and what kind of training they needed to reach the high Ranger Standard. During this deployment my platoon, 3rd of Charlie Company, had about 80 percent veterans with prior overseas experience.

Unlike other units, our mission success was not measured by the body count on target. Do not get me wrong, whacking bad guys was great and taught you about your own abilities in combat. It teaches you how you would do in a fight, which is crucial to know in our line of work. But the single biggest problem with killing them was that no intelligence for other targets was secured. For us, then, the game was to secure new intelligence, which meant bigger risk to the force when you want to capture instead of kill the target. This risk was acceptable to us, as it continued to drive the targeting train for new and better targets.

We attempted to be as surreptitious as possible to get into the target unobserved, secure prisoners, and glean intelligence, so that we could find more bad guys to chase down. Our learning curve was extreme, and we were taught and taught ourselves the tricks of sneaking into buildings without the enemy ever knowing we were there. We woke them up as we rolled them over to flexicuff them. Usually there was an AK or some type of small arm right next to them. During this type of op, we had one Ranger provide security as the others tied the bad guys up. From there they were loaded onto trucks and sent back to the base for further intel.

We typically ran four, five, sometimes six missions a night, but we were really setting up the next platoons of the next Ranger battalions by building the intelligence and target net. We created new SOPs on entering buildings silently – things like how to climb over fences, how to get the assault force into a compound without smashing and blowing our way into the target building. Eventually, we perfected the art of getting the assault force into houses fairly quietly. All our new methods and experiences were rolled into a new way to breach the building instead of our traditional door charges combined with our screaming and yelling like we had done in the old days.

Army Special Forces also spent a couple of hours demonstrating various techniques on ladders and climbing which would prove to be crucial, not only in Iraq, but also in Afghanistan, where compound walls surrounded most buildings. We didn't have ladders and we solved this problem by building our own old-fashioned ones. To be sure they were ugly and nothing like the high-speed ladders we eventually used, and yes, we looked like bums carrying them around during our missions, but they provided us with what we needed. We also learnt body techniques and equipment setups, including how to handle rifles during infil. Army Special Forces operators had spent years perfecting the ins and outs of these techniques. The Rangers normally did not have that time during our training cycles, but teaching us would prove to be beneficial to us all.

The command allowed Army Special Forces not to worry about the number of missions they pulled and increasingly gave us more lower and mid-level targets to hit. We pulled a number of missions, especially in Mosul, while Army Special Forces just sat around. Rangers were running and gunning every night!

Mid-deployment we received new ear protection, as the Army could no longer ignore the damage to our hearing during combat and, eventually, because of the number of exploding IEDs. It was more cost effective to get new protection than it was to make disability payments. The new ones were amplified hearing protection earmuffs with speakers built in. Anything shooting over 80 decibels shut them off. Our comms were hardwired into the headset. Our original ones were not comfortable at all. They were manufactured of thick plastic instead of thin steel, and we had spent a lot of time trying to make them suitable for long-term wear. We managed to wear them for about two to three hours before a migraine set in. Rangers experiment and we moved pads around within our Kevlar helmet, and removed the crown pad and adjusted the oval pads. Some guys attached Velcro to the old K-pot bump-outs for the ears. The newer MICH helmet, when it was introduced in 2012, also had the same ear bumps, which led to a permanent Velcro contraption for the whole thing to be held in place inside the helmet. In effect, the new ear protection with comms and helmet became a one-piece item. It always drove the first sergeants and command sergeant major nuts. There were thoughts by higher command that this might change the ear protection's ability to "seal" during an explosion.

After this deployment we received two different plate carriers as part of improvements to our body armor. One was the second-generation plate carrier system in camouflage, whereas the previous one had been "Ranger Green." There were no big Velcro straps around the sides, which we preferred, as it allowed the body and the clothes to breathe while the plates stayed where they needed to be. The MOLLE system was gradually getting replaced by our own regimental changes. There was one more releasable plate carrier nobody liked and it lasted maybe two years. This four-piece system was always good for a laugh with those who had to wear it and was usually based on the non-availability of the correct size. Can you imagine the look? The system had a "quick release" cable that ran inside the carrier. During the "inspection," a squad leader or platoon sergeant often pulled the release cable. This became a classic joke with the non-commissioned officers that never got old. They would have this puzzled look and question the "functionality," which led to the "Hey, you come here" kind of attention best avoided by junior enlisted personnel. They had their fun. But the growing trend was for mobility and the ability to dump the gear quickly. This was tragically illustrated by an incident in Iraq when a few soldiers in their vehicle ended up in an irrigation canal and drowned because they were not able to easily get rid of their combat gear. Hence, a releasable system with a cord, similar to an H-harness we used for parachuting with a quick-release system.

Our use of HUMVEEs in Iraq in 2004 was an eye-opening experience, as we were trying to teach Rangers how to drive in chaotic city traffic. Strykers had not yet been transitioned to us. Although there was a fairly decent road network it did not help because nobody obeyed any traffic laws whatsoever. We spent considerable time and energy learning how to drive during normal day-time traffic. Things were crazy but mostly just annoying since nobody stopped at intersections, stop lights or signs.

• • •

During our deployment we had a day strike force and a night strike force. It was always easier to operate at night – that was our specialty. Catching bad guys in daylight was far harder. We had no gunfights in general since sneaking in was a lot safer. There was a lot of positive in not getting into gunfights; it was not only safer but far more effective. The Ranger "smash and grab" was gone since killing people was no longer the dynamic. Accomplishing the mission and gathering intel were of the utmost importance. And that's how success was now measured by Rangers. We had been forced to perfect our craft. It was almost viewed as a failure if we did get into a fight. Intelligence gathering was the primary, most important, effort.

Once intel was back at the Task Force any pertinent information was pulled out and passed to respective strike forces. If there was an overlap – as in, near an already established target, for example – any strike force within that targeting bubble received that intel. For example, we received intelligence on cells operating in certain areas like Tirkut or Mosul, or intel on the guys who ran the entire country gamut, or specific targets north to south or out west in Ramadi.

The card deck of the most wanted was long gone and nobody was chasing the Republican Guards. Instead, the focus was on insurgent networks. Slowly it came to light how big they actually were and how smaller networks intertwined with larger ones. Every city received its own little network of targets.

There was a big target, Abu Musab al-Zarqawi, a main Jordanian jihadist and major insurgency leader, who eventually would get blown up in a building with a targeted airstrike. There had been a few foreign fighters at the beginning of the war. Fallujah and Ramadi, western cities, had bigger engagements. Things ramped up as more foreign fighters stopped there. A few trickled into Baghdad but not so many into the north such as Mosul or Tel Afar.

Late in our deployment we assisted the Battlespace Owner (BSO) in the re-clearance of Tel Afar, a town west of Mosul. Our tasking was to establish and secure blocking positions on the south side of town, and to provide "precision fires" using snipers and an AC-130 gunship to facilitate the BSO's re-clearance of the town. We planned the operation to take one day. This was to be done with Army Special Forces and a squad-sized element of Rangers. We knew it was about prioritizing intel and targeting. There was a stockpile of intel and data on targets thanks to "shelving," a system where multiple targets were tracked in 24 hours until the intel section thought they had a good enough pattern for striking. We teamed up with the BSO and shot over there and conducted building clearance, security, and sniper-clearance operations for about 24 hours in total. We drove in before dawn and established our blocking position. We dismounted the vehicles and set our security position. During the pre-assault fires we observed a lot of movement in and around a shipping yard, so we cleared fire with the AC-130 and had them open up on the shipping yard. During the pre-assault fires one of the rounds hit a fuel storage tank and sent up huge "Hollywood" fireballs. A few precise rounds from snipers over the next few hours and that was mission complete. From our position outside of town and on the high ground, it was, in my opinion, painful to watch the BSO clear through the town. It was slow and seemed to stall and lose the initiative several times. Mainly I think this was due to not having a strong delineation of sectors between the ground units and the officers in charge of the operation. Late in the afternoon, we packed up our blocking position and started our vehicle movement down away from our blocking position. But our op ended on a stupid note. We decided to go a different route back, a straighter one, and shot back to the highway. The vehicle driver decided the best way to navigate through a wadi was to just punch the throttle and launch the vehicle straight through the wadi. Unsurprisingly, we got a flat tire and our vehicle had to get trailered back to Mosul because we didn't have a spare. So, what did that mean? Double the amount of people crammed into one truck. The drive took about 45 minutes. Not fun.

A word on our snipers. We had a higher turnover of snipers than Army Special Forces, and we had far less time to get specifically tailored sniper training within our training cycles. Army Special Forces could perfect their snipers, while our Rangers had to deal with basic coursework and a combination of numerous other classes. There was always a push to get snipers to Special Operations Command Sniper School, but there were only so many allocated slots per class, and our numbers still had to remain at an operational level. However, most of our snipers were capable and competent to hold that job title even if they had not attended Special Operations Command Sniper School. They had attended the Army's Sniper School, but getting guys cycled into the Special Operations Command course, with its limited spaces, lasted a full eight weeks, which was difficult when operational manning levels still had to be maintained.

Our designated marksmanship course was run by snipers who had a couple of years of long gun experience, and they taught team leaders and privates the finer arts of shooting tailored to specific missions. For example, a target in Iraq was usually well within 300 meters. You shot once, missed, but the second shot would hit. In Afghanistan, on the other hand, 600–800 meters was common, but this is an extremely long shot for an M4. But it is not impossible if the shooter understands the limitations of optics and ammunitions. You had to combine that information and figure out how to fine-tune it all. Afghanistan FOBs had space and you could put ranges anywhere, so if there was terrible weather to launch a mission we might have the day off and conduct trigger time on the range. The guys had to be sharp on what it took to shoot first and hit first. We started with CQB 25-meter battle drills, then moved on to 600–800-meter targets, where we worked out the finer fundamentals of marksmanship, including aiming, trigger control, breathing, and squeezing. A lot of it was teaching limitations and capabilities of the weapons. But the most important thing taught to the individual Ranger was understanding their personal limitation on the weapon. Another platoon executed this in combat. There was enemy contact within machine-gun range, and the Rangers placed all machine guns online as the platoons moved to within rifle range to kill the contact. This kind of thinking was great. The platoon sergeant figured out how to use both the machine guns and the low ground to allow the Rangers to close in and execute the fight.

There was exponential growth from 2002 to 2004. The individual had to have the ability to learn and adapt on the fly. Before the war, it could take an entire Army career to become a sergeant first class or a platoon sergeant (E-7), but by now you achieved that rank in seven to eight years, although no one can make E-7 faster than seven years because of time requirements in previous grades held. But you had to have the maturity to think outside the box and be able to interpret what was going on. You had to have the mental cues to read the situations as fast as possible, and the opportunities of war made this readily available. This huge learning curve was referred to as "drinking from the firehose," the process of changing TTPs, observing areas or techniques that needed change, making the change, training the change, and implementing the change.

Going to Iraq for a deployment, versus Afghanistan, was sometimes the deciding factor for a Ranger who was on the bubble about reenlistment. Iraq had the excitement, the high-octane mission tempo that we all loved. Iraq, no matter the year, was fun, fast-paced, and had all the thrills. In comparison, Afghanistan was considered boring, with maybe one mission every week or sometimes you had to wait even longer. Afghanistan was great for the guys who liked weight lifting and working on their beach muscles, as they got plenty of time to do that from 2004 to 2006. Afghanistan "boredom" was due to a lack of targets. Technology hadn't caught up over there yet, so it was still very slow going in terms of collecting targetable intelligence.

The time had come for us to go home. We would see a lot of Mosul over the next years. Those would be some of the best and most exciting deployments for us.

PART THREE

STAFF SERGEANT – SQUAD LEADER

CHAPTER SEVEN

THROUGH THE LOOKING GLASS

Afghanistan, 2005

Our deployments were routine by now – packing and unpacking. Every six months we deployed for three. I was the squad leader, a 24-year-old staff sergeant, for 3rd Squad, 3rd Platoon, Charlie Company, when we headed back to Afghanistan in April 2005. It rained and snowed in the early part of that spring and it was one of the most boring deployments to date. Nothing happened. The conventional Army guys did not get up to much either. Our mood was not the best and we conducted a lot of training and spent considerable time on shooting ranges at Bagram. Our company had two rifle platoons in place. One was on stand-by for quick-reaction TSTs; the other was tasked with CSAR. CSAR used to be a platoon task trained at the start of every operational cycle. However, with the GWOT taskings and training, CSAR got pushed aside to open up time for other, more urgent, training tasks. CSAR training essentially started with the inventory of equipment, the explanations of each items and their intended use, and included things from lift bags to crash axes. You also learnt to walk around the various aircraft, identifying emergency exit handles and locations as well as destruction points for the aircrafts should that be needed in case the aircraft and equipment were at risk of capture by the enemy.

In Afghanistan, my platoon started as CSAR for the first six weeks, and then at the mid-point of our deployment we switched tasking with 1st Platoon.

One of the good things that came out of this slow operational cycle was that we had a solid CSAR tasking in-theater and we spent quality time handling the kit. We conducted rehearsals and worked through some of the tasks we used to train on before the GWOT had interrupted the training schedule.

Six weeks later we switched to time-sensitive tasking and ran the gamut from planning rehearsals to dry runs, from alerting to standing up the guys for "timetable checks." For certain missions there were preset standard timetables detailing alerts to mission launches. Every platoon had to conduct rehearsals to make sure they met those set timetables. We planned, prepared, and executed to hit TSTs. We even launched a couple of missions but nothing came out of them. TST planning and prepping took between one and two hours, while traveling to the target, using aircraft based at Bagram, would take at least a couple of hours. Targeting was good but nothing like it was in Iraq. Targets moved during the day and it was a lot harder to track. We began to track these moving targets by integrating the Intelligence, Surveillance, and Reconnaissance (ISR) platform. At the time there was a one- to two-minute time delay in the video feed. A Predator strike depended on good communications to avoid collateral damage, with the pilots having to wait on the go-ahead to engage. It was important to integrate all the assets. Up until recently ISR stayed only on stationary targets, but it became mobile as technology and integration advanced. New SOPs were drafted yet again.

We had to bide our time and occupied ourselves by going to the gym or by buying a lot of crap off the internet, like Harleys, since Army Air Force Exchange Services had overseas deals and you bought directly from the manufacturer with a huge discount. It turned into the middle of June and still nothing had happened. We wound down and we were ready to go home. We checked to see what training cycle we were to conduct back at Lewis. Some of us even planned and booked tickets for our annual block leave. We were ready to put this deployment behind us. One day we found a big turtle and painted our platoon's logo of a skull with a tan beret and crossbones on its shell. Like I said, things were slow, real slow.

But in the final days of our tour a SEAL team went out on a reconnaissance mission in Kunar Province. We did not receive the actual mission brief but we subsequently got word of their operation, *Red Wings*, once the SEAL team was already out on the ground. To us it didn't seem like the smartest idea to use such a small team when you had the ability to hide a far larger friendly element easily enough in the terrain, especially given that the JOC had estimated the enemy fighter threat to be in the region of 12–15 men. Our regiment's recce guys stated that they would have gone in with a rifle platoon in support based on the intel available. The platoon could have hidden maybe 1–2 klicks away and established a patrol base to support the recce team if it became compromised. We discussed this while eating chow. We continued to question the planning of the operation in general but not the mission itself. We also knew that they had their own internal QRF.

Nothing happened during the first night of Operation *Red Wings*. First Platoon was on the short string for CSAR and we, at 3rd Platoon, decided to go shoot for a couple of hours at a range about a 30-minute drive away. To go shooting almost required an operation order in itself. On June 28, 2005, we unloaded our targets from the pickup trucks and were ready to set them up. Before we began we checked in with the smaller Tactical Operations Center (TOC) and were ordered to return immediately. The JOC is the large command center usually headed by a colonel or above, while the TOC is smaller and usually headed by the platoon leader for a platoon TOC or by the company commander for a company-sized TOC. Clearly something bad had happened. We grabbed the range box, leaving the targets on site, figuring we could always build more. We raced our HUMVEEs back to Bagram.

Here we found out that the SEAL team had reportedly been in heavy contact. Their SEAL QRF had launched virtually immediately but its Chinook, Turbine 33, had been shot down. It was almost unbelievable.

At Bagram we immediately started spinning up on prep. It took a little bit of time to line up assets for us to launch the second rescue operation. We then heard that the original SEAL element had since dropped out of comms. We had already lost a helicopter in the area and that called for restrictive planning for all personnel involved. This meant that it was almost impossible to commit additional aircraft into the same area. This did not mean that air assets would not be committed at all, but it was crucial to ensure that sufficient air cover was committed to avoid taking further loss of aircraft. These were the lessons learnt from the Roberts Ridge incident at Takur Ghar in March 2002 during the early days of Operation *Enduring Freedom*, when helicopters had been shot down piecemeal.

First Platoon, on CSAR duty, was tasked to come in after we had cleared the way up to the crashed helicopter. They would be carrying a lot of gear. Contrary to popular belief, a body bag weighs about

35 pounds. I remember how surprised I was the first time I picked one up, expecting it to weigh just a few pounds. They are made of thick, durable, rip-stop material and are waterproof as they are designed to handle bio-hazardous remains. Unsurprisingly, 1st Platoon would be weighed down and slowed down by the amount of gear they had to transport.

We thought we might get into contact and modified our gear to the altitude driven by a necessity to move fast and not to be unnecessarily encumbered. Regimental SOP at elevations higher than 10,000 feet allowed us to request changes to our gear. We dropped the back-armor plates, which saved a few pounds, and slid the frontal plate directly into our chest rack instead of carrying the armor-plate-holding chest carrier. Our chest rack also held our ammunition. We packed our light assault packs for the original mission template for a 12- to 24-hour mission. Anything past that on the ground would be a problem. Our packing list included one meal, a few days' worth of water, and a couple of cans of Copenhagen. Our uniform had also been modified. The previous year a Ranger patrol was told by Pakistani guards that they had spotted them a long way out because the uniform did not break up the colors of the terrain the patrol traveled in. On this rescue our platoon wore the greenish-brown battle dress uniform (BDU) top with desert camouflage bottoms. The top blended in far better with the foliage of the trees and the trousers with the ground colors found in higher elevations.

We loaded onto the aircraft and we were ready to go, but at the last minute we were told to cut a squad's worth of Rangers before we would be able to lift off. It turned out that we needed to drop weight for the altitude we were to fly in and everyone wanted to cycle the troops in as fast as possible to avoid increasing the helicopter's exposure time. Every rifle squad was comprised of one squad leader and four Rangers, a machine-gunner, and his assistant gunner. Half of our platoon stayed behind. That sucked for them. The decision was about picking the best Rangers, the most senior in each squad, who didn't need extra attention. In the end we had about 30 guys for the platoon, including machine-gunners, medical personnel, communications, and other personnel add-ons.

We launched straight into the target area over the mountains, which could have been any mountain range in the U.S. It was not uncommon in Afghanistan to have mountain showers during the summer because clouds needed to drop water to clear over the high mountain ranges. And, of course, this blocked us from getting on target. Instead, due to the fog and poor weather conditions, we landed at Jalalabad for more intel briefings. Back then you needed Top Secret clearance for the JOC and so information filtered down slowly to the junior enlisted personnel. Later on in the war intel briefs were based on platoon-level TOCs open to all personnel.

The crash of Turbine 33, our aborted insertion and subsequent move to Jalalabad all occurred on June 28. We spent several hours there getting the bigger picture and by this stage ISR footage was up. We continued to receive the latest information overnight and through the next day, including target updates. We were finally given the green light to launch. We loaded back in for the 30–45-minute flight into the target area. We launched at dusk on June 29, 2005.

We had planned for the helicopter to land in a clearing which had looked suitable as an HLZ, but as we approached a large woodpile in the middle of it forced us to quickly adjust. The pile had not been evident during our planning stage so now we would have to fast-rope in. This would prolong the offloading and would expose the helicopter to potential threats for longer than we cared. But Rangers are fast at clearing a helo. In general, we could empty a Black Hawk within ten seconds and larger helicopters in less than 60 seconds, but it always felt like an eternity when in a combat zone. Nobody likes inserting into a potential beehive.

It was Afghanistan-black and we hovered at 60 feet. My NODs were flipped up for the fast-rope because using them created a depth-perception problem. I felt the helicopter drift slightly during the hover as was the norm. So far so good. We tossed out the 4-inch round-blended rope to begin our descent. Red and green chemlights at the bottom of the rope allowed us to see that the rope was long enough to reach the ground properly. Otherwise one could easily freefall if the rope was too short. At the top of the rope was a blue chemlight. It was the marker for us to reach and grab the rope safely. I reached for it, swung out, and slid down, squeezing my boots together to slow down my descent. Your hands should act more as a guide than a brake. Some of our guys had never fast-roped beyond 30 feet. In Iraq we had roped in from 10 to 30 feet straight onto the rooftops of our target buildings. In Afghanistan, on the other hand, we looked at 60, 90, even 120 feet. On this insertion we used 90-foot ropes, which allowed for insertions between 60 and 90 feet. It was hard on our leather work gloves, hard on our hands. Some Rangers carried a 27-pound machine gun and three to four 100-round belts of 7.62mm ammunition, each belt weighing in at 7 pounds. There was a ton of friction for the machine-gunner but it wasn't much better for the rest of us. Some guys fell off the rope because they simply could not hold onto it any longer – their hands burnt up over the long distance of the insertion. I used my lightweight shooting gloves, which also meant I did not squeeze the rope as hard as if I had worn leather gloves over my shooting ones. Nonetheless, my hands still got very hot as I slid down the nylon rope. I managed to avoid blisters but definitely felt the heat.

We had no major injuries during the insertion, so we pushed on, up the side of the rise. We moved north, and when we looked east across the big draw we were walking up, we spotted the crash site. It was burning. We all felt a rush; we were close. We made our way to the top of the mountain and then across it to secure the site. It had taken about five hours of continuous climbing.

In the meanwhile, 1st Platoon cycled in but they fast-roped at a higher location – badly. The weight they humped was substantial. It meant less of a climb for them, but their 90–120-foot fast rope had some Rangers fall off. The heat created from the friction had burnt through some of the leather work gloves. These were not just a few men with cuts and bruises. Their radio telephone operator fell off and landed at the base of the rope on his back like a turtle, and before he could scramble away his very large platoon sergeant crushed down on him and broke the radioman's forearm. There were ankle injuries and broken arms which needed medevac, but they were just patched up and moved on. Ranger! There was no exfil that day. The next day the radio telephone operator was physically escorted onto the aircraft – he didn't want to leave.

We followed a small, nasty, goat trail. It was hard finding the trail with almost no illumination in the inky blackness of a rural Afghanistan night. And it was even harder to follow and keep on it. The terrain was full of fields riddled with nettles that stuck in us, stinging and burning for hundreds of meters. It sucked. Bagram was at half the elevation of where we were now. The crash had happened at about 10,000 feet at the top of the ridge of the mountain. We had fast-roped in at 7,500–8,000 feet, and breathing to keep up the constant pace was difficult. Our gas tanks were on empty. We had no stops all night but did slow down to keep the heavily loaded guys, like the gunners, apace. Those Rangers would be vital in any gunfight and we needed them to remain combat effective. We spent most of the night traveling to the top of the ridge. Then we moved across it and around the bowl on top of the ridge. Two of our squads over-watched the first squad's "movement-to-contact" as they cleared the objective. We hunkered down in a loose patrol base around the site and waited for 1st Platoon of Charlie Company.

Eventually everyone showed up around the site. First Platoon arrived at sunrise. It had taken them a lot longer to make it since they carried the heavy body bags, their regular combat gear, and the mission essential equipment for CSAR. Even though they chopped down their gear it still weighed an awful lot. They went right to work and the recovery of the remains had priority. All the bodies were on the side of the mountain. There wasn't a fuselage left; it had all burnt. The only recognizable parts left of the helicopter were the rotor blades and the turbine engines.

We had a solid location but no idea what was going on with the missing SEAL recon team on the ground. While 1st Platoon worked on the recovery of the site, we, 3rd Platoon, provided security, established good lines of sight, and conducted small patrols, within eyesight of our larger element, to recon the surrounding area.

On the north side of the top of the mountain there was a naturally occurring cave about the size of an average living room. This was my first experience with caves. In it we found a bed, a small handmade desk for laying out paperwork, and a place to eat. A cave in Afghanistan was a simple place to hide without any real infrastructure, nothing like what the Viet Cong had constructed in Vietnam. Some caves in Afghanistan were used as caches for weapons and ammo. In the cave we found a section of the fast rope the original insertion team had used. We thought it was an odd thing to find – it really was kind of eerie.

As the morning progressed we realized that this whole mountain was dedicated to fighting. The Afghans are not stupid and had plenty of experience of fighting against invaders. We found stacked rocks and natural-looking bunker systems, both of which were hard to identify on the ground and impossible to spot by fly-overs and our ISR assets. You simply did not see these types of fortifications from the sky – we barely did on the ground. By early afternoon 1st Platoon had accounted for 15 out of 16 remains. We were out of water and food and arranged for a combat delivery system resupply. Our radio telephone operator went down and relieved some of the guys of 1st Platoon. He carried a walking stick which he used to roll the turbine engine over, where he found the remains of the last man missing – not a lot of him was left. The remains easily fit into an MRE box – a section of spinal cord and ribcage. My guys were taken aback by this and we thought about how much heat had been cranked out of this fire – enough to incinerate bodies! This was the first crash we ever worked to this extent. Usually it was a simple crash, a hard break leaving the helicopter inoperable. But nothing like this. Most of us had expected something more intact like at Roberts Ridge or in Mogadishu, Somalia. Everybody had thought this recovery would be like it was in Mogadishu in 1993 when a Little Bird had crashed intact. A hard landing, with the guys either hurt or killed by the enemy. This was completely and totally the opposite of that. The helicopter was shot down, caught fire and burnt for 36 hours... it was bad. We accounted for the 16 men and lined them up at a small clearing by our Command Post (CP).

●●●

We then began combat patrols, with 1st Platoon assigned to clear a village down the hill and us moving back to the top of the mountain. Charlie Company's first sergeant, Bryan, grabbed hold of me and my buddy Jason, who was also a squad leader. Jason was a great Ranger, a Puerto Rican from Brooklyn, always slightly angry, and always quick with a comment whether you wanted one or not. He was an excellent tactician with a "lead from the front" attitude. We had both completed the Regimental Master Breacher Course a week earlier. This is an in-depth course about explosives and how to best use them for our purposes, particularly the math involved in the charge construction using explosives inside and outside of buildings, along with the traditional uses from World War II. Bryan ordered us to clear an area for an HLZ for the evacuation of the remains. We requested a pallet of explosives to clear the mountain and to accommodate several CH-47 Chinooks. We carefully built charges based on the math we had learned, but Bryan said not to waste time and to simply put a ton of explosives on the trees and pop them one after the other. But doing one at a time would take even more time, so in the end we daisy-chained the trees to blow them all up at once. There was a large tree stump in the middle of the clearing, perhaps 3–4 feet tall, where an animal had dug it out. We placed explosives into the burrow and blew it off the mountain like a Roman candle. Within an hour or two the HLZ was completed and the Chinooks were able to land safely.

As soon as we blew the last tree a radio telephone operator grabbed us for a new tasking. Two squads were to push off the mountain. All day we had heard something about someone pressing a talk button on the net but there had been no actual communications with the missing SEAL team. Our tasking was to go out there to confirm or deny whatever it was. Possibly the enemy had captured the radio equipment and American personnel. We packed up and checked on what we really needed to take with us. I was trying to think ahead as a squad leader to what we might encounter. We decided to leave our chest plates behind with the rest of the element. I was the only one who had brought an assault pack so we put all the plates in it. I took some Copenhagen and a couple of water bottles. And, just like it was done in Ranger School, the first sergeant counted us out of the patrol base as we began our patrol into the enveloping blackness of the mountain.

We moved down the trail side of the mountain as 1st Platoon came back up from their excursion of checking out the village. We high-fived and saw how badly they were sucking. At the time all I could sarcastically think was, *How awesome that we are going to walk that much if not more!* To make matters worse, we were hit by monsoon-style rain for the entire night. Our visibility was reduced to 1, maybe 2 meters. The trail turned into a river. We slipped and fell and laughed at one another, because if you do not find humor during this kind of miserable suck you should not have joined the Rangers. Inevitably, one of my guys disappeared into the night having slipped on the trail. "Hey, hold up – stop. We lost Nathan," I said. Suddenly I spotted the top of his helmet over the nearby rocks. Nathan is 6 feet tall. I asked him if he was okay and he said he was but that he was standing on a tiny lip with a hundred-foot drop. Mountains at night – not a great thing. We pulled him back up. I then radioed the platoon leader and said we needed to stop, that it was simply too dangerous to keep going. We moved a bit further down from a 10-meter-wide ridge trail to about a 20-meter-wide area, where our element spread out underneath three pine trees. Though it was summer, the mountains were cold. We tried to sleep. I wiped off my NODs and looked around. Unbelievably, I saw a lot of camp fires dotting the ridges around us – nothing so close that we could engage. The camp fires seemed hundreds of meters away. It was striking to think that they were either simple goat herders or Taliban keeping an eye on us. There were about six to a dozen such fires littering the ridges. Our forward observer marked the general locations with his GPS – you never know when you might need that information. Luckily, we did not have to sit there for an awful long time before the sun came up and the rain stopped. We took a moment to collect ourselves. We heard that a Green Beret ODA team was coming up the mountain but had somehow gotten lost. So, we stood there and waited for them to tie in with us since they clearly did not know what they were doing. As we waited, most guys took off their equipment to allow their BDU tops to dry. We also tried to dry off our socks. We looked like a gypsy camp for a short while before getting cleaned up.

Our platoon leader requested a resupply drop of water, chow, and batteries. The resupply duly came and the pallet landed in the only tree in the clearing, of course. It was stuck about 10–12 feet in the tree. The platoon leader wanted to request another drop to come in, but we didn't want to wait for them to build a new pallet at Bagram. Instead, I climbed the tree with my knife clenched between my teeth. As I started to cut away at the pallet, Mario, a tactically and technically competent Ranger team leader in 2nd Squad, came to help. The pallet overhung the ridge edge a little so we tried our best to cut in a manner that did not allow for the rations to roll down the mountain. We only took the minimum we needed. Pallets in general needed to weigh a certain amount to be dropped and this one had an excess number of MREs to make up the weight and we simply did not take them.

We were eating when the ODA team finally showed up. They explained to us what they saw on their trip up the mountain. That we should not go here or there, but we told them that since they had been lost for two days it did not matter what they had to say. We offered them the opportunity to tie in with us and come along on our mission or to follow the trail we had taken, to the left, to get to our element's CP at the crash site. They decided to stay with us.

By now two to three hours had passed since sun-up. It was a clear, beautiful day as we pushed down the mountain's side. After about 45 minutes we came onto the location we were supposed to explore. We made our way off the ridge, hopping boulders across a wash. When I write "boulders," they were in fact the size of small mobile homes. Our knees hurt from absorbing the impact of each leap.

We were a 13-man element and the ODA team had about eight guys. Jason and I spotted a village in our field of view. It was an average suburban city block size. There were probably about 20–30 buildings in this village. Jason and I discussed how best to approach the village. "Hey man, how do you want to hit this?" he asked. I suggested the best way to enter the village was for us to split up and clear from the ends of the village to the middle. I cleared from the top down with my squad while Jason took his team to the low side of the village and cleared in. We intended to meet in the middle. We were excited. Our pride swelled; we were going to get an American back under our control, so he was no longer alone. And we were finally getting to do "what we do" – clearing stuff the old-fashioned Ranger way. The ODA was all about hearts and minds and did not want to smash in doors, preferring to drink tea to talk about the missing American. Well, I was not going to do that. I said: "I'm an alpha male, Ranger, and we are going to look for the missing man and I am not going to have tea with people who may have killed Americans earlier. By all means go ahead." Green Berets – hearts and minds and all that stuff. Why not.

We cleared eight to ten houses in total, speaking simple English, explaining that we were looking for an American. We pointed to our

OPERATION *RED WINGS*

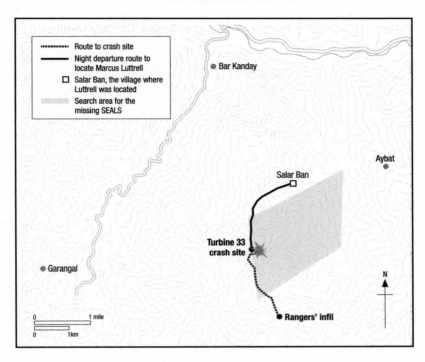

flags on our shoulders. It had been relayed to us that on the morning of the 28th, which now seemed a long time ago, a SEAL called Marcus Luttrell had written a short message, which had then been taken by a village elder to Asadabad about 32km away. This was apparently the village he was in.

Jason was at the bottom of the village and had cleared four to five buildings. Then he made the call – he had Marcus Luttrell! Marcus had, in fact, been hidden by the villagers in a kind of primitive cold storage cave near the river. He had sought refuge in the village, and thanks to their *Pashtunwali* culture – which states that all Pashtun are obliged to protect any guest, even at the risk of death – here he had remained, safe from the Taliban. Some villagers helped Luttrell walk up to meet the Rangers after the villagers had seen us arrive. It was at that point that Jason went down with Mario and took over. We apologized to everyone for smashing up some houses and informed them that the ODA team would supply the funds to cover the costs of repairing any of the minor damage caused.

We ran a number of challenges for soldiers missing in action to confirm that it was in fact him. After establishing his identity, we naturally asked Marcus where the rest of the team was. He then recounted his story of what had happened to him, the rest of his team, and the contact with the enemy. We discussed with Marcus the details of the SEAL mission and our own operation. He told us how the SEALs had shifted their observation post early on to better see the target they had been assigned – a sound tactical decision – but that he and his team had then been compromised by goat herders who had stumbled upon their new observation post. Their decision to release the locals would, Marcus informed us, have dire consequences.

We asked questions like, "Can you tell us where you had made initial contact on the mountain?" A rough location would have allowed us to focus our search efforts more precisely. I even offered to pull an azimuth to get a position where they had patrolled previously. Yet he was unable to give us even the most general location. We struggled to understand how he didn't even know the general area of his patrol.

My platoon leader and I wanted as much clarification and as many locations as possible. We really wanted to find the other men. Marcus could only give us some detail on the firefight. Under attack from a larger insurgent force, Petty Officer Danny Dietz had been the first one killed. Team Leader Lieutenant Michael Murphy had disengaged to make a call for urgent assistance from a nearby clearing. He was forced to use his satellite phone because their regular comms did not work. He called the JOC to request an immediate QRF but was killed shortly after placing the call. Meanwhile, according to Marcus, he and Petty Officer Matthew Axelson kept fighting. Axelson was shot in the head but was still alive. Marcus didn't know for how long Axelson stayed with him but he knew they had to keep moving down the mountain. Eventually Marcus looked back and could no longer see Axelson. He was all alone.

We found it infuriating that throughout the entire engagement he did not recall a single terrain feature or identifying landscape that could have helped track down his comrades. The only issue for us at that point was the missing members of his team.

All we had to go on was that they were in the general vicinity, unfortunately an area with a vertical gain of several thousand feet covering two major valleys as well as a ridgeline. It was a daunting task.

The ODA and Ranger medics took a look at Marcus and assessed his injuries. He had cuts, bumps and bruises. He even had a bullet wound – through his butt! Marcus was sore from having falling down the mountain in his panic, but he was able to move slowly under his own power. Throughout all of this we maintained communications with the TOC at our CP. The assessment was that Marcus was not able to travel up the steep mountain back to the CP at the crash site and he would need to be evacuated out. A medevac was due to come in just after sundown so we had to find a suitable HLZ.

We sat in the village for the day. As the day progressed we continued asking Marcus about what happened and we told him "know everything is great, and that Americans got you now." Marcus said "yes things are better" but he was "disappointed" that he "will never able to let it down that a Navy SEAL was rescued by Army Rangers." It didn't go down well with us – we had spent a lot of time trying to find him

A medevac was coming in just after sundown so we had to find a suitable HLZ. We held security while we waited for the medevac, with our SAW gunners holding blocking positions to ensure that no enemy was maneuvering toward us. The platoon leader was happy that we had successfully completed this particular mission. He got off the radio when Jason and I walked in to discuss updates and plans. The decision had been made that after Marcus Luttrell's medevac we were to climb back up the mountain and tie in with our main element.

We preferred to operate at night, and joining the CP could not be done before it got dark. We estimated that our small group needed two nights to move back, because we had a lot of banged-up Rangers so we would be moving slowly. I suggested that we patrol the area from where we found Marcus to the crash site. Somewhere in there the other three SEALs had to be. Our CP agreed.

Marcus was successfully medevac'd and we moved out of the village and set up a patrol base at a different location. We were temporarily joined by some SEAL team guys who stayed for a day, searched and cleared one location, and then they were called off the recovery mission to conduct another tasking. We were totally unimpressed by this – after all, it was their guys and equipment that we were searching for – but then cynicism runs deep within Ranger ranks. The two weeks after June 28 were tough to endure. Every day we became more frustrated and embittered as to what was going on, trying to find a needle in a haystack. The more we cleared the harder it got to find the missing. We were enormously frustrated by Marcus's inability to provide exact details of what happened and where.

Early on we shared intel with the SEALs just after we exfiled Marcus and they had joined us in the search efforts. The SEAL team informed us that they found nothing over at a particular draw at a main valley running east and west. A spur ran north and after a couple of klicks split, with one draw going left, and the other one right toward the crash site. We had found Marcus on the left draw. The next morning, and at this point still with the SEAL team, we continued the search. Based on their information we focused our search on the left while the SEAL team searched on the right. These directions were from the crash site looking down the mountain from a southerly view. Our sweeps were methodical and slow because the terrain was wide and about 2km long from where it split into the two draws. It was a solid morning walk to where the mountain and the valley came together. The rest of our platoon patrolled from the CP to us and they were way west.

We patrolled at double intervals, double-arm spacing between us. There was always the possibility of contact, although we felt this was unlikely since there was such a huge presence of Rangers on the ground and we had now been joined by elements of Marines. The 82nd "All Americans" also became involved, as support slowly filtered in up to our area of operation. On the Ranger side, 1st Platoon, B Company, 2nd Battalion trucked in as many hands as possible when the crash had occurred. Once at the base of the mountain, they started the arduous climb and it took them the better part of three days to reach the top. In total, it took about five to six days for the other elements to finally tie in with us to increase our footprint.

We pushed back up the valley and the mountain as the rest of our platoon came down. Nobody had found anything so far. We combed the entire area carefully, and the terrain was so steep it literally took most of one day to complete one single pass. We had split our element into two squads by now; one was led by the platoon sergeant and the other by our platoon leader. We swept, we combed, we searched the bottom. It was like trying to find a needle in a haystack. The platoon sergeant-led squad searched back and were nearly at the top again, when one of the team leaders slipped into a draw. He literally came face to face with two dead bodies when he landed on top of them. It must have been something for him but we were all pleased to have found two of the three missing. We all assumed that one more day and we would find the last SEAL. But, in reality, it was a case of one more day for two whole weeks – one more day, one more day, one more day. At the time it was immensely frustrating, as sheer exhaustion set in and we struggled up and down the unforgiving mountain, our lungs drawing in the thin mountain air. But there was no way we were going to stop until all the remains had been found and were on their way home, back to American soil and their grieving families.

Amid all the hardship and exhaustion we did have a great boost to our morale – new socks and toothbrushes were finally dropped in. I know it sounds stupid, but when you have only packed for a 24-hour mission and you are days, weeks, into it, with unbrushed teeth and filthy, slimy feet, it is like heaven. Clean socks and a toothbrush can make you feel like a million bucks and give you a mental boost as you push on.

We continued our pattern of searching and sweeping from the bottom of the valley while other Rangers swept the rim of the bowl. We covered a 100-meter-wide swath each day, while our platoon sergeant kept meticulous track of what was cleared and patrolled.

We were on the top of our redeployment window, and the next battalion had already rotated while we were still on top of the mountain. Our relief in Bagram was fully briefed and was on par with everything that was happening on the ground.

On the fourteenth day on the ground we received a radio call that we were to be relieved in place that evening. We got all equipment and everything ready to go. It was time; some of our guys had started to get sick. We had been warned not to drink the local mountain water. Jason inadvertently had. He had slipped on a rock and fallen into a creek where he got a mouthful of dirty water. He had diarrhea for a couple of days and our medic did not have anything packed to help him out. At this point we all wore shredded pants, with crotches worn out, nobody shaved, and we basically looked like a bunch of bums with guns. The Marines who had climbed up the mountain to join us in our efforts, and especially their gunnery sergeant, had gone nuts about our appearance when they first caught sight of us. We didn't care. After a couple of days, they said nothing more and nobody, not even their gunny, cared about appearances any longer. Rangers Lead the Way!

Our platoon sergeant was proud of the map he had drawn of our extensive search and the areas that had been thoroughly checked. He handed it over to the relieving platoon sergeant, and at long last we exfiled from the bottom of the valley. We were so exhausted that I think absolutely everyone was asleep shortly after takeoff and stayed asleep until the helicopter landed back at Bagram.

By the time we landed chow was over, but our company's executive officer had asked the kitchen personnel not to throw out any leftovers. We came straight off the flight line, dropped off our stuff, and went to the back entry of the chow hall and ate. Everybody looked terrible – we were ragamuffins and we smelled even worse. This was while sergeant-majors and colonels, who are usually the last to eat, were having coffee so they could talk semi-intelligently while the privates were gone and not annoying higher ups by being stupid. The stares and looks we got… "holy crap where the hell did they come from." I think I heard someone say "Oh my god, they stink."

We stuffed our faces, swapped stories and high fives as the platoon filtered in, and discussed the events of the last two weeks. Some asked what Marcus was like. The consensus was that he was ungrateful and the most important thing to him seemingly was that he would never live down the day he was rescued by Rangers. We couldn't help but have questions about the lone survivor of the lost SEAL team, Marcus Luttrell. We had been frustrated by his inability to remember clear details which would have aided the search for his lost comrades. We also questioned the accuracy of his claims for having been caught up in such a large firefight. Intelligence reports pre-insertion had indicated an enemy force of 12–15 enemy fighters but nowhere near the numbers Luttrell would later describe which amounted to a force of 200 fighters. Certainly, we found no forensic evidence of such a large-scale fight over the two-week period we stayed in the area.

We did find a lot of 7.62mm WARSAW ammo for AKs and PKMs in a couple of locations, indicating support by fire, but only a handful of 5.56 NATO brass. The Afghans do not care about their mountainside that much that they would have picked up American brass and left 7.62mm shells untouched. We conducted a loose after-action report, making sure all the info was shared and pertinent intel passed along for subsequent reports. Then it was time for us to go home.

CHAPTER EIGHT

FAST AND LESS FURIOUS

Mosul Part Two, Iraq, 2006

Back in the U.S., at Grey Army Airfield we continued with what is by now the "wash, rinse, repeat" of our training cycles and it was also "Special Operations Standard Operating Procedures" week. We conducted a company-level training exercise in preparation for a battalion fixed-wing exercise. Everyone went through parachute pre-jump instructions, which included the DZ safety brief, who the jump masters were, and who the drop zone safety officer was. This was followed by the "Actions During Descent" briefing, followed by mock door training, covering proper exits and emergencies, and the procedures for each. The company drove to McChord Air Force Base, loaded into C-17s, and took off for the drop. Ranger Blake Samodell had a bad exit from the aircraft, causing him to flip upside down with the "opening shock" of his parachute at the end of his four-second count. The T-10 parachute takes a four-second count to open upon exiting the aircraft – translated into feet, it is a 235-foot freefall from the aircraft until you are under a fully deployed parachute. Our drop altitude for this operation was 800 feet above ground level. Blake had been positioned early in the line, one of the first ten. I was on the same door, at about number three or four. My squad was spread on both doors, facilitating everyone out in the same general 180-meter area, so we could assemble quickly and clear the leading edge of the hammer head where the numbers are painted to give aircraft direction, and down the main runway. The hammer head is the convergence of the taxiways, and the main runway, at either end of a runway. Contrary to popular belief the safest place to land when doing this type of operation is actually on the runway itself – hence the mandate for ankle braces which operated as a kind of air cast worn over our boots. Ankle braces were the "standard" for jumping onto what we call "Hard Stand" (asphalt). If we were jumping onto a dirt DZ, ankle braces would not have been required. Think about all the stuff at an airport – the small storage and facilities buildings, antennas, the radar, all this stuff is in the grass – so I always taught my guys to aim for the runway or taxiways, because you know exactly what you're going to hit: a hard, flat, smooth surface.

At ten minutes, the jump commands started as usual; at three minutes, the slow down, and the doors opened. This was always the best part, as the cool night air started pouring in through the jump doors with the faint aroma of jet exhaust. Jump masters took the door and began the checks and "the hang," looking out of the door to spot the DZ. The one-minute call was issued, followed by the 30-second, and then, "Drop zone coming up." "Stand by," which is the command for the first jumper to step into the door, was immediately followed by the green light, then the "Go!" command, and it's all business!

But Blake flipped upside down; he wore mandatory ankle braces and they had got caught in the risers. While trying to get his feet free from his risers, the cords that attach the parachute to the harness, Blake was pulling on his legs, in turn pulling "slips," which is when you attempt to steer a round parachute. This "slipping" caused Blake to steer into Trevor and the two Rangers became entangled and unable to separate. Normally jumpers will bounce off each other. Blake and Trevor began "trading air," meaning each parachute was stealing air from the other, causing them to entangle with Ranger Anthony. Anthony later said he saw the incident and attempted to steer away, but it was too late and he became entangled as well. Anthony did attempt to deploy his reserve parachute, but they were under the minimum opening altitude needed for a full deployment of the reserve. At 200 feet they all lost air in their parachutes. Blake hit his neck on the landing and was killed on the drop zone. Anthony landed on his side and broke a femur, pelvis, and ribs. Trevor leaned back and landed hard on his heels, shattering both of his legs. Anthony eventually recovered from his injuries, returned a year later for one more deployment, and then left the Army. Trevor still has trouble to this day. He had a ton of surgeries. Two years after the accident the Army passed him off into the Veterans Affairs system.

This was an extremely low point in the platoon's morale. After the jump, the entire company assembled outside the barracks, and our company's first sergeant, Brian, told us that if you do this long enough, it's inevitable to see this happen. You lose friends not just in combat but in training as well. Brian is about 6'1" and 240 pounds, from South Carolina, and a huge Harley enthusiast. He is exactly what you imagine a first sergeant should look like. People listened when he talked. Cutting-edge battle training will always cause casualties because of how hard we pushed ourselves to meet and exceed the Ranger Standard.

The following week would see us successfully conduct the Battalion Airfield Seizure Exercise at Grant County Regional Airport, in central Washington. We mourned our losses by conducting a military funeral, closing ranks, and continuing the mission – that is the Ranger way.

●●●

Our training cycle then saw us cut away most of our weapons squad to attend the month-long Stryker driver course. Then it was the usual working through SOPs and TTPs to make everyone understand how the platform worked and how to get the most out of it. Things were continuously evolving.

Our deployment to Mosul would be our first trip operating from the Stryker platform. Our guys had comfortably operated the Stryker platform at Fort Lewis, mastering first the Army and then the Ranger Standard. We were trained on how to use the Forward Looking Infrared (FLIR) and drive using the monitor screen instead of our night vision. You were able to select what was called "white-hot" or "black-hot," meaning if you picked white-hot the heat signature showed up white and the background was black or vice versa. FLIR was not affected by brown-outs, which happened when helicopters kicked up dust and dirt, greatly reducing visibility. The only drawback to the FLIR system was when ground and ambient air temperatures were the same, which occurred around sunrise and sunset; then the FLIR became inoperable. We had to crack the hatch open and resort to our NODs. This slowed driving down while transitioning but it still worked.

The mechanics of a deployment entailed a certain pattern. The first 24 hours of any overseas deployment were always madly chaotic as soon as we hit the ground, with unpacking, getting guys into their rooms, sorting things out to get the platoon TOC working, loading ammo, and prepping demo charges, to name just a few things. Our weapons squad provided the vehicle crew and was responsible for not only their machine guns but also the vehicles. They placed the machine guns on top of the Strykers and conducted PMCS. Communications were installed and spread throughout the vehicles. The radio telephone operators then fixed any issues, such as bad wiring, to name but one. It felt like we were running around at 100mph with our hair on fire. There was a universal sigh of relief once all of this was done. As soon as we were good to go we tried to sleep to combat jet lag and to ensure a smooth continuation of operational capabilities. Anytime we relieved in place, we were not allowed to have a gap in combat operations. We had to be combat ready instantly and remain so until the very last possible moment, when the next chalk was inbound. During our first 24 hours in-country and after having set up everything, we usually had a little bit of time for dry runs, or getting the trucks set up and the ammo uploaded, and we had time to go through our tools and rehearsals where we ironed out some outstanding issues. Dry runs were also good because it got people to wake up and shake off the mental cobwebs.

Upon departure it was the same thing, just in reverse. We packed a lot of stuff into the last few hours of a redeployment home. The last thing was always pulling off the big guns from the vehicles and storing them in the ISU-90s, large Air Force shipping containers. We also accounted for all ammunition and grenades. We always emptied out all our pouches and pockets because things are always overlooked. Military Police, who were also certified as customs officers, would always check both us and our homeward-bound pallets for contraband.

●●●

This deployment turned out to be one of the most fun ones I had been on so far. It was our second deployment to Mosul itself but now we had a new vehicle platform. Jason was no longer a rifle squad leader; instead he became the weapons squad leader and with that he and his squad were in charge of our vehicles. He was our convoy commander and he was excellent at remembering sections of Mosul where the Strykers could or could not operate, usually because some alleyways into the city were simply too narrow. At times we forced the issue, leaving but a few inches around the vehicles as we navigated the streets. The Stryker is a bit wide and the anti-RPG net-cage hung over, taking up more space. There were a couple of nights when we turned a corner too closely or hooked a car. Sometimes this meant we unintentionally shredded them, drove over them or even dragged them down the street until they untangled. We did always leave a few hundred Iraqi dollars on the windshields with a note apologizing for the damage.

As usual we executed multiple ops at night. Our air assets, all rotary-wing, had to refuel during our operations and we would be stuck without any air support. During those times we set up security perimeters. This was always done while we were still on a target building where we could "circle the wagons" around the block if the need arose. While we waited our TOC sometimes decided to add new targets. Images and anything we needed were placed into an empty ammo box with a chemlight attached to it and then dropped off by the returning helicopter. We did a quick ten-minute plan and onto the next target we went. After the successful execution of the next target we would inevitably have no room left for the detainees we had captured thus far as well as ourselves. There were times when the question was raised with the JOC as to whether we should leave detainees or Rangers behind. We usually got the standard reply of "just tie them to the top," meaning bring everyone, and make it work somehow. We sometimes became so seriously overcrowded that we told our smaller TOC that they needed to decide who was to stay behind and who was to be brought back for interrogation.

We had a good time – no, we had a great time. We perfected our craft and executed silent entries; by now 98 percent of our targets were hit silently. We tried to keep our enemy guessing. Often, we hit the wrong house because the homes were so close to each other that it was

141

impossible to delineate them and get the exact location. When we bumped into the wrong house, we thought it was a good idea not to go downstairs and then reset everyone. Instead, we jumped rooftop to rooftop to the next building until we hit the right one and then we cleared it top down. All this in the middle of the night! Sometimes the intel was so off that our platoon spread out and hit 15 wrong buildings until we found the correct one. This sounds like a large number of incorrect building clearances, but this has to do with what's called a "signal bounce" and was quite common when the building material of choice is concrete.

I remember once our first sergeant, the big fish in our little pond, came along, and, accustomed to being in charge, he simply walked straight into a building where 15 males were asleep. He walked straight back out and said to us, "Haven't you cleared the building?" Ha! We called this "pulling a Leeroy Jenkins," after the character in the World of Warcraft video game who repeatedly ruins best-laid plans by pulling crazy stunts. Well, even our command sergeant major wasn't above pulling the occasional Leeroy Jenkins. But woe to the squad leader who threw the plan into the trashcan with a similar rash move. Rank, after all, has its privileges.

In Iraq we did become victims of our own success. The typical mission day started with an abrupt wake-up that we had a solid target with a refined targeting location. This prompted the morning scramble to get everyone up, in uniform, and the leaders into the TOC. Here we began the planning process. At this time the mission standard was 20 minutes from the warning order that an operation was going to happen, to getting out the door, with the plan briefed. I don't think there are other units out there who could do this. Most of our operating procedures were standard, which made the briefing short. We grabbed our gear from the Ready Room and threw it over our heads while walking out the door, literally snapping Fastex buckles while we moved to our vehicles. We conducted a quick ramp-side Final Manifest Call to make sure everyone who should be was there.

We then loaded up and drove off the FOB into Mosul itself. Usually it was a short jaunt through the city to within a few blocks of the target. We then dismounted and confirmed targeting data for any changes with the JOC. After we moved into assault positions, we breached either silent or explosive, depending on what was briefed, entered, and cleared the building. This was the basic day-to-day. It became "cookie cutter," as each plan was essentially the same and we were able to transfer the mission template to any target. If there was a follow-on mission, we received intel over the radio and target imagery via ammo can drop from our rotary-wing armed escort. It was awesome.

There were also times when our air assets could not operate, and during those down days there were plenty of shenanigans, including numerous pranks. It was a welcome reprieve from continuous operations. A favorite prank was when some Ranger privates created a dump bucket and tied it to the company commander's door so that when he answered his door he was dumped on by a bucket full of water.

Once our camp within the FOB flooded and we couldn't get enough rocks to keep from walking in the water. Our trailers were elevated, but the knee- to mid-thigh-high water leaked in. We found a dirt pile and filled sandbags. We felt a bit like National Guardsmen doing flood recovery work.

Day and nighttime missions were always vastly different. We primarily conducted ramp planning at night while keeping the exposure in daytime limited. Nighttime operations were always better. On missions we broke our squads down into the following teams: isolation provided by the vehicles and the .50cal machine guns, assault team one, assault team two, and near site security. We also had translators by this time.

Since we now operated on the smaller platoon level instead of at company level, as we had done earlier, everybody was briefed at the same time. The privates who were needed to prep the vehicles knew about the basics, such as where to drive to, and they did not need to attend the briefings, while the other privates did always attend. Computer use was now in full swing. Much like our equipment was upgraded, so was technology and with it our operations changed. "Death by PowerPoint" is what we called it. Air assets received their intel briefs with emailed slides. The pilots took a quick look and spun up their aircraft. Usually the slides detailed the actions of who was going to be where to avoid any blue-on-blue incidents. The briefing always ended with us shouting, "Rangers Lead the Way!" Soon all the other personnel caught on and shouted out our motto with us. It was awesome. Then there was a mad flood out the door to get into the Ready Room for our gear and then to the ramps of our vehicles. On our return journey the medical Stryker always had more room because we took no casualties and the stretchers inside remained upright. We crammed 14–15 people into it – mostly detainees. We would execute a mission and then the JOC would call us with a six-digit grid to get us going onto the next target's planning. We used our computers to detail the route and brief a basic plan. This helped keep the speed going forward because our SOPs were also so refined by now it was relatively easy.

Blocking positions were always the hardest to find and emplace. They affected air support in case of engagement, and if we shifted, then we had our platoon leader give an update to the aircraft so they were able to track our movements. The outside of the target building was marked by infrared strobe lights set by the squad leaders at their respective blocking positions. Once we executed a target, the blocking positions collapsed to our entry point of the target. This did usually involve knocking out one or two streetlights – well more than that…

Silent entry was often done by scaling near the exterior gate of an 8-foot cinderblock wall with a ladder. As a squad leader I felt it was my job to climb over because my team leaders had three other Rangers, chomping at the bit to get into a fight, to control. I knew my teams handled everything ever thrown at them, so it made sense for me to be the lead over the compound walls. This never took longer than one to two minutes.

As the technique of silent entry developed, we would go from 2x4 handmade wooden ladders to off-the-shelf ladders from the box stores and finally to sectionable $3,000 and $4,000 systems that could be carried in four to six sections and assembled on site. These ladders allowed us to climb to the roof on multi-storey buildings without making entry and were quite handy for emplacing rooftop security teams.

It also saw us rethink the way in which we approached our pouch set-up. Instead of loading everything on the chest section, adding 4–5 inches to our front, we considered how we could use the extra space under our arms and on our backs. In addition, we had to keep the chest slick for climbing and that meant only a minimal amount of pouches. The thinking was that we didn't have to personally be able to reach all items; I could always ask someone else to hand the items, such as extra magazines, to me. There were, of course, a few pouches we couldn't move. The administrative pouch, worn centered and at the top of the carrier, would hold pens, markers, and a small notebook. The bleeder kit was always worn on the left and this could be attached to the kit under your arm or as a "stand-alone" attached to your belt. Personally, I preferred it on my belt as it afforded me extra space on my kit.

Climbing to gain silent entry in the beginning would test our patience, as we were not used to such a slow and quiet approach. It was the hardest thing not to just rush forward. It would generally work like this. Identify the target, then approach the target in a calm, quiet way to the compound wall. Emplace the ladder security. First task was to check the gate pins, to see if the gate could be unhooked from the ground and pushed in, thereby popping the deadbolt open. That would be the quickest point of entry. If not, then it was time to climb.

I would ask a ladder security man if his location was clear to climb, meaning no large obstructions were in the way, then he would climb down and I would climb up. Then I'd step off the ladder and scoot onto the wall, taking a quick look at the obstructions below to see if there was a way to avoid a complete drop to the ground. Then I dropped in, making sure to unsling my rifle and hold it in one hand before a quick tactical pause. I have seen guys drop in with their rifle slung and then the barrel hits the concrete, with the buttstock coming up to hit them under the chin. Not good and not quiet. Although squad leaders usually took the lead, it was also essential that climbing was left to the more agile individuals, because not everyone was coordinated enough to breach silently. After the tactical pause I would move to the gate, find the pins, pull them, and attempt to open it. If it had a padlock, it was a quick hand signal to the breach team leader for his bolt cutters to cut the lock and gently push/pull the gate open. The worst scenario was if you dropped in and you simply couldn't get the gate to open. This would then require a second man to drop in, find a secure place behind a wall, the side of the building, or a car, and the breach would have to be opened explosively and this was always risky. Besides, it's never fun to be on the inside when that gate charge goes off!

If the gate had been opened silently, then entry into the compound and securing the enemy came next. We occasionally used a SWAT-type battering ram but more usually a hydraulic press called the "rabbit" to gently pop the door. We slid the rabbit into the door jamb and pushed it open by breaking the lock. You had to carefully place your hand over the door for counter-pressure to avoid it popping open and making a racket. This did happen occasionally. The rabbit tool came in two parts – one mechanical and the other the hydraulic pump. We always put it together in our Objective Rally Point (ORP) before the assault. It weighed about 20 pounds so it was not the easiest thing to drag around but it was handy. At other times we used the Hooligan tool – the fireman's forcible entry tool. If all this was successful then a radio call of "breach is open, entering silently" was made. Not a word was spoken during silent entries; it was all hand

and arm signals directing the internal room clearing. If the room was occupied, and no one had woken up, a quick count of the males present was made. We then gathered enough Rangers to cover all of them, and then on a head nod or a quiet "Wake'em up," that would be that. If there were as many MAMs in the room as there were assaulters, then half of us would put a foot on their neck or chest to ensure submission while covering the assaulter next to them with their rifle. The most MAMs I ever encountered during a silent entry was 13, whom we woke up from their sleep. In this instance we actually had to borrow a fire team from the second assault squad to get the right number of guns in the room.

If a MAM had a weapon near him, and no one had woken up during the initial entry, we would simply remove the weapon from his reach. During the "Wake up," if he reached for the location the weapon had been, then that individual received a little "extra attention." The idea was always to capture personnel for intelligence, never to shoot them because you could!

In general, we only used rooftop climbing and entries after we had gained access to the building and then it was used to hit another nearby building or even a building further away. This "push to next door" was easier than to relocate the entire element. But once you had been on a block for 45 minutes, undoubtedly you will have made some noise. We had security snipers on the rooftops and they monitored the entry and exit points as well as guiding us when we did do rooftop entries. The most unnerving aspect was always walking across the bridging ladders when you were three storeys up using NODs which caused perception issues. You got to see how people reacted, whether they crawled on their butts or walked across to the next rooftop.

Our use of K-9s began with civilian contractors. They were only armed with pistols and we had to keep an eye out for them as they were not really part of the team. We had to learn how to effectively use both them and their dogs. Handlers always gave us capabilities briefings. For example, they told us about how the other battalion had used them and how they could be used better. It was all a bit sketchy at the beginning because of the unknown civilian along with a new asset. How could we best use it? Some of us put on bite suits for training and were shown how best to employ the dog. Some dogs were also trained to sniff out weapons and explosives. If, for example, we operated in a historically bad IED area, we'd run the dog out front on a long leash. This didn't always work. In 2007 we had a platoon sergeant step on an IED while moving to the target. In 2008 another platoon sergeant also stepped on one after the dog had gone through. The K-9 is lovingly referred to as a "four-legged fur missile with teeth." We were never going to catch someone running with a 200-meter head start – but the dogs did.

•••

Unfortunately, Alpha Company of our battalion suffered casualties after a suicide bomb attack in Fallujah. They also had one of their squad leaders and one team leader, Ricardo Berrazo and Dale Brehm, killed by barricaded shooters. These were the fourth and fifth KIAs that 2nd Battalion had suffered since 9/11. After so many years it was easy to allow that feeling of invincibility to creep into your mindset. We had felt that nothing bad would happen and it hit us hard when it did. We had grown up together in different companies. Charlie Company's platoon sergeant and James, a solid Ranger tactician and squad leader from Arizona, were hit hardest since they knew both of the guys killed from their time at A Company. It was a big reality check on a lot of guys. Bad things can and will happen, nor are we completely invincible. Their deaths ended the deployment on a down note, although we still executed and operated a few more missions. We were finally stood down in March 2006 and headed home.

CHAPTER NINE

NOT QUITE THE TITANIC BOAT OPERATIONS

Ramadi, Iraq, 2006–2007

We deployed back to Iraq during the winter of 2006/2007 but this time to Ramadi, a city in central Iraq that lies along the banks of the Euphrates River. It was mild during the day and around 70 degrees, but at night the temperature dropped to a much colder 40–50 degrees.

This was the first time we operated outside of Baghdad and Mosul. By this point the Marines had swept and cleared through Fallujah and Ramadi. Despite this the IED threat was bad and vehicles got repeatedly pounded. Insurgent fighters became increasingly adept at hiding them. Remote-controlled IEDs were the popular way to detonate them. Command-detonated mines required someone close by, but by switching to remote control the trigger man could be a long way off. He could just sit at a roadside or a tree and detonate without incriminating himself. IEDs were everywhere, as the BSO of conventional forces briefed us on our arrival. But it was obvious; we could hear them going off both day and night.

We had done a few ground assaults with our Stryker platform but the risk of getting the force into the fight wasn't worth it. We decided alternative insertions were the way to go. We figured out that a SEAL team had boats that they were willing to share. We flew to their location and staging area by helicopter on a day when no operations were planned. We received a briefing on the boats' capabilities and on how to operate them. We conducted some dry runs to get comfortable using their boat platform, although we didn't operate the boats ourselves; we got chauffeured! Ah, the comical thought of SEAL personnel driving us to target. Well they didn't, support personnel did but still... The basic operations went like this: we loaded into the boats and the trailer was submerged into the water where it was then offloaded. We learned how to get comfortable sitting in the boats and how to back out and a few other things to become proficient in infil.

A couple of days later we executed our first-ever water infil into Ramadi. There had been a cold snap and it was rather chilly on the water. Our mission planning revealed that we could get the boats to within 3 klicks of our target and that was not a horrible, long walk. We jumped into the boats and traveled down the river. The boats were crewed by Special Warfare Combatant-Craft Crewmen who were top notch in driving and navigating the boats. We found out that there had been earlier attempts to IED the river but the enemy had never found a successful way to do that. They tried hanging

IEDs off the bridges or the sides of bridges and banks, and also placed IEDs in the beaches, but ultimately abandoned the idea. We traveled for half an hour and arrived at our disembarkation point. Underwater sandbars did not allow the boats to get to the actual beach, and the crew assured us the water was only a few inches deep. Our company commander was having none of it and insisted on maneuvering the boats further up or back down since nobody needed to start a mission wet. There was a bit of a power pull between the crew and the commanding officer. His boat was moved to a better location; the rest of us, well, we jumped off the boats and you can imagine what happened when a 280lb, heavily equipped Ranger – in this case Casey – jumped off into a knee-deep hole and struggled to move onto the beach. The sand he stirred up beneath the water created an even bigger hole, which saw me sinking up to my waist in the river. I gave Casey the dirtiest look; he just gave me the "sorry dude" look. Casey and I had been team leaders at the same time, and he went on to a support position in Echo Company for a year. He is a friend and a great Ranger who hails from northern California. Every Ranger looked back at the crew guys with a "thanks a lot, you big jerks" look. We directed a ton of sarcasm at them. We finally offloaded everyone and we were all dripping wet and cold. We had wintertime Ranger School flashbacks; it sucked.

My squad was the lead element and we snuck though the terraced fields on our way into a village on the outskirts of Ramadi. At this point we had pretty much perfected the art of silent entry and our missions still ran at about 95 percent of us employing that technique. This would be no exception. It is an incredible, awesome feeling for 15–20 Rangers to get quietly into the target building while the inhabitants remained asleep. On the count of three we jumped on the sleepers, and secured and contained them. If we had used vehicles we would not have been able to get this close.

●●●

Ramadi was cold and nasty, and many of the roadways were impassable for our heavy vehicle platform composed of Strykers and MRAPs. It was not a lot of fun to get vehicles stuck because conducting vehicle recovery is never an enjoyable task, especially in a place where the IED threat is through the roof. Infiling by boats and exfiling with helicopters was a fantastic way to operate. After the first success this was how we conducted the majority of our missions. We spent considerable time trying to incorporate the boats and making our infil as perfect as possible. For example, we always tried to improve and shorten the timing of execution, from planning to execution of the mission to how much time the crew in turn needed for their planning and execution. We had a lot of fun during this deployment because of the boats. It was a new mode of infil, different than anything else, and a ton of fun.

During a typical boat operation we traveled for approximately 45 minutes. We coordinated with the crews and gave them the warning order by telephone. We made and briefed our plan, moved to the HLZ, and waited for the helos to arrive. They flew us to the boats, where we did a quick route overview and expected the drop-off point. Once loaded, we took the insertion ride on the river to our drop-off point. We then covered the boats with our weapons until they departed our sight.

We then moved toward the target area, which usually was a 1–2-km walk. At the target area it was a "cookie cutter" process for emplacing the security and assault squads onto the target. This would utilize the acronym ASS – Assault, Security, and Support. Moving into a target, the order of movement would be Security, Support, and Assault, as the support and security elements must be set before the assault can commence. When leaving the target, Assault would depart first, followed by Support and Security, bringing up the rear. We breached by plan unless a quick glance told us we needed an explosive breach to gain entry. Mostly, we entered silently, cleared, and exploited the target then moved to exfil or to conduct a follow-on mission based on the information gathered at the current target. But due to the complexity of using the boats, we only conducted one planned operation a night.

● ● ●

On Halloween we lost one vehicle and that was the last time we drove. It was our commanding officer's and it blew up with a "catastrophic vehicle kill." A football-sized hole breached the skin of the Stryker and shrapnel hit it as well, but fortunately no one was injured. The IED breached the hull behind the driver and the shrapnel stuck into the plywood of the seat back. It was a testament to the vehicle platform. The vehicle died upon impact and the breakers blew, but the driver just pushed them back in and drove all the way to the base with three flat tires. The Stryker didn't quit until we were attempting to navigate the chicanes at the gate, when the steering arms finally let go and the front wheels each went their own way. So, we blocked the entrance to the FOB waiting on a wrecker to come get the Stryker and drag it back to our camp. Our commanding officer at the time had a horrible track record with IEDs. He had literally been IED'd on every major U.S. holiday. Needless to say, no one wanted to be in his vehicle.

It was always fun to take on a problem area of the BSO. This time it was a small outpost with platoon- to company-sized elements staging out of what was known as a Combat Outpost (COP). The problem was that the foreign fighters would see the units coming out of the gate of the COP to conduct a dismounted patrol in the marketplace. This allowed the foreign fighters plenty of time to hide or to retreat before coalition forces could close with them. The location of the COP acted like an early warning system for the enemy. The BSO's units were simply not fast enough to be effective because they were always seen upon departure.

We received a briefing about the problem area and during our planning phase found one location that was accessible by a boat infil. We planned to use the boat infil and silently move into two different locations as a pre-staging point. When ISR spotted that the market had opened, Charlie Company would conduct a rolling ambush. The plan called for 3rd Platoon to run forward and to block off the market while 1st Platoon provided a rolling push. This essentially meant rolling down the streets and clearing the area from one end of the market to 3rd Platoon's location about three to four blocks away. We used a whole rifle platoon for the operation. Third Platoon would push out via the boats, while 1st Platoon conducted an off-set helicopter insertion to walk into the area.

We predetermined that two compounds were large enough to hide one rifle platoon inside of each and that both buildings were close enough to the marketplace we planned on hitting. From the compounds our plan was to depart the front door basically in a sprint to close as quickly as possible and to set up as the other platoon began its operation toward the marketplace, pushing potential insurgents toward us. We silently cleared the compounds and tied up the occupants. We told them that we had not come for them, that we would only stay for a short time. We conducted light interrogations with interpreters we had on hand. Command had finally figured out in order to operate effectively we did not need to fill detention areas with everybody we got a hold of; instead, interpreters proved useful for quickly ascertaining if someone captured was worth detaining or not. Both platoons had set up successfully, silently, sneakily, and we did get some intel from the owners that certain shops in the marketplace were being used by insurgent fighters. They also confirmed that the insurgents had vehicles nearby to escape in whenever coalition forces left the COP in their attempt to clear the marketplace.

We had about a block and a half sprint from our compound to our actual staging location. The sun was about to go up. We staged at the door, waiting for the "trigger" to release us forward. Once that happened and the command to execute was given, we sprinted out of the compounds and raced to our staging area. Rushing out of a building actually does require a little bit of a plan because we needed to make sure that we, the assault force, actually all got out of the compounds before we sprinted. I would later, as a platoon sergeant, refer to this as "compressing the slinky." If everyone were to sprint right out the door, you would end up with some Rangers on target, while others were still trying to get out of the Last Cover and Concealment of the compounds. We needed to ensure the maximum numbers of shooters appropriate for the location. I told Casey, my team leader, that I would be the first man out but then would stop until Ray, our platoon sergeant, appeared and then I'd begin my sprint. That was the cue for the platoon to follow at a dead sprint together. Ray was a comical Ranger leader. He always found humor and sarcasm in anything, but was calm and collected. He was not the tallest of Rangers, at about 5'8" and only 160 pounds, but a great platoon sergeant none the less. Although he was originally "raised" in Alpha Company, fortunately he did not conform to the Alpha Company "norm" – but more on this later.

The SEAL commander, whom we were working for since he was the regional boss in our area of operation in Iraq, came along for the ride and was alongside our own company commander.

There was a small footbridge about 50 meters away from one compound that was only wide enough to accommodate one man at a time. Our entire formation was out by now and I spotted Ray so I began my sprint, which led me directly to the SEAL commander, with both of us going for the small footbridge at the same time. I stiff-armed him and yelled, "My bad; gotta get out of the way!" I think he landed in the water. Rangers Lead the Way!

My squad and I, along with snipers, got to a large clearing which doubled as a parking lot but was mostly occupied by trucks. This was our blocking position for the op. In the back window of a navy blue or black BMW I saw a 7.62mm Russian PKM machine gun and other weapons; this was grounds for us to be able to prosecute the target. There were four men in it. We had been briefed in our Rules of Engagement that weapons were considered a hostile threat and we were cleared to engage.

One of the most awe-inspiring things I experienced as a Ranger was to see a Ranger rifle squad of about 12 men come to a sliding stop from a dead sprint as weapons came up and engaged the enemy. We heard the starter of the car we were about to engage – the vehicle's driver slipped into gear and was about to move as we opened fire. The BMW launched itself out of the parking lot and crashed into a nearby ditch. We got into our blocking positions and I sent a team across to clear the crashed vehicle. Meanwhile 1st Platoon, Charlie Company rapidly cleared the market, firing warning shots to get people off the streets. We heard sporadic gunfire from both sides. They captured about 20 MAMs during the raid, who were sent to detention. They rolled into and cleared the shops and left security behind. By the time the clearing force showed up there were just a few dudes left. It was a funny sight. We spent a little bit of time in the area and cleared other compounds where some people had fled to, based on ISR intel. We knew the enemy liked to hide things in orchards because they were in the open, accessible, and an enemy fighter could easily mark a nearby tree. The leafy trees prevented ISR from seeing exactly what they were doing. The enemy ain't stupid! At one small fruit orchard we found a small weapons cache which we blew in place.

The BMW we had shot up had a trunkful of RPGs, grenades, and other weaponry. It looked like a mafia car. It carried lots of bad stuff for people to do bad things with.

We came up with a supposedly brilliant idea. Since most of the weapons were trashed and the four occupants dead, we thought, *Let's blow it up*. Rangers like big explosions – a lot. Our commanding officer, first sergeant, and platoon sergeant were cool with this idea, but Platoon Sergeant Jeremiah, who was the battalion master breacher from 1st Platoon, said, "Hell no." And at 6'1", weighing in at 220 pounds, few people disagreed with him. He was one of the most knowledgeable master breachers I have ever known. This would create too big an explosion, he stated, and asked how much gas was left in the car, to which we honestly answered that we had no idea. There could be a lot of fragmentation and possibly someone from the assault force could get injured. It was an unpopular call but the correct one. But it would have been so awesome. To this day we still talk about how awesome of an explosion and massive fireball it would have been. In any event, we emptied the car of its weapons and the dead and blew it in place. Just a small explosion.

But it turned out one of the "dead" guys from the BMW had a faint pulse so our medic immediately worked on him. Our doc stabilized the fighter for two hours but he died later during surgery. Doc always rendered aid regardless of combatant status – everybody was treated using his great medical skills. We would see these medical skills shine more during future deployments.

●●●

After this operation we continued to do more of the same. We infiltrated by boat, entered silently, and hit targets. Unquestionably, we were really very good at it. We pulled off missions within the hour: breached a target, entered, tagged and bagged, marked and cleared anything to exploit, including media, documents, you name it, and snatched it all up and were off the target within the hour. Once again, we became victims of our own success and we began to hit multiple targets at night, to follow on targets, and even more. If you got one bad guy, you might as well get the guy down the street too. It made sense. Almost nobody knew we were around because typically no shots were fired. So it was possible to walk down the street, down the block, or even several klicks, with both detainees and materials, and to then set them aside and execute another target. All this was done before it got light. And not just by us; the entire Ranger Regiment operated like this now across Iraq.

We had a good working relationship with the SEALs at this point. Occasionally we felt like we were regarded as the poor relations, but whatever – we executed more missions and more targets, brought in more detainees and more intel than they did so we looked at it as a win. The boat crews were not part of the team per se but a support element and so they didn't dish out any grief. They were great guys to work with. Our only complaint was that they never let us operate the onboard guns, .50cals and MK19s, even when they were short of crew. Rangers are, of course, qualified to operate these weapons; the only difference was that they were mounted on boats instead of vehicles so it seemed kind of stupid to us.

One night in early December of 2006, we were sitting in the back of a Special Operations Craft – Riverine. Three Rangers sat on the engine cover in the back and one or two were on the sides by the driver and bow. Everybody else of my squad of 10–12 filled in the gunnels on the sides. Since they didn't want us to operate the MK19, Casey, my team leader, was also on the engine cover. The boat made a hard right, starboard, and the unmanned weapon just hung there. The strike shield of the weapon acted like a giant scoop and Casey and three guys in the back got soaked. We conducted an overnight infil on foot and they were still wet by the time we got back. I had to listen to Casey bitch and whine about how he would man the gun the next time. We hurled abuse back and forth. Our exceptionally fun, but taxing, deployment ended shortly afterwards in early 2007.

●●●

In 2007 I attended a Basic Non-Commissioned Officer Course as part of leadership training at Fort Benning, Georgia. The eight-week-long course was required for the promotion from E-5 sergeant to E-6 staff sergeant and you cannot be promoted to E-7 sergeant first class without it, which is the rank required to be a platoon sergeant. Part of the promotion required requalifying in Army Combatives Level 1. I should point out that by 2003 even privates were certified with this straight out of basic training. Originally this was a 2nd Ranger Battalion driven program of Jiu-Jitsu combatives that the Army adopted hook, line, and sinker. I needed to pass the combatives course that I had been doing since I was a private. I had to horse around in a gym just to get a piece of paper. Horsing around meant conducting combatives with Mac, a 6'2", 240-pound line-backer-built beast versus me in the other corner at 5'9" weighing in at 165 pounds. Mac was at the time a Ranger instructor from the 5th Ranger Training Brigade and we quickly hit it off as friends. I asked him at lunch why, as a good Ranger, he wasn't in the regiment. This led to an after-class trip to the regimental shop at Fort Benning where Mac filled out the "recruitment packet." Six months later he stood in the Quad as part of 2nd Battalion. Ranger!

We were on the mat, doing some test wrestling, and on a move I felt something tear. I was diagnosed with a hernia and missed the deployment in 2007 and had to serve in the rear detachment. Charlie Company, together with the battalion headquarters element, went back to Mosul. It sucked to miss the tasking.

Rear detachment was awful. Everyone thought you did nothing at all but the reality was you dealt with a lot of trash and the accompanying drama of Rangers who did not deploy, and sometimes their wives. We dealt with Rangers who were released for failing to meet the Ranger Standard, DUI, or had been arrested for whatever reason. It was not like you had a platoon-sized element waiting to go to Ranger School. Oh, you had those too, but you also had privates who did what privates typically did. And if you did not hold their hands and if you did not try to keep everyone busy for an entire work day, five days a week, things got messy... Guys who screwed up got tagged and were given "fun" corrective training, such as mowing our massive Quad field situated between the various company buildings. We gave them a 5-gallon gas can and a mower and told them that once completed they could go home or be off for the rest of the day. They always underestimated the task and would spend considerable time pushing that mower.

I was always on the phone, including weekends, having to explain to our deployed first sergeant why Rangers X, Y, Z had made massive mistakes and gotten into this trouble. This was especially eye-opening since I did not have a platoon sergeant around who was experienced in dealing with this. If I asked a master sergeant or an officer at staff, I always got the "why are you such an idiot" look. This would lead me on a personal quest to learn the information required because I despised the thought of being the dumbest individual in the room.

I did manage to watch the combat ops and listen to the radio comms of the deployed battalion. I also read the JOC's logs and reports so I had a fair idea and understanding of what was happening back in Mosul. I visualized where my friends were but it sucked not being with them.

We also had to deal with the protocols of our casualties. This was difficult, especially given that we had few quality people remaining at the battalion and that only certain ranks in the Army were allowed to be involved in the process except for the firing squad detail and pallbearers. There were certain requirements in dealing with casualties. For example, an E-7 had to go to the family, and if an officer was killed it required an equal or higher ranked officer to be the casualty officer.

During the deployment, Corporal Jason Kessler of 3rd Platoon, a vehicle commander for one of our Strykers, was killed in action on July 30, 2007. An RPG gunner had snuck in behind him and hit the vehicle hatch he stood in. He was killed almost instantly but the medics still desperately worked on him throughout the trip to the hospital where he died. We waited for Jason's remains in

Philadelphia and relieved the overseas escort. It was not the quickest process and took about four to five days. We also inspected his uniform before it left the mortuary. It was mentally taxing. Dealing with Jason's arrangement was hard, and then we had a training accident in Afghanistan and had to do it all over again. There were the grieving families, escorting the remains of Ranger buddies, and the crushing realization that we were starting to lose people. It was awful. Casualties occurred more often and this was part of the ever-changing, fluid fight we were in.

Finally, the battalion returned.

CHAPTER TEN

TIPTOE THROUGH THE DEADLY TULIPS

Mosul Part Three, Iraq, 2008

At the end of 2007 a few of us, including me and Jason, submitted our promotion packets for sergeant first class (E-7). All were accepted – Jason moved to Alpha Company later and I to battalion staff. This would be my last deployment to Mosul as a staff sergeant (E-6), age 27, squad leader of 3rd Squad, 3rd Platoon, Charlie Company.

Our platoon had been in Mosul more than any of the others and we joked that we should buy a summer home there. We did not even need a map to drive through the city since we had it memorized by now. Frankly, this was awesome on our part because in the event that the navigation system failed we were still operable and we could give route directions over the radios. This deployment pushed us to our limit mentally as well as physically. Between our two platoons we conducted over 160 combat missions within our 90-day deployment cycle.

During our first few weeks my squad was tasked out to support Army Special Forces. They had a small troop deployed and we drove their vehicles and navigated the city on the way to their targets. Our squad had dropped from an all-time high of 13 to about nine or ten. I broke off four senior Rangers to accompany me on this tasking, and we were sad to leave our platoon behind since they were going to have a lot of fun. After all, who wants to chauffeur other units and never get off the truck? We did get to do a few helicopter operations with them, which was fun, but blocking positions on most of the missions were always boring. But Army Special Forces was small and needed some additional muscle.

About a month later we rotated with another set of Rangers from 2nd Platoon. Within the first week of that rotation, they got into a gunfight and suffered one Ranger KIA. Specialist Thomas F. Duncan III, age 21, died of gunshot wounds suffered during combat operations in Sinjar, Iraq, on June 9, 2008. They had taken a helicopter flight out west of the city to a typical small village. They were sucked in and baited into a gunfight from barricaded shooters along a half-crumbled wall. The fight ended with a tragic blue-on-blue KIA. What had happened, it seemed, was that once the gunfight began, the Ranger blocking position shifted its location to put accurate fire onto the target location but somehow this was not properly understood or communicated. Through either miscommunication or misinterpretation during the fight an aircraft ended up strafing blue elements along with the enemy force. Such is the fog of war. It really sucked and put the guys into a funk early into their deployment. This happened alongside Army Special Forces and questions were asked about their operation. During the investigation a few things came to light but all one can say is human beings make mistakes and will always make mistakes. It reinforced that you always needed to make sure everyone knows where everyone is, especially if you are using a non-organic asset – be that a gunship or helicopters flying support. One way to do this is by calling and checking in with the platoon sergeant to confirm everyone involved in the mission. That is his job and it helps paint a complete picture for ground and air assets. Accountability of people is especially critical during combat operations.

We had day and night platoons to execute our tasking during this deployment. It was a lot of fun but it was also exhausting. We refined our craft more and more, mission by mission. The target refinement was better and, as a result, the targeting sequences were a lot smoother on the ground. I would say it was a tenfold improvement on what constituted a target. Our guys became very good at delivering intel using the ammo can distribution system dropped off to us by gunships in the middle of our missions. We conducted Stryker "ramp side planning" in the back of our vehicle platform and reviewed the imagery and intelligence provided. Jason, who was the convoy leader, worked out the route to be taken to the follow-on target. Planning took maybe 10–15 minutes. We drove, entered the compound, and cleared it within an hour. Another ammo can was dropped off, and onto the next target we went until there was no space in our vehicles for additional detainees. The continued succession of targets wore on the guys and we needed a break. Finally, thanks to some inclement weather, we got one. Oh, thank you break. A storm clouded the sky and our air assets were grounded. But we were back in action far too soon.

A typical raid in Iraq involved driving vehicles into the target area, where we dismounted and continued the mission on foot. We usually stopped about two to three blocks away from the target to stay out of vehicle noise range. We searched for the correct target compound and checked both sides of the block.

On one mission and about a block away from our objective there was an impromptu Iraqi police checkpoint. We were in the process to deconflict – basically letting everyone know who-was-where to avoid friendly fire when exactly that happened. The Iraqi police engaged one of our guys, Erich, who carried a ladder. At 5'10" and 200 pounds, Erich was a sniper team leader and one of the most knowledgeable snipers to work with. He went down. Mitch, Allen, and I had been waiting for the final deconfliction of the target area when this happened. Mitch was one of my great team leaders from 3rd Squad. He was quick thinking in a fight and an all-around solid Ranger. We took a few steps ahead of Erich and laid down a base of fire onto the police post. We were on the crest of a hill that led down to the police forces. Mitch grabbed Erich and moved him away and down the street. Allen and I fired downrange while the entire platoon ran to the sound of the guns. I was about a foot away from a cinder wall on one knee and Allen was above me. We poured on more lead. More and more guns showed up, machine guns, then Strykers, and we all shot at the Iraqi police. It was a gunfight back and forth, but as we believed them to be green forces we directed our fire away from them, instead hammering everything around them. We simply wanted them to stop firing at us. Our massive platoon leader, Walker, 6'2" and 220 pounds of him, was on the radio still trying to deconflict the area. But once the .50cal guns opened up the police finally stopped shooting and one of our interpreters used the bullhorn to shout at them that we were friendly forces. The fight ended and the whole action had lasted no more than five minutes. It was a bad night for Erich, who had been clipped on the outside of his knee. We completed the mission, conducted our actions on the objective, cleared, searched, and found nothing and then we took him to the hospital. But, as luck would have it, the bullet had missed every important thing in his knee, and he was released from the Combat Surgical Hospital (CSH) a few days later. Erich was more annoyed at having a bullet hole through his new pants than he was about his knee. Much to my amusement or annoyance, he kept griping about his pants. Ranger! Green on blue. Blue on blue. It happens. It's war and it is unavoidable.

● ● ●

I served in Charlie Company from 2003 to 2008, and one particular gunfight inside a target building stands out to me as a testimony to our perfection of our craft and our silent entries. The tasking was named Objective *Crescent Lake* and it involved the interdiction of Abu Kalaf, the emir of al Qaeda in Mosul, who had been accidentally released from prison by the Iraqis in an attempt to purge the overcrowded detention facilities. Abu Ghraib was shut down because of detainee abuse and it was during the merging of detainees into one larger facility that he was allowed to leave.

Recapturing Kalaf was a personal issue for our battalion commander because he had been wounded during the gunfight to apprehend the emir the first time around. Our battalion commander was certain that the fugitive would return to Mosul. He knew Kalaf well, knew that his house was within the city, and so we used local national assets to run a recce down the street in front of his house to confirm or deny his presence. We didn't want to burn the target and be forced to chase after him in a hostile environment. Our local assets conducted a route reconnaissance and confirmed Abu Kalaf was on target.

Our challenge was how to best approach the target compound without getting compromised. Kalaf had a good personal protection system set up so we knew we couldn't simply drive up without being seen or heard. This was based on intel from our battalion commander who had captured him previously. We were certain we could drive HUMVEEs into the area but not the Stryker platform. I suggested that a dismounted patrol was the best approach to the target compound without the emir's early warning system kicking in. We decided not to take any risks whatsoever on this particular mission. We agreed on a dismounted patrol and knew that it would take a lot longer to set all the pieces before taking down the building. The reason for the more cautious approach was simple: Abu Kalaf had only been out of jail for about seven to ten days and naturally would be skittish. We had intel that prior to his arrest he had had a personal security detail of two to three bodyguards with him all the time. We also knew, based on his previous capture, that he had a suicide bomber within his protection circle. We assumed that we had one to deal with now as well. We therefore planned on possibly being compromised and, if so, that there would be a firefight with his security personnel and a suicide bomber. Our commander was not too keen on a roughly 1.5km walk to the target within the war-ravaged city, especially since we were going after such a high-profile target. But our briefing was very detailed and our confidence was high that we would be able to set the pieces unseen. He believed in us and gave us the okay.

Our plan called for the assault force to drive up to a nearby Iraqi police station and then conduct the dismounted patrol. Recently we and other U.S. elements had been engaged by the police but had been ordered not to shoot back; instead, they had to wait until their headquarters was able to call the police to have them stop firing. To avoid a similar situation we drove our Strykers off the main supply route, across a bridge, and to the police station. After we deconflicted with them, we left our liaison officer and interpreter with the police to listen to radio comms alerting the police to possible crowd disturbances during the mission. It would be the police's responsibility to deal with any potential mob.

We continued a little bit farther down the road where we dismounted. The route we followed was along a main artery for a little over a klick. We made a sharp left, then a right, and, on our final approach to Objective *Crescent Lake*, we held up short and crossed a large drainage ditch running through the city using the typical one-person-wide footbridge. Our assault element moved across, turned left, then right onto a road where we held back about a block away from the target compound. This was our release point. So far, our walk in had been perfectly uneventful; nobody had tripped or fallen, no metal had clinked. It was more or less a quiet night. We had alerted no one.

The target block was about five houses deep with around a dozen houses around. We set security on the west side of the block. The release point was one block away from the road we needed to turn right on. The target compound was smack in the middle of it. We released the isolation squad, including our sniper teams. They made a right turn from our main travel route and followed along the block's near side, continued until the end of it, and then turned around – basically a U-shape movement. Five Rangers, composed of two snipers and a small security force, slowly and quietly hopped over the wall and climbed with assault ladders. People in the Middle East often sleep on the rooftops in the summers because their houses are too hot at night. During our planning process we felt there would be a high possibility of civilians up top so we had to be aware. If we encountered anyone, we would secure them by tying them up temporarily. In a 360-degree urban combat environment it was always nice to have guns up high, so they could deal with any and all threats. We knew that we would not be shot at from someone up top without a response from our sniper teams. Knowing that people were asleep basically meant our guys had to tiptoe around the sleeping bodies and then hop-scotch across various roofs to get to their location. They proceeded to cross rooftops on their way back toward us, halfway down the block, to their position near the target building.

Meanwhile, the other elements involved in the assault got antsy because the movement of the isolation teams was so slow. I thought, *Holy crap, what are they doing? Drinking tea?* A call came in asking if one element could move in closer to the next intersection so they could get eyes on the target building. The answer was, of course, a no. A few more minutes passed and the same question was asked, but with the add on that if something were to happen now they could offer no assistance or interdiction to the isolation team. Still the answer was no.

The rooftop team called in the building numbers as they made their way across them. That way we knew where they were at all times. Later I heard that while they hop-scotched across one rooftop an Iraqi woman woke up, sat up, and stared at Team Leader Mitch, a.k.a. Catfish, an Oklahoma boy from 2nd Squad. He calmly put his finger to his lips and whispered "shh." She went back to sleep as though nothing had happened. Tiptoeing through the tulips.

At this point I felt that the isolation element was too far away to support them if something went down. So, this time I asked if we could move a team up to the target street "just in case." The answer this time was yes. We moved forward another block and finally put eyes on target. Our briefing called for a shock and awe entry, not our favorite since we had perfected the silent entry technique, but we needed to surprise and disorient the enemy within the compound.

The rooftop team was in place and the assault force placed breaches on the gate. We gave out "set" calls that we were ready, and waited for all the blocking positions to report. We were on the left side facing the gate. As the set calls came back the command to execute was given. We blew the gate charge. My E-5 team leader from 3rd Squad, another Mitch, not Catfish from 2nd Squad, was the breacher for the gate. He also expected the front door to be locked so it needed to be breached almost simultaneously to the explosive breach of the gate. The gate blew and we "flowed" in and immediately there was gunfire on the rooftops. Without missing a beat Mitch rushed to the door and shot-gunned the door handle and lock with one round. He kicked it in and we pushed into the house.

We split into quick-clearing teams by twos, per room, and flooded the house. The front door swung open, covering the doorway into the kitchen, but we could not really see it. I was the No. 1 man

OBJECTIVE *CRESCENT LAKE*

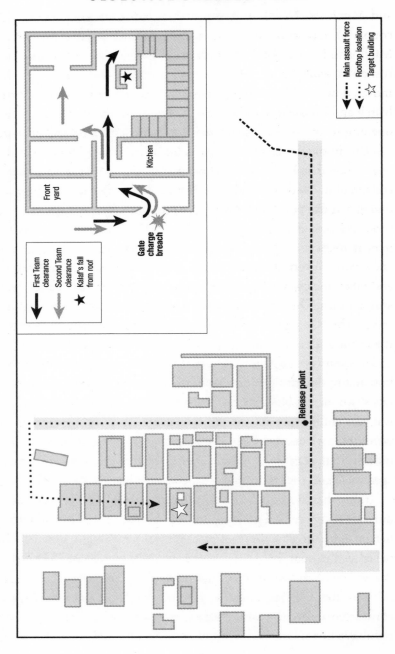

and Mitch the No. 2, as he transitioned from shotgun to rifle. A couple of Tabs completed the rest of our four-man team first in. Mitch and I saw an open-door threat in the back of the house as we rushed in, while maintaining site picture on any possible threats. We moved down the doorway. The two guys in the back broke left, while Mitch and I pushed straight across, past a room on our right with an opening to the roof for a gas-fired water tank. Some kind of noise came from the room as we passed it, but we moved straight on to the open-door threat. I was deep into the room at its far wall, and I collapsed my sector of fire, back toward Mitch, who, although designated the No. 2 man, took the position of the No. 3 man in a room-clearing diagram. When room clearing is taught the No. 1 man is never wrong, and makes his choice to go left or right and takes two corners. The No. 2 man goes the opposite of the No. 1 and takes one corner. The No. 3 man goes the opposite of the No. 2 and steps into the room, just far enough to clear the door by about a meter. The No. 4 goes opposite of the No. 3 man, and also just enters the room to clear the door at about a meter. This is how it is trained and it is very choreographed, but combat and building size determines how many shooters can actually fit. The key to remember is it only takes two men to actually clear a room. In this instance, there simply was not enough room to properly conduct room clearing. But we were where we were supposed to be, so he had adjusted mentally very quickly. In the opposite corner from me we encountered one military-aged male and one woman.

It was an odd situation we encountered within the split second of our entry – the male and female were hugging – the male had pulled her in tight. In all my deployments in Iraq and Afghanistan I had never seen this kind of "show of affection," if you will, at least not to that extent. Also, the male was fat for his size – well fairly fat, actually he was obese. Being that fat in the Middle East is sometimes considered a sign of wealth. I immediately knew something was not right. We had memorized a number of Arabic words and phrases so

I shouted at them, "Put up your hands, let me see your hands!" But to my three challenges there was no compliance, no compliance, no compliance. Everything went down in split seconds, from entry, to clearance, to encountering this couple, to me thinking that I knew my Arabic was terrible, but it had served me well in hundreds of missions and other targets. By now I had asked for compliance four or five times. The situation was tense; gunfire had been exchanged seconds earlier, and we knew about the personal protection Kalaf had in place.

It didn't feel right but what was I going to do? Drop my rifle, engage in a fist fight, or flip the safety – yes, the safety is always on – and shoot? I thought about the briefing about the potential for a suicide bomber; it's called a "judgment decision." I asked for compliance once more as I flipped my weapon off safe to semi. From my angle, my perspective on the couple's embrace, I could only get a clear sight of half the dude's face, not his body. All the years of training, all the lessons learnt not only in training but in combat... decisions had to be made, tough ones, and, if wrong, there were lifelong repercussions – from getting kicked out of the regiment to possibly being charged, to feelings of remorse and guilt... split-second judgment calls that change one's life forever.

I adjusted my sight picture on the rifle to compensate for the distance – he was less than 5 meters away – while I shouted out the final compliance request in Arabic. I calmly compensated for the optics over the rifle bore center line, which was about 4 inches, and raised the sight picture to where I wanted the bullet to impact. My sight picture centered to the base of his hairline; I depressed the trigger and fired as I finished the last statement. I hit him off the left side of the nose. Immediately his tense body position relaxed and he slumped over dead, but I immediately and very quickly put a second round into him. The female was released from the man's embrace by now and she fell forward. She cleared Mitch's line of fire and Mitch engaged the dead man with eight to ten rounds and I put seven more rounds into him as well. I called the room "clear." The female held up her dead companion. Her back was still to me. Mitch yelled for compliance in Arabic yet again but I did not clearly see her actions. But Mitch did. He saw her reach under the dead guy's buttocks, so Mitch fired off two rounds, then three more, as part of a failure drill – two into the body and then one into the head or neck. I engaged with about five rounds – two pairs to the body, and the final round to the head.

The entire sequence from entry to clearing the room took maybe 60 seconds if that. Meanwhile Rangers had cleared up to the first floor, while other assault squads on the stairs began clearing up the stairs to the roof.

Our platoon sergeant, Justin, another big Ranger at 6 feet tall and a solid, tactically sound leader, came in and now was a lot less stressed and angst-ridden than when we had been setting the pieces in place. Our doc and another Ranger swept in as well. They cleared the kitchen. Our battalion commander wanted to be part of this mission to recapture Abu Kalaf and he too burst into the building. This was his last deployment before a change of command to another job elsewhere. Incredibly, we also had the incoming battalion commander on target as well just as we had barely cleared it. This was a pain when the battalion commander wanted in on the action. Why? Because he was the senior ranking guy on the ground, and he didn't have to listen to anyone if he didn't want to. And it was not yet secured! Our outgoing commander, with the self-proclaimed call-sign of "Big Eagle," as he just been promoted to "full bird" colonel, wanted to fist-bump with me. I responded with, "Hey sir, I'll give you as many fist bumps as you like but let me finish clearing the building first."

"Right, right, right," was his response while laughing.

I moved upstairs and tied in with the rooftop teams and secured the target building within three minutes. Our rooftop guys had killed the target, Abu Kalaf. After getting killed he had fallen down the ventilation shaft into the gas-fired water tank room. This was the mystery sound that Mitch and I had heard earlier as we entered the building.

We conducted a battlefield interrogation on a female detainee; we had killed all the men. The only information we received was that the couple we had killed had shown up that day and that they were from Syria but she did not know who they actually were. While moving the bodies we found out what the deal was regarding the "show of affection" that had me alerted. Turned out the male was sitting on a suicide vest composed of about 7 pounds of Semtex and it was rigged with a couple of Russian hand grenade fuses. Upon discovery of the suicide vest we received a call over the radio that explosives had been found, and that Explosive Ordnance Disposal (EOD) was coming in to deal with it. We were told to avoid the room it was in. The code word was sent for us to move out of the house quickly. The EOD guy came in and left the building sometime later. He moved to a blocking position by a drainage ditch and blew the explosives in place.

Subsequently we picked up a flood of intel traffic about this target. It had stirred up a lot of things and led to more executions of other targets over the next few days. Biometric system intel such as detainee fingerprints helped build the military data biometrics system, useful not only for future missions but also for Homeland Security. We were now able to send digital fingerprints over the internet and if it was in the database you could get a hit. We would get a name, location, and past objective where the individual was fingerprinted; it would also tell us if he had been detained, or just entered into the system as a male who had been on the target area. Since we needed a clear line of sight for the computer, we had to drag all three dead bodies, Kalaf and the Syrian couple, to the driveway to run the biometric system.

As we walked back out of the target building we met Jason who, upon breach, had brought the vehicles to within four blocks and turned the "wagon train" around. He had got it ready so when we had finished the exploitation we were ready to roll back out. The sun slowly came up. This one op had taken up most of the night, but it had been an extremely worthwhile surgical strike. The execution took time but it was the right amount of time.

The "judgment call decision" concerning the mystery couple had turned out to be right and it was a good feeling. I had listened to my gut and paid attention to the culture, as in what is normal and what isn't. We wrapped up the target and moved off the objective. We called it a night.

Back at base we conducted a debrief. It always sucked when you did not capture the target alive since no additional intel emerged. Although possibly the battalion commander had wanted him dead. But Abu Kalaf had been a foreign fighter – an emir, essentially the head of the mafia in Mosul – and handled not only weapons and ammunition but was also the key organizer of foreign fighters and the ratline networks running throughout the area. Fighters came through those lines along with everything else usually from western Syria, Turkey, or Iran. Now we were not able to exploit his intel. Kalaf had his hands in a lot of these networks. How current would his intel have been because he had been in jail? Well, just because he was a prisoner did not mean he did not run things. The television show *Sopranos* was big at this time, and Jason, who hailed from Brooklyn, always said, "If the guy is in jail and you think he is not running things from jail you are so wrong."

The rooftop snipers had killed him right at the go. Kalaf had grabbed a Glock 19 from underneath his pillow. He tried to get to the edge of the rooftop to engage us on the ground where he was killed instantly.

We always tried to teach Ranger privates about judgment calls. A private probably would have erred on the side of not shooting. Mitch later said that I shot half a second before the suicide bomber was going to detonate. So far, all my judgment calls had been correct.

A lot of our success was based on not being complacent and taking every target for what it was – its own beast, and it could be

175

sleeping or rear its ugly head. You always had to snap everyone back to reality because any target that erupted created total chaos. But complacency can and did happen, even to me, a veteran of hundreds upon hundreds of missions. It would only take one night that could change everything and affect everybody.

Some of us talked about the shooting of the couple. Adrenaline was a huge factor in the emotion. Everyone asked how I felt – was I okay? By the time we got back to the FOB the overriding emotion was that I was simply pissed off that someone had tried to blow me up. It is only ever later that the reality of the situation hits you, but in this instance it was definitely a valuable lesson. Anything can happen and will happen. This all sat with me for a couple of days but then I pushed it off to the side; there was work still to be done.

On the same night 2nd Platoon had been looking for one of Abu Kalaf's moneymen. They successfully netted him and over $100,000 U.S. dollars in their own raid. These two raids put a serious dent in the foreign fighters' funding and operation capabilities. We executed ten more missions before the end of the deployment. Thanks to this key operation the deployment ended on a fairly high note; all the bad guys had been taken care of and nobody was injured.

No deployment was ever complete without some of our stupid shenanigans. There was some childish stuff early on when some Ranger privates wanted to see how many pairs of ladies' underwear, found on various objectives, they could stick into the platoon sergeant's backpack. I think it was 26 by the time Justin, the platoon sergeant, finally opened his pack and the underwear exploded out of it with him yelling, "What the…?" Another time they would hang a pair off the platoon leader's radio antennae. Finding humor in any situation was important and nobody was better at this than Ranger privates, who were, of course, goaded on by tabbed specialists and team leaders. It was time to go home.

PART FOUR

SERGEANT FIRST CLASS – PLATOON SERGEANT

CHAPTER ELEVEN

DON'T LEAD FROM THE FRONT, PLATOON SERGEANT!

Afghanistan, 2009–2010

Charlie Company had been back about a week from its last deployment to Iraq and with my pending promotion to sergeant first class I moved to S-3 Operations at Headquarters and Headquarters Company (HHC) across the Quad. I spent the next 11 months as a training non-commissioned officer responsible for securing all the ranges and training grounds for the battalion. Originally each company had its own training non-commissioned officer, but it was moved to battalion level for greater control and centralization and to alleviate errors at the company level. It wasn't a lot of fun but I loved listening to the whiny executive officers and platoon leaders. It was a good, eye-opening experience, learning what was required of platoon sergeants as far as administrative work went and how the system operated. Basically I learned how the wizard worked behind the curtain. If everything was done properly it was a thankless job, but if it got fouled up you definitely had officers breathing fire at you regardless of who was actually at fault.

So far we had been focused on fighting the war, and as Rangers progressed in leadership positions we learned a lot about warfighting but a lot of the administrative knowledge got left behind. Basically, leadership evolved but only tactically. I spent long Army days pounding the keyboards, staring at screens, and wasting my own gasoline driving around in my own not so fuel efficient late '70s Ford pickup truck to talk with other units and components to get signatures on a ton of paperwork. Why? Because I am a red-blooded American and I love Ford.

The S-3 shop at HHC had the hottest room in the battalion and it was rightly called "the house of pain." Our office was situated directly on top of the boilers and we had no air conditioning. We could not have doors, blinds or windows open as we were a secure room utilizing a classified computer system. Oh, the joy.

After the latest deployment a couple of platoon sergeants either reached the end of their commitment or it was time for them to move out to a different leadership position. Some were promoted to master sergeant and had to move on to other jobs. By early spring I had been promoted to platoon sergeant (E-7) and had just finished the Maneuver Advanced Non-Commissioned Officer's Course at Fort Knox, Kentucky. I was now in line for a platoon sergeant position. To what position and where I did not know. In my mind, as long as it wasn't Alpha Company, I would be happy in any of the other companies. The Ranger companies have distinct tribal personalities. For example, Alpha was called "Alpha-bots" because they are to this day the most regimented and strictest of all the companies. Charlie is considered the most lax or casual, whereas Bravo fit right in between the two personalities – it was perfect. Alpha-bot Company was just not for me. I didn't fit its personality.

Our operations sergeant major had come back, and together with the company first sergeant and battalion sergeant major worked out that I would be moved back to 1st Platoon, Bravo Company, as a platoon sergeant where I had started out as a private! In fact, the operations sergeant major had been my platoon sergeant when I was a new Ranger. This was totally awesome. He had kept his eye on my entire Ranger career. He also thought that I would be the best fit for that particular platoon and that I could help finish bringing it out of the "funk" it had been in for a few years. Pride was always at stake.

The hand-off at HHC and at Bravo Company went very well. I inherited a great group of squad leaders and team leaders. There was no head-butting except for the rare Ranger private drama. My leadership style was simple and effective, which worked for me. We discussed anything behind closed doors but ultimately when the door opened everyone went along with the decision that had been made even if there had been some disagreement. I had kept mental notes of what my own platoon sergeants had done well, and not so well, over the years. I grafted all the good into how I wanted to lead as a new platoon sergeant.

We had another good training cycle and since we were due to deploy to Afghanistan in the winter we conducted training in the snow-filled mountains of Washington. Who can forget our previous winter deployment to Afghanistan? The big suck. We were to conduct movement-to-contact en route to our objective, clearing any possible Command and Control nodes. These can be anything that acts as an early warning for the larger enemy force – it can warn them to flee the area, or arm themselves to fight. Whatever it was we had to deal with it.

Real-world injuries occurred, such as bad ankle sprains, because in Washington it was never just snow. It was a snow-rain mix, until we got to elevation, which always made the trail a slick, wet mess, and, coupled with 150-plus Rangers carrying combat equipment, it became a slick, muddy mess. Injuries forced us to sit and wait to pass the injured back down the line while the rest of the company kept moving. We talked medevac vehicles in and by then we were at least two movement cycles behind the company. Each cycle was a 50-minute walk, followed by a 10-minute rest period. The question was how to catch up and be combat effective once we reached the objective on the top of the mountain. We were supposed to have kept pace and we were supposed to have taken regular breaks. But being the last element in the order of march, we had to conduct the medevac. We decided there was not enough time to stop and take breaks; otherwise we would not make it to our objective and be able to join in the assault. We then would fail this training objective. We pushed on but at a slower and steadier pace and were able to compensate for the time lost. The battalion air officer accompanied us to evaluate and to observe me in my duties as a platoon sergeant. He said he had never heard of anybody take such a common-sense approach. I know it sounds simple, but sometimes the simplest things escape you. So, we moved slowly but continuously.

We caught up and my platoon was in good shape despite the uninterrupted movement. The company had set a good clip and taken its breaks but they were worn out. We arrived on time and everyone was overly impressed by our common-sense approach. They probably figured we were not going to make it. We then ran around in the snow, cleared the objective, conducted our company and force-on-force objective, then it was back to Joint Base Lewis McChord for the platoon live fires. The Army had restructured and merged Fort Lewis and McChord into one administrative component. We packed up and took two weeks' leave and then deployed.

• • •

We arrived in Afghanistan in December of 2009. This was my first Christmas spent in the country. Second Platoon of Bravo Company had rotated in about three days earlier and had already ran ops since combat operations are never allowed to stop. Everything was ready for us at 1st Platoon to run our own ops.

We weren't slotted to conduct a mission and we were in the process of getting our vehicles ready but then suddenly were told to stop and be on stand-by as a QRF. We listened to the briefing and made sure the privates and team leaders received their combat ammunition load. After inspection we waited to see if we were going to be called into action. Second Platoon was after a Targeted Individual (TI) who was a car bomb builder, and he had been tracked for days before any of us even arrived in-country. In fact, their tasking was the first or second operation since they arrived in theater. The operation order was completed and I was sitting loading my ammo into the magazine and getting myself ready to go when needed. My radio telephone operator dealt with crypto and communications. We watched the screen as the mission unfolded and I was simultaneously finalizing the chalk manifest, a name-list of who will be riding on a particular aircraft. This is important because if an aircraft is shot down, or broken, the JOC has a list of each individual on the aircraft manifest of the Rangers and other personnel who came into country and, in this case, who might be going out on the QRF. I had learned it is always best to have a complete and accurate manifest already constructed when you arrived in theater. Suddenly the TV screen exploded into a plume of dirt. The TI had detonated a vehicle inside the compound while our guys were setting into position to "Call Out," similar to a police hostage negotiator on a bullhorn.

We immediately spun up and for 15 minutes we were trying to get as much intel as possible on the ground and have the helicopters on stand-by so we could be lifted into the area. But, sadly for us, the targeted building was not that far away from the battlespace owner's COP so they launched a ground convoy QRF instead. We stood down.

But 2nd Platoon was incredibly lucky. The most prominent injuries were a dozen concussions. One Ranger was critical but he survived, and after two years of rehab and therapy he returned as a squad leader to B Company. He lost a finger and suffered some severe damage but nothing that could not be fixed. It was a wild ride to our first 24 hours in Afghanistan where usually nothing happened, unlike the pulse-pounding operational tempo of Iraqi missions. We stood up the rest of our equipment that night after 2nd Platoon returned. They had known the target was a bombmaker, just not that he was sitting at home with his car bomb.

We rolled out the next night. When things like this happened guys could react in different ways, but I was proud that the previous op did not affect our mission in the same area. No doubt it was in their minds but it had no impact. We successfully cleared our targets that night.

Every other day there was an operation and we rotated with the other platoon. It was close to Christmas when we were called upon to an objective requiring several platoons. First Platoon launched a GAF. Some platoons preferrred not to load and drive the trucks because of IED threats. No one liked the thought of being blown up when you can just fly instead. The bombers in Afghanistan had gotten good at hiding IEDs and better at detonating them. But my weapons squad leader of 1st Platoon was not concerned and he was in charge of the vehicles. That being said, my platoon decided early on that we had an under-employed mortar section and we offered them the opportunity to do more than get coffee for other people. Instead, they could actually go out and do something. We used them as drivers and, as a plus, they brought their mortars along as well. And let's be honest, who didn't like bringing a big mortar cannon to the fight? This was a win for all, as they were more than happy to man and crew vehicles. In total we drove about eight to ten missions. In the grand scheme of things this was not a lot, but considering the daily IED attacks it still represented a fairly high number of operations to be driving on. For us it worked out though; we had extra Rangers, an organic 81mm mortar system on the objectives, air assets, and more guns in the fight.

On this particular operation we set up the mortar firing point in the Vehicle Drop-Off area (VDO). Our two objective compounds were about 1 klick apart and that was plenty of separation for our two different strike forces to not endanger one another should bullets fly. Our two organic strike forces did not have enough air assets to fly us both at the same time; that is why we drove in, set up the VDO, and walked 3 klicks toward our objective in a big arc. We even passed the target vicinity a little. We also refined the target with better intel gathering and were able to pinpoint it more exactly. We set the pieces around the compound with blocking positions and sniper teams. And then, wouldn't you know it, while setting the pieces, we were compromised.

We were lying undercover around 100 meters away. Our last line of cover was a small tree line and a ditch, with a large plowed field separating us from the target compound, waiting for the pieces to get emplaced. But I got this funky feeling while I watched the snipers getting in place on the target roof closest to us. The roof was not as high as we would have liked and was therefore exposed to fire from inside the compound. The drop from the wall to the roof inside was only about 4 feet and this meant that it would not allow the roof team easy egress should rounds be exchanged and they were forced to get off the roof quickly. I told Austin that he needed to be ready to run and explosively breach the compound's gate because the snipers might not get out of there should they be compromised. Austin was my 1st Squad's squad leader and a big man at 6'1" and 210 pounds. He was a little eccentric at times but light-hearted and could always be counted on to pack a sandwich onto target. Yes, a sandwich! He was a great Ranger. The only way out for the snipers would be if we breached the gate and provided cover fire. As we were discussing the situation a two-way gunfight suddenly erupted. Our snipers had got compromised, just as I had feared, and the team radioed in. They were engaged at their 10 o'clock from enemy fire from an elevation about 3 feet higher, making it impossible for them to get off their rooftop. The command to execute the breach was given and stupidly, still in the mindset of my previous E-6 squad leader position, I led the charge running to the sound of the guns. As a platoon sergeant my job was to oversee the various elements and control the fight from the breach, the "friction" point in most assaults, not to lead from the front! My job now was to press the assaulters with direction.

The rest of my assault squad followed me. On the ISR video you can see one lone idiot, me, ahead of the assault force, running by himself across the open field to the target. It didn't seem to be such a big time-gap but, in reality, I was alone at the target for a full 15–20 seconds. Finally, the assault squad joined me, and explosive charges were blown. The entire sequence took less than a minute. But in a gunfight, a lot can happen in just a minute.

Inside the compound was a separate guesthouse. First Squad's No. 1 man, in room-clearing terms, went straight down the long wall, and Squad Leader Austin turned and went into a doorway to the left, not knowing it was a separate sub-compound. He immediately became engaged in a gunfight with the TI of all people! It was the same fighter that had been engaging the rooftop team prior to our explosive breach.

Another Ranger joined the fracas within less than 15 seconds. Nobody knew what was going on. Dust and dirt, explosions, screams, and moans littered the area as Matt, a SAW gunner, laid waste somewhere. The resulting dust cloud obstructed everything as though it was a smoke grenade. That was the major drawback to blowing explosive charges to gain entry in Afghanistan.

It turned out that an AK-armed enemy, our TI, was inside the guesthouse. Austin had gone to the doorway parallel to the direction his squad was going to clear. Austin and the shooter exchanged gunfire, but the fighter was not able to see Austin during the fight other than his muzzle flashes. Austin managed to hit him, and the insurgent shot along the wall in response, creating a lot of ricochets. He then peeled into an interior doorway and threw a grenade, which bounced off Austin as he tried to spin away from it and back out into the courtyard. He managed to avoid most of it but caught a nickel-sized piece of shrapnel in his cheek. The shrapnel piece knocked out two teeth on the right side of his jaw, which was at the point of impact. Then, like a coin standing up on a table, it severed his tongue and knocked out three more teeth on the left side of his mouth before creating a massive exit wound. Austin looked like he had been shot in his face. What a mess.

Matt had figured out what was going on and ran up to the front porch where Austin was now on the ground in the near right corner of the compound. He had ended up there after trying to avoid the grenade and most of the shrapnel. Matt was rapidly firing continuous short round bursts into the doorway as suppressing fire. Austin meanwhile got up and walked out while Matt covered him. Matt tried to get out but was stuck reloading a drum as Doc and I popped in and covered him. Doc covered Matt while I broke to the right and put rounds into the bay of windows. We were now outside in the little courtyard shooting suppressive fire into the house. I helped Austin and called Doc and Matt back to the gate. It always sucked withdrawing from a fight even if only momentarily.

I left Matt covering the doorway with his SAW and moved Austin outside of the compound where Doc began to treat him. I turned around, found Eddy who was Austin's Alpha Team leader, and yelled in his ear that Austin was hit and that he was now the acting squad leader, to which I got the standard reply "Roger." Eddy was squared away, a solid Ranger who knew his job.

Austin tried to communicate his 15 seconds from the breach to the actions on the objective but because of his severe facial trauma he could not speak. He just mumbled, spitting and drooling blood.

While this was going down, command net on the radio informed us that 2nd Platoon was three minutes out from their helo assault. I tried to abort the mission as compromised while Platoon Leader Greg had already spun up a medevac. Greg was 6'1", 200 pounds and a

West Point grad. He was a great Ranger leader, a solid tactician, and a great friend. Seemingly Rangers come in two sizes, small-to-medium like me or large. I should have been dealing with the medevac – that was my job and another learning experience. The platoon sergeant deals with casualties and the classification of the wounded, and not the platoon leader.

We also had our battalion physician's assistant on target who had wanted to tag along. Now he and Doc were working on Austin. I also learned that any facial injury could not be classified as walking wounded. The physician's assistant informed me right then and there, which wasn't too bad an ego blow for not knowing the classification for facial trauma. The physician's assistant and I had been friends during his enlisted days in B Company. Anything on the face was considered urgent and required surgery because if the throat and mouth were damaged it could result in an airway problem. Live and learn. Additionally, Austin's tongue was halfway out of his mouth and something might have lodged in his throat. There was a brief discussion between the Doc and the physician's assistant about doing a cricothyrotomy – an incision into the skin and membrane to ensure the airway wouldn't collapse. Austin replied with the universal sign language of the middle finger. Funny guy, Austin. But he needed to be emergency medevac'd.

Greg and I were still trying to get 2nd Platoon to abort their infil, to which the first sergeant, who had accompanied us on target, said 2nd Platoon wasn't going to abort and to just work on my casualty evacuation.

We also had to deconflict the area with all the assets on the ground and in the air. It was a total mess and the medevac was flying to the wrong objective HLZ. During planning we had inadvertently given two of the HLZs the same name. Both platoons had used the same name for a different HLZ on each objective, something we didn't realize until the operation was over. The forward observer had to "rope" the medevac in due to confusion with the HLZ and the close proximity of the objectives. The "rope" under night vision looks like a giant laser lasso with the individual doing the rope as the point of origin. The forward observer used a handheld laser and made circling motions with his hand, "roping," to guide the helicopter in to the correct HLZ. As this was going down the platoon cleared the compound. By this time the air asset had also arrived to medevac Austin. It was a fairly wild night.

Austin was medevac'd to the CSH for surgery and three hours later he departed for Bagram to have another surgery, and then through Germany to the U.S. He would be back just three weeks later. Austin is, in a word, awesome.

We had cleared the original big compound and we still had Ranger privates in the courtyard of the guest facility. Eddy and I took a team to clear the guest compound. We cleared it and the fighter that was engaged by Austin and Matt certainly looked dead. But, in fact, he was not. Doc took a look but I said that we could not risk compromising another medevac crew. Doc needed to do what he could and we would ground medevac the casualty when we left the target. Doc felt strongly that the wounded man would not make it either way. Our battalion physician's assistant agreed. The man was riddled with bullets. I told them to do what they could for him and we would be ready to drive off target shortly. After another 25 minutes we pulled off the target, and here was another testament to the skill and dedication of our medical personnel. The fighter made it to surgery, lost an arm because it was shattered, but survived. It was unbelievable but our docs ruled.

We had found three or four more hand grenades, his AK, and tons of ammo in a knapsack. The insurgent had been passing through the area and had asked if he could stay. The locals had, of course, agreed as it is their culture and custom. We took two detainees off the objective and did nothing more than ask them questions. We called in the atmospherics to try to discover what the locals were seeing and hearing, how the bad guys were affecting their area, and to see if what we were doing was making a difference. We kept them for a couple of days and released them together with monetary compensation for their loss of time. This had all taken place in the weeks shortly after we had arrived in-country and before Christmas of 2009.

●●●

Never in a million years did I think I would hand over the actions of a platoon sergeant on an objective. Greg the platoon leader and I had discussed how we would handle this if it ever happened. Before deploying we came up with our own "code phrase" for this, where I would call him on the radio and say, "high five," as in "tag, you're in." Usually it is the platoon sergeant's job to control the flow of traffic in and out of the target area, thereby allowing the platoon leader to communicate with the JOC, updating them with reports. Having handed the clearance of the target off to the platoon leader caused him to slow down his reports to the JOC, prompting them to call him instead for updates. This makes the platoon leader's radio telephone operator act like a little kid continually tugging at their parents' pants, asking for everything in the store, because the JOC needs updates too. That night the platoon leader did a lot of my work.

I learned a few things about my leadership level that night. I asked my first sergeant questions based on the situation and the outcome of the mission for my own edification and knowledge. I never let go of these lessons during my time as a platoon sergeant. The lessons learnt came back to pay dividends down the road in future deployments. Part of the knowledge base gets lost as generations of Rangers are too busy training and going to war. Platoon sergeants pass on the knowledge during training and a lot of it was gleaned from previous platoon sergeants who took maybe seven or eight years before receiving that rank, whereas now a squad leader could be promoted within two to three years. This led to a loss of administrative fieldcraft and, as such, there was no ability to hone something that had been lost. We were so successful, and almost never took any casualties, that we almost never dealt with those issues in the field. In the ten years I had been in the Army I had only been on two objectives that required medevac. Not that you would want to deal with it – losing an important member of your element was terrible – but you need to be adequately prepared nonetheless. In this mission I failed to evaluate situations properly. For example, I didn't think about all the moving pieces involved in calling in medevac during a large-scale operation. There were a lot of details about the various issues and deconflicting the space. Another example was that our vehicles were in the way for a medevac HLZ. Knowing the deconfliction plan, in terms of moving all the assets and moving parts of the operation, is crucial for my level of leadership. The leader requires the maturity and the experience to see these issues and address them during planning so the plan can be refined to have the least amount of complications due to human error.

Over the next few years this was always in the back of my mind. I was determined that from now on I had to be able to deconflict quickly and to see what was urgent and what was not. Of course, the commanding officer learned that he should have aborted the air assault to clear the air space instead of pressing on to the target. It was easy to abort 2nd Platoon since they had not yet infiled. But they wanted to execute their mission, and what Ranger would not want to get into a fight? Lessons relearned sucked and could, and did, create heated Ranger discussions. Of course, one can never plan for everything no matter the level of experience. So we had a conversation about mistakes and eye-opening lessons. When 2nd Platoon had executed the mission to capture a car-bomb maker and they were blown up, nobody had planned for that either. We just did not think about scenarios like that – we are Rangers; we smash in doors and shoot people in the faces and nothing ever goes wrong. Now we had two separate occasions where things went wrong in a single deployment.

Back on the objective Austin was gone, there had been one enemy casualty, and we handed the target back to the original BSO. We worked with about four to five different battlespaces. The conventional owners were the face of the battlespace and smoothed out ruffled feathers before we drove back. We dropped off the detainee casualty and went back to our camp to debrief the operation. Austin was doing great but he was unable to talk, so he had written a message stating that it was nobody's fault, and not knowing the exact layout of the target compound was just one in a million possible scenarios. He also let me know which of his two team leaders he thought should be the squad leader in his absence.

We always coordinated and worked with the BSOs to avoid problems on all fronts, though we always had priority over the battlespace. We also tried to coordinate with the Afghans as well. We gave them basic intel, but nothing too detailed. For example, we would tell them we are going out tonight, roughly here and for this guy. They wanted to feel included and to have a say in how we executed ops in their country. They would let us know if we offended them and, if and when we did, we had to project a suitable sense of humility when we apologized. Relationships could be difficult, but like any organization there are good guys and there are bad guys – some were decent and others were not. As a rule, they did not agree with the U.S. deployment although we were only trying to help them and their country, and especially to set things up for them once we left. Going after bad guys created stability.

● ● ●

When I was on staff during the previous deployment the use of conventional airlifts began. We had a limit of Special Operations aircraft to deliver people on target and we prioritized targets, including the terrain where the targets were. The choice to use conventional air assets was simple. If we sat around waiting for SOAR assets to become available we probably lost the ability to strike at the target, who might move in the interim. We figured out how to work with the BSO, specifically how to use his air assets and his pilots' abilities to infil onto our targets. We off-set infils, for example, when the pilots were a bit hesitant to land too closely to the targets. The conventional pilots were not always fully employed, usually having to wait for the conventional units, and then to provide them lifts. They also flew "ring routes" – looping and dropping off mail or supplies to various COPs. So naturally they were fighting hand over fist to fly for us and be actually part of a fight, a mission. It almost turned into auditions for them and Rangers gave feedback to the pilots and crews regarding how did they perform, did they land correctly, on the right spot, and a lot of other things. They wanted feedback and got it. If a pilot was not good enough, bearing in mind his limited equipment of the air asset such as not having all the avionics and tech a SOAR aircraft had, commanders and flight officers received our feedback during the debrief. They had a simple rule – three strikes, screw-ups, and he was out.

We were fairly nervous at the beginning because the conventional guys had to use seats and seat belts whereas Special Operations did not. Instead we used safety lanyards which, of course, had to be cleared through their aviation chain of command. Think of it this way: if you drive a Ferrari to work every day and it breaks but your wife has a Prius, you're gonna take the Prius to work. Some transportation is better than none. After all, a ride to work is a ride to work. But for the most part we had great pilots and overall it was a clear 9/10 for the conventional pilots and their aircraft. But sometimes, for particular missions, you simply needed Special Operations aircraft.

There were only a few times where the pilot got a little skittish on an HLZ and moved the air asset a little. Once a pilot moved on the HLZ when there was a full brown-out, dust and dirt everywhere, and he was at 50 feet flying solely on instruments because he could not see. The insertion was a lot slower and we came to a flat static hover and then straight down, unlike Special Operations aircraft which came in like we were used to – a sort of flare. It worked out fantastic though because we could do a lot more and basically had a direct airlift asset.

We also asked for their guidelines and recommendations for their criteria for a quality HLZ. We always informed them what we would ideally want in terms of infil and exfil on targets. If the conventional unit disapproved of the plan, then they always came back with alternatives they could execute comfortably. We adapted and changed a few plans, meshing SOPs and TTPs. When this happened, it took maybe an extra hour of revising our plans but it was totally worth it.

The conventional direct support assets were a big success across Afghanistan, allowing us to operate continuously. We used them to the best of their abilities and they were happy to be part of our missions.

●●●

I never thought the Taliban regained the upper hand in Afghanistan. However, they did enjoy some regional and local successes. We had a handle on the key areas, but we did not expect or anticipate the speed with which they were able to shift to other areas we were not paying attention to. In 2009 there were certain places along the main route from FOB Salerno in Khost to the COP that were always color-coded "black status." Traveling required clearance patrols with EOD because there were tons of IEDs. But we put enough pressure into this valley, Khost, and struck at enough targets that for a whole week that route did not have a single IED. Our ops made a huge impact and it was a feather in our cap.

From the start of our deployment we had a continuing target called Objective *Kraaken*, a "piss-me-off" target. Seemingly this guy was uncatchable; no matter how good the intel or the planning or the tracking was, he always slipped out at the last minute. Once we missed him by just 20 minutes. We finally tried a middle of the daylight raid to get this guy. We almost never conducted daylight raids because targets do not move as much or as effectively at night and we owned the nights. We studied his patterns and daily life. We were continuously talking with the JOC in Bagram as well as our company and battalion TOC as to what qualified as a trigger to launch a mission. He needed to be at a location for so long, during daylight, and the air assets had to be able to shift HLZs on the fly because of the additional risks. After a few days all the criteria were met, and although we had just returned from an op, within an hour we knew we had to go. We had a plan already on the shelf, a back burner, which everyone knew. We conducted a ten-minute brief to add small changes and launched immediately. We missed him but the daylight allowed us additional opportunities to observe him. We chased him across the Khost Valley bowl and we hit a new series of building objectives. Each time he stopped at a new compound, and we cleared it, it got a new objective number. We launched on Objective *Kraaken 8* and ended on Objective *Kraaken 12*. We began a foot chase, smashing through targets, from target building to target building, until we lost him running into the bazaar, a large open-air market. He probably weighed a buck-forty, no body armor or combat gear, and in flip flops. The average Ranger probably weighed about 170, plus gear. We never got closer than about 600 meters to him, but we chased him until we got to within 800 meters of the bazaar. Given the number of people in the bazaar, we went back to the last target building he stopped at and asked to exploit it. I had led the chase squad with a forward observer, medic, and the rest of 3rd Squad, so about 13 guys in total, with easily 400 people in the market. We called for an exfil and were satisfied that at least we had given him a big scare and broken his pattern. We almost caught him once again when we intercepted comms with his other bad guys, saying he was going to Pakistan to hide for a while. We tracked him when he returned to a section of a small town 2–3 klicks away from the FOB. We did not take any vehicles and walked out the side entrance of the FOB's fence, thereby avoiding any early warning from the noise of our vehicles or our air assets. All our air assets were at "level one" with full-speed rotors and they would be able to jam immediately, going from take-off to arrival within one minute. This was a great response time in case we needed it. We raided Objective *Kraaken 13*. We walked in and silently entered and cleared the compound and finally captured him. He was what we called a "mid-level pipe swinger." He wasn't the guy who transported war materiel but the guy who took what he needed to supply himself and others, akin to a broker. He was responsible for a smaller area, not the province as a whole. Hence he was a mid-level player, but one who could give us the lower-level layers; more importantly, he could lead us to the top end of the network. A mid-level player gave us access to everything. Our first sergeant had accompanied us on this objective, while our commander was with 3rd Platoon, which had been spending the deployment detached from the company. After we confirmed we had the TI, the first sergeant came out onto the porch, got mine and Greg's attention where we had been discussing the exfil, and decided to make fun of the commander's basketball moves! It was such an odd show of excitement from the first sergeant that it took a second to be funny but it was and still is one of the most talked about goofy moments. Rangers like to keep things funny especially if the commanding officer is the butt of the joke.

•••

Our company operated into the new year. There were still a lot of legacy targets, such as Osama bin Laden and others who came into Afghanistan from Pakistan from time to time. One particular night, two Afghan nationals came to either a COP or an FOB in Paktia – we didn't know the finer details. These were two separate individuals who both said that a legacy target, Objective *Duck*, would be in a particular village at a particular time. Even if their information was wrong, you would still want to take a swing at the target. We got every asset we needed right then and there, including Special Operations aircraft. Not only was it a better flight but the flight lead had the authority to adjust and change HLZs on the fly. If an HLZ was fouled, he'd hover and let us fast-rope in, or we identified a secondary HLZ and landed there. The battlespace conventional assets couldn't do this.

The briefing included whether or not to sit and observe or to take the target down. But as it was a legacy target, the decision was made to swing for it. Our company commander, who commanded an independent strike force at a different FOB, was at the location where SOAR was so he jumped in and brought more Rangers in as a QRF. Our company commander thought that since finally all three platoons were here that this operation should be turned into a larger company-sized one. This didn't change my platoon's mission. We still were to walk in, isolate the objective area, and secure the village, while 2nd and 3rd Platoons were to clear the rest of the village and provide a large security element and enough men to clear the entire village area. We had enough Rangers to do this easily.

In the mountains was a snow line with sporadic snow banks which we saw from ISR but we would have to fight the knee-deep snow for about one klick. During the planning process, Brian, our weapons squad leader, had a great idea. Brian was another big boy at 5'10" and 200 pounds, nicknamed "the Badger." He was the oldest Ranger in the platoon, a great friend, a superb tactician, and always grumpy. Why walk uphill, when instead we could land on a secondary separate valley, which connected to the valley we were going to raid? We could off-set higher, making anyone in our target area think we were after something completely different and then walk downhill, which was easier than the uphill struggle to the target. This was a testament to Rangers being involved in making plans and not just executing them. Common sense rules when applied properly. It was a flat-out scoot downhill and we moved faster than the company thought. We set up an isolation squad on the objective area while the rest of the company brought in Phase Two – the other platoon and the rest of the company. Waiting for them to finalize their movement was not too bad, although nobody had dressed for the 20-degree weather up in the mountains, meaning our winter over-parkas had been left in our deployment bags at the camp. We had dressed for the mid-forties and we generated a lot of body heat carrying our gear, having walked, and walked, and walked, and sweated, and sweated, and sweated, but we now sat in the cold. Some of us might have gone down with cold weather injuries as the emplacement took longer than we thought but it all worked out in the end.

Unfortunately, we hit the wrong valley. The village had looked like the target village that had been described. It is always difficult to plan and strike accurately simply from word-of-mouth reports because most Afghans do not know the names of the valleys. They give a walking distance and point to a general area. Nor do they use maps and have rarely seen one.

We missed the legacy target but we had fun. It was really fun for the company commander who got to bug all three platoon sergeants instead of just one. We did clear the village and took atmospherics and some detainees but nobody knew anything about our legacy target or Taliban in the area. All the platoons cycled back out via our air asset and we had a lot of fun laughing at the Rangers earlier who had to walk around 700 meters up the hills while we watched them from our security position. They started with a sprint and slowed down to a jog, then a fast walk, and then hit the wrong target. Too funny. Finding humor in these situations was always key to good morale. We always knew that no matter how much it sucked there was always someone who sucked more...

Another thing that made us laugh constantly was when people wearing NODs fell down – we knew that eventually it would be one of us. Brian, my weapons squad leader, would always look around to see if anyone had seen him fall; if no one had, he would pop back up and dust himself off, as if it hadn't happened. It was always the best to tease him about it later, because, well, that's what we do! It's not a matter of *if* you'll fall, only *when*, and who will see you and laugh.

* * *

Although General Stanley McChrystal, commander of U.S. forces in Afghanistan, said in late 2009 that the Taliban were gaining the upper hand, I think the Taliban did not. During this time more restrictions were placed on U.S. forces. The rules changed and became tighter and more restrictive. In Iraq, high civilian casualties, loss of life, not affiliated with a target was treated differently. In Afghanistan, if one civilian was killed the entire strike force was shut down, ending its operations for anything from seven days to a month. A bad shoot, or bad judgment call, could also lead to repercussions because of the Uniform Code of Military Justice (UCMJ) – the military's version of law – though it probably didn't mean going to jail. Squad leaders could be demoted or even removed from the regiment altogether, even though they were only trying to do what they thought was the right thing at the time. The issue often was that when the shooter engaged the bad guys the other Rangers opened up on the surrounding buildings without seeing or identifying specific targets. They were doing what they were trained to do, but civilians were sometimes caught in the fire. From Iraq to Afghanistan, from deployment to deployment, it was vital that we made sure that our men understood the different Rules of Engagement every time.

Being a platoon sergeant, I saw how government and local political restrictions led to issues that played out on the battlefield. By now we worked with local Afghan units who volunteered for more training to operate in conjunction with us. This was a new requirement – to take new local faces to objectives with the strike force. There was a trust factor involved since they were armed and part of our strike force, but no matter how well they were trained the cultural differences and the mentality of Army Ranger versus Afghan was always an issue. The Afghans always erred on being kind and courteous to their own people. We tried to make them understand their job – they were the local face – we were not just going out to randomly hit someone's house. We had actually targeted him, and this was a seriously bad guy in this house. Why was he there, where was he before, what was he doing? Those were the questions we wanted them to understand. It took years and there was a back and forth to try to get them to understand this. We tried to convince them that they needed to let the Afghan police force be the nice face, while they needed to know that if we were going out on operations it was for bad dudes, and they needed to explain that to the locals on target.

Whenever we rotated into country we never had the same Afghan Partnering Unit (APU). They had different rotational cycles. We inherited one for a few weeks from the previous platoon and then they also rotated out and went back to their own base. They had a similar rotation like the Rangers, but they did not get to leave Afghanistan. At the platoon level we had to recertify them every time, from marksmanship to room clearing and making sure the boxes were checked for them to be ready to operate with us. This always took a few days during the transitions.

By 2011, every deployment saw more APUs attached to us from team size up to squad level. We had to have them all in order to operate; if one became sick a medic had to write a report why and what prevented him from going on this mission. And then this report had to be sent to the big JOC prior to our operation being approved. Working with them could be incredibly frustrating and aggravating as it was another load of political and cultural sensitivities we had to consider when sometimes you simply had to smash something, and they always demanded compensation for the people whose properties we went through. In theory it was great to have local faces in front of the assault after 10 years of the U.S. being in-country. Now Afghans were responsible for their own country, or at least in theory.

We rotated home in the middle of spring 2010. We would be back before the end of the year.

CHAPTER TWELVE

BAD SANTA

Afghanistan, 2010

We conducted another normal training cycle before we deployed to Afghanistan yet again. This time my platoon was going to be detached from the rest of the company, as platoons started to do more away from their companies. We were to operate independently with the executive officer acting as the ground force commander. We arrived in-country in October 2010 and we were stationed in a little FOB called Lagman out southwest. It was a small battalion-sized FOB for the BSO. We had a small camp within it large enough for two platoons but usually only one operated from there. We had flown into Kandahar, unpacked our body armor, loaded up on helicopters, and flew to FOB Lagman, which was about a 45-minute flight. We had everything we needed to operate for 24 hours. The Air Force-approved shipping containers, called ISU-90 – filled with sensitive items, extra weapons, comms, squad boxes, and pallets – were to arrive the next night by C-130 onto a nearby desert landing strip which was located a couple of klicks outside the wire of the small outpost. We secured the area for the C-130 to land and to forklift the containers onto the flatbeds. We had to do this every time we needed resupply of anything that was deemed unable to be transported by helicopters. During the deployment we had to waste four or five nights to secure the landing strip instead of executing missions.

We had a new platoon leader. Our old one, West Point graduate Greg, had decided he had fulfilled his military obligation required by the contract and had left the military. It was always hard but fun to break in a new platoon leader and find one you liked. Sometimes there was head-butting and the platoon leaders were not always on par with how Rangers wanted things done. Those situations had to be worked out. Being a conventional, regular, platoon leader is a far cry from leading high-speed Rangers. However, on this occasion we ironed it out quickly, and the new platoon leader Jake and I became great friends. Jake was another monster at 6'2" and 225 pounds' worth of fun. He was fun-loving, always open and receptive to platoon input, and overall a great Ranger leader.

We worked well together, especially after coming to terms with our unconventional way of operating, although sometimes Jake made me feel like beating my head against the wall. I explained to him the reasons why things were done a certain way. Jake had, in a previous deployment, been commanding a small COP which Rangers used for operations, and we handed over the battlespace to him so he knew some of the ways we worked. But it is always different when you are part of a new team. Every platoon leader went through the same transformation if he wanted to be integrated.

We operated by ourselves with the company executive officer in command out of the Zabul Province. It said a lot when the company commander and the company's first sergeant picked our platoon to operate independently. It meant they had confidence in our leadership and our platoon. They believed in our daily decision-making process and that we would make the best call on the ground regardless of the situations we encountered.

We never once used a Special Operations air asset in direct support during this deployment; instead we relied on our conventional airlift. We conducted 35 missions during the deployment. Sometime in November we had a decent target and the sergeant major wanted to come along. He called and told me to put him on our manifest and he would fly conventional using our assigned lift asset out of Kandahar. We took off for the target after briefing the colonel by video teleconference. By now our tactics in Afghanistan had evolved to what is known as a "Call Out." Our tactics no longer called for the highly successful silent entry technique. This was mainly due to the changing political influence of the Afghan government. And this was the safest way to put the Afghan face at the front of the assault.

A Call Out for us meant isolating the compound, setting security around it. We then had our interpreters use a bullhorn to call the people out of the target compounds. Over the last three to four deployments, be that in Afghanistan or Iraq, higher command agreed that we needed them at strike-force level. In layman's terms, the new tactic was similar to a hostage call-out scenario used by police negotiators. We communicated to the people inside that they were surrounded and had to give up. Technology had improved greatly by this time and so we were able to use ISR, which provided a 360-degree view, and accompanying software helped us identify the height of walls or buildings and so forth. We also used Google Earth for our imagery and planning.

This new technology was very useful to our mission planning. We were able to tailor our equipment exactly to what was needed. For example, on previous missions our ladders had been either too long or too short.

Typically, we called out the men first and made them lift up their shirts, ensuring they were not armed or wearing explosive devices. Then the women and children followed. We made them leave the courtyard and move outside of the compound where we then contained them and occasionally tied them up. We never tied up the women and children, just corralled them into a designated area, and had a couple Rangers pull security. We always had to anticipate potential lies. A Call Out typically lasted between 45 and 60 minutes. The new technique was implemented to protect the strike force given the Afghan geo-political situation and it provided a bit more security, because our guys were not going to run blindly into baited ambushes – although it was always still a possibility. The war was ever evolving. We also had the ability to escalate our use of force; for example, by throwing in flash bang grenades and then hollering over the bullhorn. We could escalate from there, and if a Call Out lasted longer than 45 minutes we got antsy and escalated our show of force, the violence, even further.

In this particular instance, the plan the executive officer, platoon leader, and I briefed to the colonel was as follows. We were to fly in as close as possible to the target with conventional assets and thereby deny the enemy the ability to flee and then we were to conduct a Call Out. He gave us the thumbs-up and we got ready to go to the FOB flight line where we waited for the birds. We loaded on and took off for the 20-minute flight to our target. We deliberately landed short and ran to isolate the target building. Unfortunately, when you got close to everywhere and anywhere, people heard the helicopters all the time and that was probably how the SEAL team with Marcus Luttrell got compromised. The sound of the Chinook helicopter would be heard across 7 to 10km because of the mountain ranges and the valleys, and because there were no other ambient sounds. Contrary to popular belief, helicopters are audible for several klicks before actually reaching the target area. But I always would rather do a quick sprint to target, rather than walk a few klicks.

In any event, our target became active and people ran out of the building and only from the target building. We knew that our target assessment was correct because only bad guys ran! We always had a contingency to break off an element from our assault force to deal with that possibility. The main assault executed its mission, while others chased the runner – the "squirter" – and anybody else who might have left the target area and had been in the orchard, a wadi or a building where he thought he had the advantage to get away.

We had briefed that during the Call Out nobody was to enter the target building until we were confident that everyone was out of the building, but the sergeant major – not carrying the heavy gear like everyone else was – blew through the door with another E-7. They were armed with rifles, some ammo, and thought they only needed radios. He and the E-7 barged into the compound and all we could think was, *Oh no, here we go – he's pulling a Leeroy Jenkins.* They were now in the compound's courtyard and I tried to get them to come back out. "Hey, this is not what we briefed; you gotta come out." It was one of those moments when things could go very badly and I thought, *I gotta control this now, oh this is going to be fun tonight.*

As this was happening, my assault squad was executing the plan, laddering up, and locking down the compound. To their surprise when their weapons "dropped" down to scan the compound there were Rangers in the courtyard already. Sometimes they only listened so much since they were the higher rank. It was not deliberate necessarily, but once the target became active, the sergeant major reverted to how we had handled things a few rotations earlier; back then it meant that once there was a runner you hit the target hard. We finally managed to get them out of the uncleared compound. In the meantime, Jake led the chase team. The separation between the two elements was almost 1 klick and that was kind of the limit of comfort where we liked to pull the chain and stop, mostly because that was the maximum distance we could support ourselves using only our organic weapons systems.

We were on the southside of Paktia/Ghazni provinces where the mountains started to creep in and that elevation kicks your butt. You could easily get gassed and you did not want 25–30 Rangers running out of steam as they would have, had they joined the chase squad. Once exhausted you were basically combat ineffective. I kept 1st Squad and two machine guns with me at the target building and sent 3rd Squad with a gun after the chase squad to support them. The sergeant major and his E-7 took off along with them. We cleared the target courtyard, which had a wood and brush pile. We searched for caches and found one within it.

Jake's element in the meantime had cleared their area and found the runner hiding in a small well-pump shack. They searched the immediate area for anything he may have hidden. The chase squad radioed that they were "Clear and Secure" with one detainee and headed back to us.

It was winter, of course, and bitterly cold. The sergeant major had returned and was on the flank by himself as he walked by another large compound. Sergeant Major "Leeroy" banged on the gate demanding hot chai from the inhabitants in the middle of the night. *Oh lord, are you really going to do this to me twice – asking for tea in the middle of the night?* I thought. David, the squad leader from the chase squad, along with our platoon leader, went over and said that it was probably not a good idea to wake up people and alert any enemy just to get tea. David was a big guy too, only a bit shorter and a bit lighter than our Jason. David was a great tactician and fun to have in the JOC or anywhere for that matter. He was light-hearted and found humor in most situations. I can just imagine what he thought about our Leeroy sergeant major! I was irritated but tried to laugh it off – Sergeant Major Pete would be the only one who would do this!

We conducted battlefield atmospherics with our interpreters and ran the standard list of questions by the inhabitants: where are the fighters, do they come through here, what's the deal with the runner from your house who ran into the desert, and so on? What we had found matched our intel that we had on the target. We took two males back with us, one of them the runner. The other one was questioned and released later.

When we exfiled the sergeant major apologized with a "don't know what came over me, I got squirrely and antsy because I'm out of the JOC." I thought the JOC saw everything we were doing. Haha! But I said to keep this in mind the next time he came out with us. Murphy's law was always around. It certainly made the mission memorable, because Sergeant Major Pete pulled a Leeroy Jenkins twice and that finally made me laugh.

It was close to Thanksgiving and we received a tasking for a reoccurring target. The term legacy target was used for Osama bin Laden and his historical cronies. It was not a big one but a legacy target nonetheless. Previously we had been unable to get the TI and missed him three or four times. It seemed we were unable to put the pieces together to get it right. We picked up targeting on the guy as he was active and his pattern revealed we needed to strike him in daylight hours, during one of his meetings or at least somewhere we could see him so we could track his movements. If nothing else, it disrupted his pattern of life, which can sometimes make it easier to catch him within the following 24–72 hours.

My squad leaders, all of whom I inherited and who had been promoted from team leaders from the previous deployment, were enthusiastic to try. We watched the target for a few days. We came up with triggers and briefed the plans. We believed our historical data was the only way to get this guy. He was in a village not too far from our COP. Our commander was not always keen to operate

CAPEX 2011. Sergeant Holtz gives sectors of fire to his rifleman. Objective secure, team leaders assign sectors of fire in the event of "counter-attack." Train as you fight. (U.S. Army photo by Sergeant Marcus Butler/CC BY 2.0)

CAPEX 2011. Captain Jake leads his element during the fast-rope demonstration. Second Squad fast-ropes onto a rooftop to secure the high ground. (U.S. Army photo by Sergeant Marcus Butler/CC BY 2.0)

CAPEX 2011. I run to the Last Cover and Concealment. Off the Chinook, and a mad sprint to the street intersection to cover the fast-rope infil by the second Chinook. (U.S. Army Photo by Trish Harris-Brownlee/CC BY 2.0)

CAPEX 2011. I lead my element during the ground infil. (U.S. Army photo by Specialist Michael Spoor)

First Platoon after the final demonstration during CAPEX 2011. This would be the last platoon photo taken before the death of Sergeant Holtz. (Nicholas Moore)

Rangers conduct fast-rope training from an MH-47 at Gray Army Airfield. Rangers certify this prior to every deployment. This is an easy day of round-robin-style training, switching between the aircraft types. (U.S. Army photo by Private First Class Connor Mendez)

Rangers preparing to conduct parachute training. Loaded on the C-17 Globemaster III, they wait to take off for the flight to the drop zone. (U.S. Army photo by Private First Class Connor Mendez)

A Ranger leader moonlight silhouette – because sometimes the cameraman couldn't resist a cool photo. (U.S. Air Force photo by Airman 1st Class Christopher Callaway)

Rangers on target conducting external site exploitation, while snipers maintain the high ground for security. This is an ongoing process outside, while Rangers conduct exploitation inside at the same time. (55th Combat Camera Photo by Sergeant First Class Walter Reeves/CC BY 2.0)

An MH-47 flares, preparing to land. Rangers are waiting on a knee to exfil the target area. (U.S. Department of Defense photo by Specialist Steven Hitchcock/Released)

A CH-47 and two Black Hawks refuelling at Kandahar airfield. After strike forces are inserted, helicopters will return to base, refuel, and wait for the exfil call. (U.S. Army photo by Corporal Robert Thaler/Released)

Internal site exploitation. Rangers search through everything inside the homes, looking for weapons and information that will further the detention and targeting process. (U.S. Department of Defense photo by U.S. Army Specialist Brian Kohl/Released)

A sniper pulling security from a rooftop position. Never give up the high ground, even if it's just a rooftop. (U.S. Department of Defense photo by U.S. Army Specialist Brian Kohl/Released)

A Ranger walking to exfil during the early part of the morning. Some missions will be ongoing until the last possible minute, even if it means calling for exfil as the sun is coming up. (U.S. Army photo by Specialist Steven Hitchcock/Released/CC BY 2.0)

Passing information during site exploitation. Ranger leaders ensure everyone involved is tracking important items found on target. (U.S. Army photo by Specialist Philip Diab/RELEASED/CC BY 2.0)

This is the manifest for Extortion 1-7, removed from the pocket of USN Chief Robert Reeves. This was the only complete manifest (SEAL and Ranger). I would pen in for the aircrew to ensure accurate accountability. (Nicholas Moore)

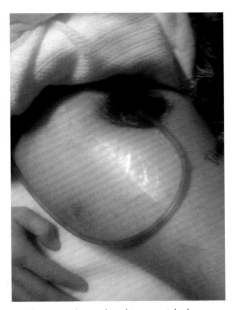

The wound vac placed in my right leg to drain the fluid swelling. This would be changed every third day, so doctors could monitor that no infection was starting and that the healing process was progressing. (Nicholas Moore)

Ranger Memorial Ceremony 2012, picture with the Cerros family. This was the hardest conversation I would have, to explain how I had survived and their son had been killed on October 8, 2011. (Nicholas Moore)

Rangers exfil the target during live-fire training. This is the final evaluation on the platoon's ability to "certify" ready for the upcoming deployment. (U.S. Army photo by Specialist Steven Hitchcock/Released)

Department of the Army official photo for master sergeant promotion packet. (Nicholas Moore)

Meeting my daughter for the first time post deployment 2012. This would be my last deployment. (Cheryl Moore)

A welcome-home kiss from my wife after returning home from my last deployment. (Cheryl Moore)

outside of darkness. We formulated a plan for triggers to launch the mission and briefed our commander. Our dedicated pilots, crew, and aircraft had to change their schedules and cycles for a few days so as not to violate their flight regulations.

The plan called for two helicopters to land to the north of the village as close as possible. Since this mission took place during the day it was easier for the pilots to navigate the terrain, the dust, debris, and dirt. We had good confidence in our flight crew and knew our strike force would come off both helos correctly. We set a rolling L-ambush – a set ambush line with crossing phase lines, laid out and based on the foot paths and roads in the village. The reason it's a "rolling L" is because everyone was pressing to target and the view from above made it look like a loose "L" shape. The plan required all elements to stay true to the sectors of fire as best as possible in order to avoid friendly fire.

The triggers for the mission were met. We brought up the birds ready to strike that day. Our company commander decided to come up since he had not had any interaction with our platoon for half of the deployment. It was always difficult for him to break away from the remainder of the company since he was the ground force commander for them. He walked off the helicopter into our briefing, sarcastically saying, "If you don't remember who I am, I am your CO." I did not appreciate that and thought, *You're gonna pull this kind of stupidity right now in the middle of a brief?* We always tried to hold the utmost professionalism during our briefings. One, this kept everyone on point so nothing was missed, and two, it helped keep them as short as possible. I was irritated. I responded with, "Sir, normally I'd be joking with you, but I have been told that sometimes our briefings are not as serious as they should be and this being a daytime op we may very well run into a gunfight so I need my guys well briefed."

We took the short ten-minute flight to the target village and scrambled out. I took my element and sprinted directly into the target objective to lock the area down and cleared through known areas of interest. But we had missed the guy again. It was simply too tough to get him with a small-sized element of one platoon and there was no back side blocking force to seal off the area because of our plan and sectors of fire. He had jumped on a motorcycle and driven on Highway One, which was close to the village, all the way to Pakistan. He stayed in Pakistan – we had scared him out of Afghanistan – but ultimately it did not really change anything.

A word about our great pilots. The cool thing about being off-set from the company and the battalion was that we had a Direct Support Package which was given to lone-operating platoons. The direct support package flight lead or lead pilot was, in this case, a former Ranger from 2nd Battalion, who was in 1st Platoon, Charlie Company, at the same time I was a team leader and squad leader in 3rd Platoon, Charlie Company. Small world! And one of the great things was that if the pilots thought the op was crazy, this ex-Ranger turned pilot pushed it a little by calling me and asking me exactly what it was we were trying to accomplish. Then he fought for us with his command to use the HLZ, which may not have met their standard for infil, exfil, or medevac. It was great to have a pilot who not only was a Ranger non-commissioned officer but also one who understood how his helicopter assets were to be used to effect the plan. He had been flying helicopters for six to eight years by now and was highly competent. I had complete trust in him, and if we asked the pilots to do something they were not capable of doing, he would explain it to us – for example, the lack of avionics equipment or their avionics limitations. He also provided significant suggestions, similar to what we needed but at the same time limiting the risk to the helicopters. He alleviated a number of issues we otherwise might have experienced.

A few bad weather days including clouds prevented us from collecting data. The down days were boring and saw us going to the gym and going through the target deck. We read through targeting reports based on the targets we were tracking. We took this time to reprioritize them. The priority strike list was reworked and based partially on who we thought we could get once the weather allowed for missions again.

There was a lot of chatter on a guy trying to make a name for himself in the Zabul Province. He was an IED emplacer and we couldn't believe the audacity of the guy. He was brazen about what he said and for how long he remained active on comms than most seasoned individuals who'd been chased by us. It struck me as odd, but it provided a great way to narrow down the target. We received the triggers on Christmas Eve. A lot of strike forces were given the day off, especially on bigger FOBs, but the decision was made to go forward anyway. We had nothing else to do. I decided to talk to my squad leaders on what my take was regarding the holiday. I told them we might get triggers to pull the mission and they should speak their minds behind the closed door, but whatever decision we made was going to be done without complaint. The squad leaders had the same opinion that the day was irrelevant; we were bored and not home with our families, so "Let's do what we came here for and do combat operations." We were the only strike force to operate that night and we said this was a Christmas present for the boys. We wanted to say Merry Christmas the American way.

Care packages had arrived from home and some contained about 50 Santa Claus hats and reindeer antlers to cheer up the morale of the boys. My team leader, Chad, another big boy, came in with his helmet, to which he had attached a cut-down Santa Claus hat to make it fit. You can guess what he was like – an eccentric, fun-loving leader, and, of course, a solid tactician and a great friend.

"Can I wear it?" he asked.

"Noooooo, you cannot wear this."

"Not even on BPs?" To which I responded with an even longer no. Chad pulled out another helmet with reindeer antlers affixed. "So, helmets with reindeer antlers are out too?" he asked, fully knowing the answer he was about to get.

"Chad, we are not doing this."

"Think about the effect it would have on the Americans – how great for morale this would be."

"No, we are not doing this; you are not doing this to me." But what I was really thinking was, *Lord, this would be so funny wearing Santa Claus hats on Christmas Eve, striking targets*. But being the professional Ranger I said no. I reminded him that the battalion commander was coming out with us on this op and we could not have 10–15 guys with Santa Claus hats and reindeer antlers. The Rangers complained, of course.

We briefed the plan to the battalion commander, who approved it, and my guys got ready for the mission. And yes, I checked the helmets to make sure there were to be no shenanigans as we waited on the flight line for our helicopters. We landed on target near a tiny village of five to six houses and sprinted a few hundred meters toward it where we set up security and assault squads. Like Santa Claus, we entered silently but unlike Santa we did not leave any presents. We took 'em.

The target there was a teenager who had been bragging to his friends that he was trying to make a name for himself as an IED emplacer. The problem for us was that with underage enemy personnel we still had to get clearance from the JOC to detain and remove him from the targets. Fortunately, as our battalion commander was with us, the clearance was not up for debate. He informed the overall task force commander about the situation and his recommendation to detain the kid. Having him on location was helpful in this case since the task force commander would not have disagreed with another high-ranking commander. We tied up the inhabitants, cleared the target, and then we further exploited the target building.

I spent a couple of minutes talking to the battalion commander who was joking around what a great Christmas present this was. I took the opportunity to ask him what he would have thought about our entire strike force wearing Santa Claus hats. He started laughing as I explained to him what might have happened. He said he probably would have had a good laugh. Oh, well!

We finished looking for hidden items and called for exfil. We moved to the exfil HLZ, and while I watched the blocking position collapse, lo and behold, I saw one Ranger through my NODs wearing a Santa Claus hat. I knew who he was. After all the nighttime missions we had pulled I could easily recognize how my men moved. I separated from my element and approached. Yup, that's right. Chad.

"Take it off," I said.

"But, but…"

"No, we are not doing this. Good initiative but still bad judgment. It's funny but no." Situation handled, or so I thought.

My security weapons squad leader moved his Rangers forward and as his guys came out from their positions, he yelled, "Ho ho ho, Merry Christmas." The battalion commander clearly heard this. And all I could think was, *Why are you doing this to me?* It was funny though.

● ● ●

We pulled a few more ops after this one. One of the last ops was targeting a fire-team size of mid-level pipe swingers who were IED and weapons facilitators. We tracked them all into one village and we figured that we could get all four targets potentially in one shot, if not at least four targets. There might be more as we hit the area. We briefed the battalion commander with the solid target. We tracked the crew all day and they had stopped in a lot of historic locations of bad-guy activity. We also identified weapons tied to their motorcycles. It was a good target to strike in order to get bad guys off the battlefield. The dynamics of landing a long way away from the target were not feasible. We wanted to prevent them from running, so our plan called for close landings, off-set a little by a few hundred meters. Upon landing, the security and assault elements on my aircraft were to lock down the target building while the isolation and their security elements pushed out to prepare our assault. Think of the target as a bullseye; each ring around the bullseye is a security bubble. The assault squad is always focused on the building to be cleared, and the initial near security squad, which doubles as the secondary assault, focuses on the buildings immediately left, right, and across from the target building. This ring keeps potential close threats from interfering with the operation at hand. The isolation squad and the machine guns are the larger ring. Their purpose is to keep others outside the village from entering and disrupting the ongoing operation.

The security team was on the left side of the target building. They spotted two individuals with AKs through a hole in the wall. The team leader and SAW gunner yelled in Pashto but they chose to run, and we had a "squirter chase." We radioed the isolation squad on the opposite end about the two runners coming their way and told them to come to this field to block their flight. I grabbed a small fire team element, went through the hole in the wall, and gave chase. We moved into a deep furrowed field with a little dyke alongside it which we ran on. By the time we had gotten through the wall to give chase, the runners were out of sight. The two runners split and we could not see them because of the crops in the field. One of the runners turned away and the other seemed to continue forward. I heard Mike, my squad leader from the isolation position, yell in Pashto for the runner to stop and to put his hands up. Gunfire erupted and we could tell it was one way and from us – the sound of 5.56mm rounds fired from an M4 is distinctive. Mike radioed one enemy KIA. Mike had been promoted from team leader in 3rd Squad to squad leader during the previous training cycle. And yes, he was a monster too but a quiet and reserved kind of guy. He was a fantastic team leader. I was a lucky platoon sergeant.

We still had one runner. My element got within a few hundred meters of our blocking position. Somewhere between our elements was the other squirter. We received an urgent call from the ground force commander, our executive officer, that the other man was behind us about 600 meters out in the open field.

Mike's squad grabbed the dead's man's weapon and marked his location with an infrared chemlight to conduct an SSE later. We were back to the foot chase and called in air assets to contain the runner. There were a lot of times when shooting from the aerial platforms had forced the squirters to stop and lie down. But not this guy. He ran across the open field and it sucked as he had the weight advantage. Typical for us. He made it into an orchard, but since it was winter there were no leaves on the trees to provide camouflage from observation. We spotted him and called in air assets to use blocking barrages to force him into a certain direction where we had our blocking positions. But there were two to three more compounds he could hide in. We double backed as he did. Later on we would be talked back to the various locations to find weapons and possibly other hidden or lost items. In the meantime, he found a hole in the wall of a little abandoned livestock pen.

My team and I were ahead of the larger squad trailing us by a couple of hundred meters. We were a minimum size force, the smallest we liked to use to chase people. The maneuvering element and I pushed to interdict the individual. Our air assets told me the bad guy's location in the pen but that he was difficult to see. We pushed in and a "strong wall" command was given – our shooters lined along it. A strong wall is a command given during CQB that means all shooters are in a line. The size and depth of the room prevents the rapid movement of Rangers to their points of domination – so a line will have to suffice.

I shouted out commands to the runner in Pashto who did not comply. I saw him with his hands in his pockets and again I had the feeling that something was not right, although I did not see a weapon at that moment. Again, I shouted commands – non-compliant, non-compliant, non-compliant... I had that gut feeling and went through the steps of whether or not I was going to shoot. I gave him one more chance to either get his hands up or to drop him. I put him in my sights, and lined him up, compensating for the 20–25-meter shot, not a long shot by any means. But I had also just run 1 klick, was gassed, and my adrenaline was flowing. I tried to calm down to take the shot. All of this happened as I shouted one more compliance command while flicking off the safety. I put rounds into him then the other guys opened up as well.

We pushed up and cleared the body. Underneath his jacket he wore a flak vest and inside his jacket was a hand grenade, but the fuse had gotten stuck inside his jacket. The runner had unsuccessfully tried to pull it free during my compliance commands. We had cleared the body and taken off his vest when we found a Makarov pistol inside his jacket pocket as well. This was another correct judgment call in the "shoot or don't shoot" situation. In Afghanistan pistols are a symbol that you are a bad guy, much like it symbolized gangs in the U.S. It was the visual representation of violence, keeping in mind that every house in Afghanistan has an AK, or some old British Enfield rifle. We finished the SSE of the dead runner, photographed everything, and handed over the material to the platoon leader while I briefed him on the actions on the objective. We knew how unstable the hand grenades were and we placed it into a hole in the back corner of the pen and blew it in place.

I had not been paying attention to what was going on around the target area because of the chase. Either someone from the other elements had to come and look for me or they had to ask the supporting rotary assets who had an aerial view of everything. I basically said, "Follow the helicopters; that's where I am at. And I don't have time to look at imagery to find my location, I'm still trying to catch my breath."

I then told Mike from 2nd Squad to go back to the other location where they had killed the other runner about 15 minutes ago and to conduct a thorough SSE. I asked him to gather whatever intel they could get from the remains. Then we tied all the pieces together to see what had happened while the platoon leader had cleared the other compound. Overall, we found half a dozen AKs and ammo and had two enemy combatants killed. We also pulled off some people from the target. We consolidated the strike force, pushed to exfil, and flew back.

Back at base my computer's messenger window was full of smiley faces and other emojis. The guys back here had been watching "Kill TV" as we, their friends, pulled off the mission. A few asked sarcastically if I had not seen the guy I was chasing. We always went back over imagery to look at what we had missed and to reconstruct what had happened. During the early part of the chase as I made it through the hole in the wall I did not see the runners split up. One squirter had hidden in the field and allowed us to pass and then taken off. We could have easily gotten stitched up and smoked by an impromptu ambush. The jokes came in fast and furious. "Hey, you run so fast that you ran right by the bad guys." I responded with, "Hey, I am only 5'9" and can only see so much over the grape rows." We all had a good laugh. I reminded the rest of the guys who had been stuck on other blocking positions about paying attention and staying switched on. Even a platoon sergeant can make mistakes by not looking left or right. I used my own stupidity to reinforce those points. This was another valuable lesson learnt.

The intel that had driven this mission resulting in two enemy dead was about a month old. A SEAL team had been ambushed and their chief had lost his leg. He had hit an IED in that area and they had abandoned the mission. That was the reason we hit this particular target, because we had intel that linked those guys to the IED. It was nice to be able tell their chief while he was in the hospital that some of the guys who did this were no longer on the planet.

The chief thanked us for everything and for not having given up on the target. It was a feel-good moment all around. No matter what you think of or how you feel about other SOF elements, when someone got hurt it always stung at every level of the SOF community. It was always a good moment when you got even.

● ● ●

During this time the number of people we took on missions had doubled. There was a minimum number of guys you needed to take to execute the actual missions, but we had to make cuts to accommodate the extra personnel of our Afghan partners. Helicopters only carried so much, so sometimes we cut privates and other staff who wanted to be part of the mission. We also cut Ranger privates to allow the battalion commander or sergeant major to tag along. I adopted the attitude that what we lost in firepower we made up for in experience. I knew if the sergeant major took over the seat of the person who had been cut, be that as a rifleman or whatever, he would perform that job. The battalion commander, of course, did whatever he wanted.

An organic Ranger strike force now included the shooters package, the APU of a squad-sized element of seven, plus another five to six non-combat arms individuals. A 45-man strike force rolling onto a target grew to 60, seven of whom did not speak English. My biggest concern was working with the language barrier. The plan was the plan until the first bullet was fired. Sometimes I had a lump in my throat once a gunfight erupted since I did not speak their language. I was concerned that our comms could be wrong or off and that that would lead to problems or possibly even deaths. I always needed someone to have physical control of those extras. The Cultural Sensitivity Team and personnel for female detainees were not on the scene at this stage but were in the works. Our small detached strike force was away from the command head shed and so we didn't have them on our missions. But if a target, based on intel collection, required one, they were sent. The system was not in place yet to implement these changes completely but we knew it was coming.

I learnt that we could operate without the Afghans. The only time we were allowed to eliminate the APU from the manifest was if intel suspected a big gunfight which, of course, never happened, or you were rolling out as a QRF to support an element already in contact because they already had Afghans on target and you were just reinforcing their numbers. All other times they were included.

Our last mission before standing down would see us chase our typical mid-level pipe swingers. The target was situated just inside the Paktia Province and since it was just after New Year's, it was quite cold at or around the snow line. We would be the only strike force in our region striking on a solid target because the deployment was winding down.

The battalion commander and command sergeant major decided to add themselves to the manifest, which was always welcome in my opinion. When the battalion commander asked, "What cold weather gear do you recommend wearing?", my platoon leader, Jake, had decided to make some wisecrack about cold weather clothing since they were coming out of Kandahar which had a much warmer operating temperature. I got one of those sideways glances from the command sergeant major. *Oh great!* I thought. After the briefing my phone rang; the caller ID said it was the command sergeant major. *Oh.* I answered, and he commenced to tell me in polite terms that the platoon leader had been a wise-ass, and I needed to "fix" him. I replied, "Roger! I will get him in check." There wasn't time between the call and our platoon briefing for the "correction," nor after that, because it was time to kit up and move to the HLZ to await the aircraft arrival.

The infil and actions on the objective went as briefed with no contact from the enemy. We grabbed two detainees. As we were wrapping up the objective the command sergeant major approached me and asked if I had "squared away" my platoon leader, to which I replied, "Stand by!" I reached down and secured a handful of snow from a small drift inside the compound, packed a large snowball, and headed towards Jake, who just happened to be standing next to the battalion commander engaged in, no doubt, a very deep and meaningful conversation. I pulled back and let it fly, hitting Jake just at the collar level and on the shoulder. Jake looked at me, puzzled, to which I responded, "That's for being an idiot during the briefing!" This caused hysterical laughter with the battalion commander and the command sergeant major along with everyone who had watched from the platoon. Needless to say, a small snowball fight started. Even the battalion commander and command sergeant major threw a few.

Ah, the joys of ending a solid deployment with a little humor and some fun. And in case you are wondering, most of the guys were wearing a medium-weight bottom, a light-weight top, and everyone packed in the big snow coat to put on for when everything went static and the assault was complete waiting to exfil.

A few days later we would send our ISU-90 and our deployment bags back to Kandahar, officially standing us down. Twenty-four hours later we high-fived the relieving platoon and flew the 45 minutes back to Kandahar to await our flight home.

CHAPTER THIRTEEN

RAGNARÖK, THE DAY OF RECKONING

Afghanistan, 2011

We conducted one normal training cycle during which 2nd Battalion had to provide one company for the U.S. Army Special Operations Command Capabilities Exercise (CAPEX) at Fort Bragg, North Carolina. Usually the president or vice-president as well a number of congressmen showed up for this dog and pony show. Other visitors included the front office people of NFL franchises and other supporters, including the Wounded Warrior organizations. They were given the VIP treatment for CAPEX. This was in May 2011.

We were in Bragg for a week for the show but for us it wasn't too bad. My platoon's mission was a helicopter assault operation into a MOUT environment. We used small explosives, smoke grenades, and blanks to let them see how we do business and to make them happy. It was fun and it gave us an extra week working with the pilots, ironing out some of our own SOPs and TTPs as a platoon before we deployed overseas again.

The boys prepped all the required charges, smoke grenades, and loading of blank ammunition for the event, before going to breakfast. As the platoon sergeant it was always my job to be the last to go and I was conducting random "spot" inspections. After completing a few I decided to go to breakfast as well. I had just exited the barracks and was walking down the sidewalk to the chow hall when the first sergeant blew out of the chow hall, jumping up and down, screaming the entire time. He was all excited and I thought that since he was a Steelers fan that they had finally got some amazing trade. I had to ask him whom they got a couple of times as I made my way into the building.

"Bin Laden. We got him."

I could only respond with, "That's all? You do realize the flip side of this coin is that in a few weeks or a month I have to work with those guys. Think about that for a second."

"Oh, yeah, that sucks," he said, laughing.

"They will never let this go; it's never going to die. It's gonna be another catalyst for who the best is in Special Ops and they already think they are." I added that they probably just whacked everybody.

"Probably," he said. "But, finally, the biggest legacy target in nine-and-a-half years is down. The No. 1 target is down!"

We finished the dog and pony show and it provided us with an extra week's worth of training using different facilities. This was great because it broke down the repetitive pattern of training when using familiar ranges at home. New ranges, although similar, made the guys think a little bit. We redeployed home.

Young Rangers about to deploy to combat ops and without the years of experience were always excited to work with the other SOF elements. I had other stuff to worry about like manning requirements, getting the right guys to Ranger School, planning who would be going home on the rotator to go to schools, doing Non-Commissioned Officer Evaluation Reports, and all the other administrative tasks a platoon sergeant dealt with.

We were victims of our own success from the previous deployment as an independent force. Our ability to operate outside the company command group without tactical or personnel issues, the maturity of the entire platoon, and the seniority of the leadership within the platoon were key. Not many Ranger platoons were lucky to have all these things at the same time.

We were attached to a SEAL command group and unfortunately were stuck working for and with them out of FOB Shank. Sometimes it worked out well but not always. A lot depended on the personalities involved. Did Rangers and SEALs find common ground? Did their chain of command mesh with our platoon, or were there moral and personality conflicts? The SEALs were notorious for bending the Rules of Engagement to fit what they wanted. That is why I had made the crack about the SEALs whacking everybody during the raid on Osama bin Laden. It gave Ranger privates bad habits and set very bad examples. Those things were hard to break from any platoon; it could really be a bad thing within a Ranger platoon if left unaddressed. Working with SEALs was also always a roll of the dice because we would get one of two treatments, either as equals or not. You never knew until the missions were passed out. Would we get equal treatment for targets that had a probability of turning into a gunfight by chasing relevant targets, or did they stick us clearing garbage targets like old historical "named areas of interest"? These are locations where the individual may have stopped or stayed in the past but did not meet launch criteria as a solid target. Hitting these can sometimes help provide valuable information for future targeting through interrogations of individuals in the area. This was my observation from over the years. Ranger leadership and SEAL leadership did not always mesh and when they did not it could get ugly. Nothing was worse than being stuck with a command group you did not like for four months. Deployments by now had gone from 90 to 120 days. It just made everything difficult and awkward.

In June of 2011 we loaded up and deployed forward. Bravo Company was the last company in the regiment to be part of the surge in Afghanistan. We were sent in six weeks early to provide three platoons for extra combat power.

It was summer in the Logar and Wardak provinces. We primarily worked the security bubble, keeping IED emplacers and weapons facilitators on the run and away from Highway 1. We were like the last line of defense before weapons and equipment could get into Kabul. Our targeting and missions had a great influence on preventing attacks inside the city. The weather was not too bad yet, but every 7–10 days there would be clouds in the mountains or dust blowing so heavily that it reduced visibility to the point of not being able to launch our air assets. It was a bit frustrating.

Once we had settled in, Jake and I went over to congratulate, handshake, and high-five the SEAL team we were going to be working with and its leaders. It was also about feeling out the personalities. Would we work together well or was there going to be a power struggle as to who got to do something? It was not too bad. I considered this one of the better working relationships between a SEAL team and Rangers.

By the end of June and early July the targets were more mobile than they were in the winter. Simple really: you can sleep outside during the summer. Traditionally targets stopped early in winter to make sure they had a place to stay overnight, whereas in summer they traveled all night. We conducted some joint operations with the SEALs and it was not horrible. Basically, they hit two to three targets and we did too. We primarily hit areas they wanted to gather more intel on so we confirmed or denied intelligence. Basically, it was a case of "stirring the pot" to see what intel we could generate.

The last time we operated together in July there were some questionable actions taken by the SEALs on their target. My platoon leader and I decided that we were not going to do this anymore. The SEALs had engaged an enemy combatant who, in fact, was not one. Instead he tried to comply with their demands. The SEALs had an APU with them. And after the SEALs engaged this individual the relationship between the two units soured to such a degree that the Afghans refused to work with them again. Rightly so. Our set of Afghans did not know about the situation and so we swapped partnering units with the SEALs. We talked with the Afghan unit joining us. They said they were fine coming over as long as something like this did not happen again or they would complain up their chain of command. This swap came into play later in our deployment during the Extortion 1-7 mission. The Afghan government had a big say in what Allies got to do on operations and this particular Afghan unit was rightly offended by the SEALs' actions. But sometimes they were so easily offended by the dumbest things; for example, if you accidentally stepped on a Koran that was covered up by a blanket it could cause serious problems.

In any event, we got the peace worked out and changed the manifest listing all the personnel. I did not put individual names of the Afghans on the manifest; instead we used battle roster numbers for each individual like I had done on previous deployments. This avoided giving out their personal names over the radio, ensuring privacy. Instead we used a letter-number combination. The SEALs did not change their manifest and had instead retained their old APU's battle roster numbers.

The period of darkness, sun down to sun up, was the day routine for 2011. We started with a battle update brief, looking for possible targets to strike. Did it meet the criteria for a strike, did we want to take a swing at the target, or was it something we did not like? Did we want to let the situation develop for another day or two on specific individuals or targets? These were questions we asked during our decision-making process. There was always the possibility that we would pick up additional intel or targets if we waited.

We finished the brief and pulled a quick update on someone of interest – Quari Tahir, a mid-level pipe swinger facilitating weapons and explosives into Wardak and Logar provinces. He was known as Objective *Lefty Grove*. Other strike forces had pursued him during previous deployments but had always missed. We launched orbiting assets to see if he was still in the target area in a small cluster of compounds about a block in size. Jake and I ate breakfast – technically speaking it was dinner time, but we operated to a different schedule. We discussed the target and asked ourselves if we wanted to strike it. The SEALs did not want it as it did not meet their requirements. It was not the greatest target but not the worst either and we had launched for a whole lot less on previous missions. The weather had been bad and we had done nothing for three days already. Finally, we had a small good weather window so we decided to take a swing. The pitch was that this was an okay criteria for us and worst-case scenario we would at least have disrupted the target's pattern of life even if we missed him. The JOC approved the plan and we briefed it.

The planned operation was set in the Tangi Valley. We knew the population did not like the Afghan government, the Taliban, al Qaeda, or Americans. They liked only themselves, their clan, the people who lived in the valley. They were willing to defend the valley and fight and scrap every time we sent strike forces in there. There were always gunfights with the locals trying to get you back out. So, we knew there would be one and I hoped it would be with bad guys, not the locals wanting to defend their homes. Based on the threat analysis with aircraft, personnel, and vehicles getting shot at, the only safe time for air assets was during zero illum – basically no illumination. This happens during the new moon when the moon casts no light. We had that for a few days during this mission cycle. The criteria for safety for aircraft was met and we had the tactical advantage operating in the dark. In Afghanistan we liked to say that the weather or nighttime was either one of two ways: lights on or lights off. The moon was out and up, or it was not. During the new moon in rural Afghanistan it is jet black and everything is completely hidden. People back home do not understand what it means to have pitch blackness with no ambient light from cities. You couldn't even see your own hand. For us that was perfect. We could move without being seen. Ghosts.

We drew up the plan and put the manifest together. We had a standard package of shooters, our normal Afghan package and the platoon leader's antenna farm, and the non-shooters. We were a bit short of shooters in my platoon at the time. We did not have a full complement because we were just at the bottom of the retention cycle and had not had a RASP class with new Ranger privates come through before deploying. As you may remember RASP replaced RIP and went from three weeks to eight, which included a marksmanship week and a basic driver's training course. I had about 35 of 40 for a full complement manning. Not super short, but five guys make a difference for spreading the mission essential equipment. We had a couple of interpreters and the Cultural Sensitivity Team for the first time and we were trying to figure out how it all worked. It was a new mission requirement which we had not had to deal with in years past. We had a female officer with us and I sent her to my platoon leader's antenna farm element which included the forward observer, radio telephone operator, and others. That way the platoon leader shouldered the responsibility. I did not want to deal with them, and on the flip side if contact was made going into the objective, the safest place for them was with the platoon leader and his static element. My responsibility as the platoon sergeant was for driving the maneuver train to clear with the assault force through the contact and I did not want, or have the time, to deal with them.

After all, they were not shooters and they were not a combat arms element. I simply did not want to worry about them while clearing an objective. Tactically, it also worked out, because when the actions on the objective had been cleared and secured, the platoon leader's element moved forward and they then could do their job. So, tactically it made sense to have them with the platoon leader. There was another new twist for operations in Logar as well. When we operated in other battlespaces, whoever owned the battlespace would send a representative to accompany us so they could see what was going on, and how events unfolded. That way they could explain everything based on first-hand experience instead of reading reports. This was also a good thing for us as we no longer had to answer phone calls or emails about an assault and the subsequent actions on the ground to their chain of command. Usually we were to be accompanied by an E-6 or E-7. Of course, it meant one more on the manifest. This BSO non-commissioned officer traveled with my small element composed of a doc and a second forward observer. One person was better than two or three for my entourage.

Our mission plan included the ability to insert helicopters into the base of the valley. We off-set a couple of klicks from the target area because flying into the valley would have tipped our presence. We did infil into the valley, just not right on the target area. We had a standard package of rotary and fixed-wing air assets. The standard Afghan Rule of Engagement now was that it was better to be shot at first. It was a lot safer for us. I hated to have to tell my guys that, but you had to wait to get engaged. Lately some decisions to shoot had, in hindsight, been wrong considering the changing geopolitical environment. And frankly, we were not too worried about it given the history of gunfights in the valley. We knew there would be one.

Our standard plan was technically a cookie cutter plan of the general concept. We moved this generic concept from one building to the next, so nothing was really distinct in the operations in general terms. We rotated isolation, security, and assault squads once a month which also created less confusion. In Iraq we had weekly change, and some platoons switched daily to stay alert during the deployment. In Afghanistan, the platoon's internal decision called for changing every 30 days to allow us to focus and get comfortable with the jobs at hand. Shorter rotations sometimes meant forgetting special equipment because one did not think about it. A month allowed the guys to focus and to tailor the load.

Machine guns were always with the isolation squad, and the plan called for them to be on higher ridges, such as draws and spurs, elevated and set for plunging fire. The order of movement was led by a team leader acting as a squad leader, due to a company manning shift, of 3rd Squad with snipers and one machine gun for isolation up front. There was a reason for this manning shift. There was a personality conflict in another platoon. The conflict was between a squad leader, platoon leader, and platoon sergeant in 2nd Platoon. Command Sergeant Major Daryl stepped in, along with the first sergeant, and called me about the manning change. I would receive Sean, in exchange for Nick going to 2nd Platoon. Nick, a.k.a. "Nasty," was a squad leader of 3rd Squad. He was energetic and funny. He was a fantastic squad leader.

This happened the day before our operation. Nick packed up his gear, and we drove him to the flight line to await a transport to Bagram, and then he would be shuttled down to Kandahar. I had a smart team leader running the squad in the interim but it was going to be hard for him to adjust to the thinking of a squad leader in moving two teams instead of one. It was a tall order to ask of any team leader. But at battalion it was what we called operating on a "Fallout 1 Drill," when someone is either killed or wounded, and the next person in the chain of command takes over. We had experience executing this drill when Austin was shot and Eddy took over in an earlier deployment. There will always be a hiccup because a team leader is not accustomed to maneuvering two fire teams. For this operation, then, it was easiest to put him and his squad in the isolation element to alleviate the burden of leadership for him. This allowed the team leader to get used to the position until the new squad leader arrived.

Third Squad was isolating the objective area, followed by 1st Squad as the initial "close security" squad just outside of the target building and the adjacent ones, with the platoon leader package of five to six people, the weapons squad leader, and one machine gun. Second Squad was the primary assault squad. I was happy with all my squad leaders so mostly the coin flip determined who got to do what. In this instance it was Staff Sergeant Ben, who was very competent and he had two seasoned, great team leaders. They were, in fact, the most seasoned squad. Ben had been promoted from team leader to squad leader during the training cycle.

We landed off-set and pushed off the field along the road running through the valley. We moved to the objective, when suddenly our rotary-wing asset ID'd four individuals who left the target building and moved over the ridge into the next, bigger, village. It was not a quick movement for them either; the straight-line distance for them was maybe 3 klicks.

As we moved and drove the individuals off the target, the Apache providing cover for us identified eight armed individuals with AKs, RPGs, and backpacks maneuvering toward us. We held the assault force on the road. The forward observer organized his assets to engage the eight enemy fighters with two gun runs. First, he had to make sure that friendly forces and the assault force were not in-line of ricochets or strafing. The aircraft reported six KIA and two fighters fleeing so the strike force moved forward and we pressed toward the objective. We kept one asset on top of the dead to make sure they did not get back up and move toward the Ranger assault element to engage us.

We were switched on. The gunfight had started. We were not complacent. It was game on. We hit the target after we had set up the machine guns, isolation, and security and pressed our assault into the objective. We started clearing the target building and we were about 90 percent done. We had not received any fire, nor were we worried about it. The objective area was quiet. The Call Out saw almost everyone out and it was a good time for me to take a squad-sized element, the security squad minus the machine gun, to the area where the six fighters had been killed. Our assets talked us onto the site. We tried to find a footbridge to cross the irrigation ditch where the water was about 4 feet deep. We looked along the ditches and tree lines as Garret, who was our acting 3rd Squad leader but in fact was actually a team leader, slid into the ditch when the gravel gave way to his weight and he landed right on top of two dead enemy combatants. He popped back up and fired into the bodies. We had a good laugh but it was completely normal to re-engage combatants. This incident still has me laughing. It freaked him out. We found the footbridge and pulled Garret out of the water. He clearly did not expect to be in kissing range with the enemy. Now he was wet, and nobody liked to be on combat ops in wet boots and pants. He was really unhappy.

We fished out the two dead enemy combatants with four more dead near a building. We cleared them and conducted SSE, including taking photographs of those killed in action. We collected the weapons, ammo, and other items to get accurate intel. We set that off to the side to eventually take to the target building to tie in with our guys who might have pulled additional material off the objective. One of the last tasks was going to be blowing all the weapons and ammo in one place to deny them to the enemy.

But we still had eyes on the two squirters on the run. I took my element and gave chase through the open fields – well, open meant chest-high crops, and it was virtually impossible to see anything. We ran about 1 klick trying to chase them down but we had to pull the chain. I did not want to split the force further. We decided to keep eyes on them, and if a new objective came from the intel we had gathered from the original objective on the ground, then we would press on. That's what Jake and I decided to be the best course of action. We also thought that maybe the squirters would "bed down" and become static, giving them a false sense of security. Perhaps they would become complacent and make it easier for us to bring in the entire assault force to take them down.

We reconsolidated at the original target objective. We took 20 minutes to collect everything about 100 meters away from the target. Jake wanted to clear another building based on local intel. The next compound was where the bad guys had had dealings with the owners. We got ready to reset in order to clear this. We were two hours into the mission cycle by now. Just outside of the target building, Jake and I received comms about the other two individuals who had fled up and over the ridge into the next village. We learned that they were trying to rabble rouse and collect fighters to maneuver and fight against our assault force. The valley came alive like it always did when U.S. strike forces were in place – it stirred like a hornet's nest.

Back at the FOB our JOC saw all this play out. The JOC wanted to get into this potentially large gunfight. There was discussion between them and Jake, who then called me on internal comms to ask what I thought about all the enemy movement in the nearby village. The estimate was that a one to two squad-sized enemy element might fight us. Jake asked what my plans on the ground were. I was not giving up anything on the ground here and we may very well have had a potential "jackpot" on the TI on this new objective. So, I was not willing to dump this to walk into a gunfight where we no longer had the advantage. My recommendation was to continue to work and observe this objective and see what happened elsewhere as well. On this location, and around it, we owned all the high ground and had great machine-gun positions. So, if the fighters wanted to come down here and walk into our baited ambush, we would be happy to oblige – but on our terms, to our advantage, where we also could maneuver our pieces to advantageous terrain and kill the threat with the least risk to our force. Jake agreed with the assessment.

We informed the JOC of our intentions and they wanted to know if we cared, or if there would be an impact on our ground operation, if they inserted another team. Jake and I said that was fine if they wanted to conduct movement-to-contact straight off the HLZ and deal with stuff about 3–5 klicks away from our target objective. That was a good and safe distance between the two forces in terms of fire. We said go ahead and let them do what they wanted.

The JOC briefed their SEALs to move to contact based on the enemy situation on the ground. We had previously discussed exfil, which was to be executed once everyone was on the ground and consolidated, using a two-cycle exfil. So, one element at a time. It was not uncommon to cycle aircraft on larger operations since they could only fit in so many guys. The assault team was almost the size of ours and we had agreed that when one element was out, the other would be on standby as a QRF. And if launched, then the two elements were to consolidate, secure the HLZ, and exfil, cycling out. That was sort of the set plan.

Eventually we received word that they were going through final plans and would soon launch. They were about to kit up and get onto the birds in a short amount of time. While this was transpiring I told my platoon leader that the safest way to enter the valley was to enter it the same way as we did – basically, to overfly our objective and then we could see what's going on and there would be no confusion. We could even support them with ground fire if the need arose. The direct support package planner inside the aviation units' JOC, their intel analysts, and approval authority said it was more of a risk to the force and it was better to enter the opposite way. We had inserted east to west and the SEAL element was flying in from west to east.

Over comms we heard they launched. I don't remember the detailed plan, only the more general one. The SEALs made their tactical decision based on the risk to the air assets and strike force. They would load a single ship, meaning the entire team was on one aircraft, because it is faster to only have to land one aircraft and offload than landing two helicopters. Also, when landing two the HLZ selection has to be larger because both ships will land together and there are also the brown-out conditions to factor in.

Fifteen minutes prior to their launch, our forward observer had re-tasked our air asset to recon the new HLZ for the SEAL team and the surrounding structures. We basically retasked our rotary wing asset for the SEALs. This was required because all transport aircraft had to fly with an armed escort. We figured that the AH-64 Apaches would be at most one to two minutes away from us in orbit if we got engaged in a gunfight. It was not a big risk to shift assets to support the SEALs. It was good to make sure their landing zone was not fouled by obstructions that had not shown up in the imagery in their planning phase. No one wants to get on "short and final," only to have to abort because there was a piece of farming equipment on the landing zone. The other purpose was to ensure that the HLZ was in fact large enough to accommodate a Chinook. We tasked Apache gunships, part of the direct support package, to support and cover the infil of the SEAL aircraft. A fixed wing was in observance as well and the landing zone was not fouled. Contrary to some conspiracy theories, all of our aircraft, tactical and observation, were focused on the SEAL insertion. The theory that escorting gunships and assets were supposedly never released was false. Every time a transport air asset was used an armed escort was provided. Additionally, there was an AC-130 overhead lazing the HLZ.

The SEALs had a ten-minute flight and the HLZ showed no movement. They approached from a southernly loop, wrapping around to the west, to come on line with the landing zone. They were about one minute out from the HLZ and the aircraft flared using its aerodynamics to slow down to land.

We had conducted the Call Out. Everybody was out who was compliant while we waited for the birds to go ahead and then cleared the building for potential bad guys who had not emerged. We always cleared as if there was still a threat in the buildings no matter what we were told by the inhabitants. We received a time hack, the approximate time, for the SEAL infil. We waited for the birds to give us the "infil complete" call before our assault and we assumed all was good. We held our second assault to avoid any potential ricochets. We didn't want to start shooting until the air assets cleared the air space because the helos were to fly over our objective as they took off, having inserted the SEALs, or so was our assumption. We heard a six-minute out call, then three minutes out, but we didn't hear any rotor blades. Jake and I looked at each other wondering if they had decided not to fly over us. Maybe they had flown a different route. Maybe we had missed it.

We cleared the building. Midway through the clearance, the forward observer heard from rotary wing assets there was a "Fallen Angel," a downed aircraft. He passed this to Jake, who passed it to me over the command net. CH-47s always flew in pairs or threes – even if only one bird was used for infiltration. The first helicopter, callsign Extortion 1-6, had peeled off to high orbit, waiting for Extortion 1-7 to "flush" then rejoin and return to base. Jake called me and told me to join him immediately as they had a Fallen Angel. I responded incredulously with, "Say that again?" I was dumbstruck. "We have a Fallen Angel," he responded.

"You mean we have an aircraft shot down?"

"Yes."

"Okay."

I consolidated my guys immediately. I net-called all my squad leaders and ordered them to "hold the assault, back out, and everyone get a Blue Sky right now." "Blue Sky" meant they had to get accountability of their men and sensitive equipment and get ready to move their squads out. We were at 90 percent of our Call

OBJECTIVE *LEFTY GROVE* AND RECOVERY OF EXTORTION 1-7

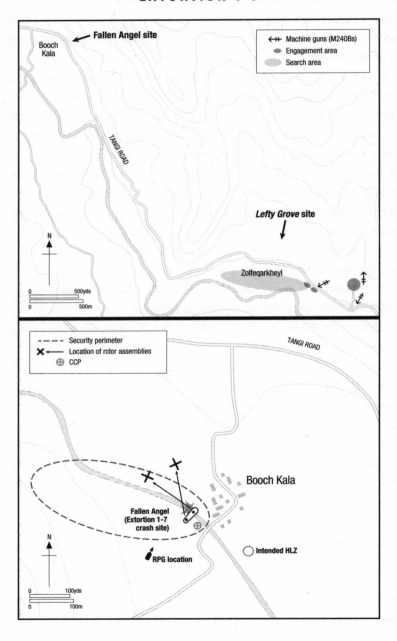

Out, clearing the building, when the Fallen Angel call came in. My sniper team leader, Ryan, jumped down from his rooftop position and walked over to me. Ryan is a big guy, a superb sniper, and a quiet and reserved Ranger.

I told him to grab Dave the K9 handler and Spencer who was a sniper and be the point for our movement. Ryan wanted to know where we were heading. "Move forward up the valley to the west. The rest of the assault force will follow suit, but you need to get going now." "Blue Skies" came in from the machine guns as they got off the ridge, as did the assault squad. The order of movement was getting briefed while we moved. "Third Squad leads with the machine gun, behind Ryan's sniper element." I also told the platoon leader that he and his package needed to get going. Then the rest of our platoon – 1st Squad followed by 2nd Squad and my element – would bring up the rear as per our platoon SOP.

At this point everything was on the objective and as we moved I told Ben, my 2nd Squad squad leader, to move the captured equipment up the road and find a good spot to "blow in place" once the last element passed him by.

Jake and I quickly discussed the detainees and decided to leave them behind. There were plenty of people here in the cluster of buildings who would cut them loose. We were not going to worry about someone grabbing an AK and engaging us from the rear because we were blowing up all we had found.

All of this was accomplished within three minutes. The entire strike force moved at a clip that could almost be called running. The snipers in lead asked what we were looking for. I said, "Once you come around the spur you will see exactly where we are going."

Ryan and his element pressed on. They were just about around the spur and saw some light in the distance. They rounded it and it was one of those "oh shit" moments. It was the first visual of a massive fire roaring. They were about 5 klicks away from it. I heard gasps on the radio as the intel trickled down throughout the force.

I did not know how many aircraft were involved. We could not get answers between the various TOCs and JOCs that now cluttered the airwaves. They were looking for personnel counts and numbers on their manifest. I had assumed that the manifest of personnel loaded the element into two aircraft but they had not. And there was nothing inherently wrong with that for the reasons listed previously. I pressed Jake for information from the JOC, to get details including how many people we were dealing with, all the while moving as fast as possible. We were already on the road; the lead element wanted to know if we were going to stay on the road or to move through the terrain. The IED threat was ever present. I recommended to Jake that we stay on the road, that the risk to force was worth what we were trying to do. He agreed.

We assumed the risk and moved as fast as possible on the road. We kept it switched on and I told our lead element that if they spotted anything suspicious to mark it and move around it. God willing, all would be fine.

Jake and I switched frequencies, trying to hail the SEAL element. It was so bright, the light and the heat, that the air assets could not make out any movement on the crash site. We closed to about halfway when we heard the staggering number of the presumed dead. I could not wrap my mind around it. I said, "Wait, there are 33 dead plus five crew… 38 on this aircraft. How many people on the other aircraft?"

"None. It was an empty ship."

Oh, good Lord, I thought. Operation *Red Wings* came to mind. I went through those awful days and took quick notes of what was needed for this recovery on an arm piece like those used by NFL quarterbacks. I had added an illumination tape to see the notes. Jake and I were on the Command frequency now, while still talking on our own assault net. But I thought, no, I knew, everyone was dead.

It took us one hour to cover the 5 klicks and we got to within the last klick of the crash site. Our air asset informed us that there was a

village on this final part of our route and I didn't want to risk the
force by going through it, so we jumped off the road to avoid it. Jake
and I made the tactical decision for two squads to get on line, 1st
and 3rd. It looked like a capital "T." Second Squad was our reserve
maneuver element with me in case we got hit. Our job then was to
kill the contact and push toward the objective. Nothing happened
and we pushed through.

We enveloped the crash site in a cigar-type formation. The
machine gun covered the southwestern edge, one squad on
the southwest side with a machine gun, the south/southeast side had
the APU. And another machine gun with 3rd Squad covered the
nearby northwestern villages. If we had to fight in a defensive
formation, 2nd Squad would fill in from 3rd Squad to the last
machine gun on the northeast.

We made it to the river bottom. The fire was so utterly blinding
that the brightness shut off our NODs. I gave guidance as to what I
needed the squads to do. I told the squad leaders on the radio that
the priority was to secure the crash site and to be able to defend
themselves in case of attack. I gave Ben of 2nd Squad some
instructions as his squad was the primary for CSAR. I did my best
to minimize radio traffic. I did not want to chew up the radio waves.
I managed to convey that we did not all run to the flames and the
crash site even though we all wanted to. Instead we formed a
concentric circle and swept it to make sure nobody had been thrown
from the helicopter and was still alive but really messed up and
unable to communicate with us.

Ben's squad and my element along with Doc pushed into the
bottom, and I was absolutely amazed to watch our Rangers risking
it all to find survivors. Some charged into the flames to see if
someone was somehow still alive in there to get them out. Our
Rangers risked themselves for even just one guy in this crash. It blew
my mind. Without hesitation, they got as close as possible, calling
out names of the guys some of them knew personally. I came onto

the crash site, having dropped off the last machine gun in position. I told my guys not to fixate on the fire; they needed to move around the area, mark remains, or individuals with chemlights, so Doc could move to each, check vitals, and render aid if needed.

We found Rob Reeves first, the recce team leader. I considered him a friend. Rob was at the bottom of the river. He looked physically okay although both legs were broken. The blunt force trauma when he hit the ground must have killed him. You knew he was dead looking into his grey, milky eyes. Living ones had a sparkle in theirs. *Damn.* This really hit home, especially since I knew him well and we had planned and talked on many occasions. *Oh man. I can't describe the feeling.*

Ben's squad continued the concentric circles on the north side by the terraced fields. On the south side was a 6-foot terrace wall to retain dirt from washing into the creek bottom. We secured it and swept the area. A couple of guys from the blocking position assisted in sweeping a small, thin orchard to make sure we did not miss anybody.

Eventually I found out that Extortion 1-7 had been at about treetop-level height when an RPG was fired, from the south side of the valley from a nearby compound. In fact, two RPGs were fired. One missed the nose; the other impacted about midline of the aircraft. Every asset lost visual of the aircraft due to the Chinook turning into a fireball. There was almost no time in between the two shots – they happened very fast. Even in the assets slow-motion video feed it was hard to see the first shot's trail. The second one was easier to spot because of its devastating impact.

The Chinook helicopter in our midst was engulfed in flames. Doc made his way around. I moved west and around the crash, trying to put eyes on my security positions to make sure all were tied in. My job was to manage CSAR so I turned around and walked back to the site when the last fuel cell violently exploded. I was 30 meters away and immediately thought about my guys within the concentric circle. Everyone within it had been blown onto their backs. Doc had shrapnel in his calf; Andrew, my SAW gunner from 2nd Squad, had a piece in the small of his back, burning a hole into the top of his blouse and blistering his back. There were sporadic smaller explosions from hand grenades, explosive demo charges, and ammo as it cooked off. But we kept at it.

I felt we had done a good job so far considering we could only use the light of the fiery crash. We found eight people ejected from the helicopter before its crash. Jake asked for a status report, wanting to know if anyone was alive. I told him that at this point there were no survivors. He was being hounded by the JOC for an update. On a side note, he did a great job of buffering the requests to let me concentrate on the task at hand. NODs were still not working because of the heat and bright flames, but we would keep searching.

We did not need recovery equipment but I requested a list of items: fire extinguishers rated for metal fires, body bags, nitro gloves, bio-hazard bags, and a dozen more things. Jake passed that up. At Bagram at the big JOC they scrounged to get everything on the list and it would be on site in about two hours. We got everything we needed except for the fire extinguishers. There were none in-country.

The sun came up and the BSO said they had launched their CSAR Pathfinder team, composed of a large squad with a company commander. We secured the HLZ for them to fly in and this was the last aircraft flying in for almost 36 hours. I sent Mike, the weapons squad leader, with two machine guns plus a fire team to deal with the HLZ.

Once the Pathfinders arrived I had them fill in our hole in the security line on the northeast side. I told their captain what the plan was and that my platoon leader was doing a good job of handling some of my responsibilities. In theory, he was supposed to be in charge but I suggested we leave it the way it was, that there was a lot of loss of life and I needed to focus on that. I was not the nicest guy to deal with at the time. I probably was the only guy in Special

Operations in Afghanistan who had previously dealt with recovery and who was still operating at a strike force level. My superiors from back then were now either retired or driving desks. Now I was a platoon sergeant, the senior non-commissioned officer who had previously worked on the Marcus Luttrell recovery. Jake and I jumped on comms with the SEAL JOC and we were able to talk to each other without the rest of the platoon hearing anything.

The platoon leader's job was to bark orders and mine was to make recommendations of what needed to be done. We always discussed this quietly and never in front of the guys or over the radio.

In any event, the sun had come up. We pulled in our Rangers from the search, received and made reports. I placed the recovery squad on hold and consolidated them. The aircraft was still raging hot. With the better light they went back everywhere they had marked the bodies. I told my guys we needed to consolidate them by bringing the bodies to the wadi at the south side of the crash for accountability. It was also the most usable spot for an additional HLZ. Tactically it made sense. I didn't think about them standing down all air assets for a while.

Any helo crash situation always became the number one priority in-country. Everything was re-tasked to support us on the ground. It was ridiculous – the air assets stacked every 1,000 feet up to 35,000 feet up. We had an insane number of aircraft in support. On the flip side, this was not a good thing either, as every single American strike force in-country was watching some kind of feed that was showing our mission.

We consolidated the eight dead men who had been thrown clear of the helicopter. The fire was raging hot still. We re-swept everything, starting close and worked to 100 meters out, concentrically, moving back towards the crash site. Most people thrown clear were within 60 meters from the crash. But we wanted to be very thorough. We did not find any bodies or remains but found the rotor mast for the rear rotor which explained to us what had happened. The Chinook's nose was facing north, perpendicular across the wadi from the rock wall; the edge of the body rested south through to the north side bank. The nose was stuck in the dirt on the north side – perfectly consolidated. It was almost like a CH-47 had been set alight on a flight line – it was that perfect. The entire aircraft was there except for the rotor assemblies but it was just a burning ball of metal. I identified everything and marked them on my map. The location, the front rotor, the rear one, the driveshafts were sporadically here and there where they broke. Marking the map made the best sense because there would be a great many questions from higher command about what it looked like and how it all played out.

After we completed our second concentric sweep I grabbed Brandon, leader of 1st Squad, and had him pull out his camera to take images of the objective.

Every squad carried a digital camera, to photograph objectives, detainees, weapons, and enemy KIA. I urged him not to take close-ups of faces or any remains. I wanted images of the wreckage, the rotor assemblies and their locations, and the surrounding area in a set of panoramic stills all the way around. This was going to play out later and the easiest way to explain everything was to have photos. I reiterated not to take photographs of the remains. I had my guys collect personal effects or call-sign patches and bag them. So far, we had only found eight bodies; the rest were in the wreckage. We tried to count the remains in the wreck as best we could. We could get close numbers, but not exact, due to guys being on top of others.

The fire had finally started to die down in the morning. The guys started to figure out how to work their way into the crash, creeping in slowly and recovering the dead, working from the upwind side, so the smoke was blowing away from them. We pulled out as many remains as possible before the fire flared up or the smoke made it impossible to stay in the wreckage any longer. My guys then waited for the fire to die again and then they went back in to work. We had problems with our casualty litter because the remains were so hot they melted the plastic rubber mesh that made up the litter surface. We tried using climbing ladders to move them to the CCP. There was not an awful lot left of some of the guys who had been in the helicopter the longest, and the experience, the gruesome work, took a toll on my guys.

The guys were worn out, we had no water, and it was hot. Halfway through the recovery we heard supplies and body bags were inbound – to be dropped off at a terraced field next to the crash site on a predetermined point. I pulled some of my guys away to retrieve the big pallets. At ten minutes out, A-10s made gun runs on the north and south of the ridgelines to show force and to allow for the air drop of two pallets. One was comprised of CSAR equipment I had requested and the other was water and chow. Both pallets hit the bullseye; the water/food pallet landed 50 meters west of the crash in the wadi, the second landed 20 meters northeast of the crash, just outside of the wadi. It was almost 9am and pushing 100 degrees plus the heat of the fire. We had been out of water since we had left our initial objective and had been fighting through dehydration and exhaustion, trying to stay on task, secure the site, and recover our colleagues. It felt like Ranger School when I requested two Rangers from each squad to come in and fill kit bags and distribute the supplies internally.

At this point, I took a hard look at the combat effectiveness of 2nd Squad who were totally and utterly gassed. I rotated them with 1st Squad. The reason I picked that squad was that it was full of senior squad and team leaders. The squad also had older privates. I believed 1st Squad was going to be able to handle the grizzly sight and smells they were to encounter more fully now. We continued to clear in the cauldron of heat. A request was made to drop some of the equipment. I told them they could ground their weapons but had to wear their helmets and body armor. It was not a popular decision, but tactically it was absolutely correct.

By early afternoon we finally accounted for all 38 members of the crash. I tried to get my guys into some shade. The squad on the high ground to the southwest resorted to stacking rocks to make shade, as there were no trees on their section of the perimeter.

All the while we had two ground assault convoys from the BSO push into the valley, one from west to east and the other east to west, from opposing ends. It took them all morning and mid-afternoon to conduct route clearances. The convoy from the west cleared six massive IEDs and made it in; the other one turned around and aborted the mission because of the longer distance to travel to our location in the valley and they had cleared an IED every 800 meters. This was an arduous task – from finding to clearing. Once one was found they had to confirm it, set a charge, back up the force to clear the blast radius, then detonate it, confirm it had detonated, and ensure there was not a secondary IED. It was painstaking work. Every hour we got an update. Jake and I joked sarcastically to lighten the mood. It was unbelievable how many IEDs there were.

Looking back at our men I think most handled the situation fairly well. I was proud of the level of maturity we showed. Rangers, typically aged 18–24, always got a lot of stick regarding their maturity. The immature tag was attached to us and, to be fair, most men that age are, but the level displayed here and the utmost respect given to everyone in the crash – it was remarkable.

We called up and let them know we had accounted for all of the 38 dead and the working dog as well. The dog and handler were found together. The handler had cradled the dog in an effort to restrain it from flying around in the cabin during the crash. We tried to be respectful, but it was a tangled mess. Electrical wiring melted into rubber and metal and with the bodies. Some bodies fell apart once they were touched. I remember the last guy we recovered, well, there was not a lot left of him physically, in fact, very little. They were so tightly crammed and burnt that during their recovery we had to break them apart to retrieve them. It was soul-draining work.

No one was left unmarked. Once we were home, after the deployment, we had a training cycle and I could see that this mission weighed heavily on some of them. One committed suicide later on, and maybe the things he experienced out there played a part in it.

The remains had been placed into the body bags and neatly lined up in the wadi. We were getting set for the ground convoy's arrival, which would take the remains to the BSO's COP and from there they would be flown by helicopter to Bagram's casualty/mortuary affairs.

The guys were absolutely gassed and waiting for the convoy. It stopped 500 meters to 1km short of where we expected them. We had hoped for them to arrive at the 6 o'clock position by the wadi about 400 meters away. This was the best place to load them. The nearby bridge could hold 20 tons so it was ideal for the vehicles. But they did not want to go through the village. Instead they stopped on the outskirts of the west side of the village. Both units carried the remains to the trucks.

Technically, the BSO's executive officer, a major, was now supposed to be the ground force commander of the site. He talked with me, Jake, the Pathfinder commander, and our radio telephone operator and he basically said that they were leaving as soon as the remains were loaded, and whatever we needed was the most important thing since he had no idea what to really do here. I was angry, tired, and hot but thought that that was a very professional thing to say. I had no patience for anyone, and we all were processing everything we had accomplished, and I certainly was not in any mental capacity for any army politics. I replied, "That's good, sir, because I was ready to give you some choice words if you had insisted on taking command."

We were now trying to figure out what the plan was for our assault force. Should we let the Pathfinder element remain in place and cycle in a conventional unit to support them? That brought up the question of whether or not we would exfil with the BSO and the remains, or would we move to an HLZ, or walk out to the BSO's nearest FOB? We had nothing solid on that but finally were told that we were to be relieved in place. We communicated back and forth with the JOC about the exfil since we did not know anything and we were asked if we could walk 7 klicks to the BSO's combat outpost, or to an HLZ or whatever.

While we waited for the plan to be refined and to keep my boys busy, I sent them to find any equipment and weapons around the site, to collect them up in extra kit bags we had lying around. I rotated them. The area in general was extremely quiet. We reduced security to 33 percent to take a break, to rest and to sleep. Josh's platoon was ready to come and relieve us on the crash objective just after dark and we were ready to move to the exfil location.

The remains were loaded onto the BSO convoy. We were now waiting on dark, and I took a look out west where I saw a weather formation happening over the mountains. I knew that there was rain in the clouds and it was raining somewhere down there in the distance. We caught the last corner of the weather as it sprinkled on us for 5–10 minutes. It was a welcome relief. I remember thinking how nice it felt. I took a deep breath. I closed my eyes for a moment. The weather got cooler as the sun disappeared behind the clouds. I heard a collective sigh from the guys. As the Washington State Ranger Battalion, we liked a mild climate.

An hour or so after the sprinkle I heard my machine-gunner on the west side radioing that he thought a truck was coming down the wadi. I instantly thought, *Holy crap, flash flood!* and I said, "Don't tell me you are in wadi." I heard an "Oh crap!" He tossed the gun over the berm and barely got himself over as 4 feet of water washed the entire crash site away. Stupidly, everything we had collected – kitbags full of busted stuff and rifles – had been sitting at the bottom of the wadi trail. Gone, all of it. *Oh man*, I thought. It wasn't anything we could have known. It had made sense to keep it there, and it was out of sight and out of mind. We radioed up and told them the crash site was now under 4 feet of water. Initially they simply didn't understand. I had to explain it a bit better: "It was dry and now it's wet."

The new platoon flew in on SOAR aircraft to the top of the ridge on the northside and there were only a couple of ways to come down to us and, unfortunately, they picked the wrong draw. They had go back up, just to climb down again, this time on the correct draw. They wasted a couple of hours doing that. We were to exfil from their infil HLZ. I did not know it was Josh until he came right up and gave me a big hug. "Sucks to see you this way but you guys did awesome. We watched the operation unfold in your TOC. We watched the whole thing unfold. We tried to help and fly in to support but within an hour all helicopter assets got grounded."

I also found out on a comical note that our other two platoons were out on a mission in Kandahar and had not finished their op so they almost did not get a ride home. They had all their assets until the crash and then lost everything. They had to abort and turn around.

In any event, our radio telephone operators and everyone else on radio tried to deconflict the area. I thought, *You'll all get brain cancer* – that's how much time they had to spend on the radios.

Josh told us to follow the breadcrumbs, the chemlight trail, back up the mountain to our exfil HLZ. I told him I appreciated that very much and we continued the handover. Josh's platoon stayed there for five more days, fishing for the wreckage that was once consolidated into a small area but now was spread out over a few hundred meters.

During the hand-off I showed him where we were tied in and what area we owned. I had my squad leaders emplace Josh's squad leaders and the hand-off was complete.

By now we were out for a second complete period of darkness without sleep and I saw how tired and burnt out we were. But we had to move since it had taken Josh longer to get down to the site, and we did not want to miss our exfil. That motivated the guys and we just managed to call for exfil before sunlight, pretty much as the birds landed for exfil.

The SEAL team commander was on the exfil waiting to fly out with us. Three aircraft were used to exfil all of us and our equipment back to our FOB. We wanted a moment away from everyone to talk to ourselves and to talk with the SEAL team commander. It was an awkward moment; I did not know what to say and how to say it. He thanked us for what we did, and I answered awkwardly. Saying "you are welcome" felt wrong. If the tables had been turned they would have done the same for us.

Buses came and drove us from the flight line to the camp. It was eerie walking back into the camp. It was empty, like walking back into an abandoned town, a ghost town, but people slowly filtered out of the TOC to thank us. But what do you say, what can you say? They had lost their entire team. We only had two wounded in action from shrapnel. Some of them simply hugged us.

We dumped our equipment and got chow. Normally we were not allowed to get chow in mission uniform but I did not care and told my men, "Go eat as you are. I don't care, eat, then clean and sleep."

I went to my computer to download emails and messages. Calls exploded but I simply looked at the personal effects we had retrieved, which were bagged individually and tagged as to whom we thought they belonged to. I had an armful of plastic bags – American flags from their backpacks, patches, and personal items that we thought the families would want. I moved to the JOC to tell the commander about them. At the time it had seemed like the right thing to do; now I wasn't so sure. But he was grateful and said the families would probably be happy to get these items.

I then returned calls and emails. My mind was spinning, trying to process everything. I received a call from our first sergeant in Kandahar. "I don't not know how to explain everything to you yet,"

I told him. He said to take the rest of the day and figure it out, including awards. I really did not know how to write awards for this, though plenty of guys deserved them. It was a big conundrum for Jake and me. Whom would we pick and how would we write them up? Our Battalion Sergeant Major Darryl called as well and wanted first-hand accounts. He was stateside as the battalion had not yet deployed. Our company had been deployed forward earlier than the rest. I answered him with an email. I wish I still had it. It said something like this: "I have never been more proud of the way the guys handled the situation they walked into. I know it scared the hell out of the young guys – this is real – how am I going to settle the nerves when it is time to get back on it?"

Jake and I were up for a few hours trying to process everything and figure out what information did we need to put into report now, versus sleeping and processing stuff in our mind? We decided that it was not an absolute must right now; we would shut down and catch some sleep.

● ● ●

There had been a back and forth between the SEALs and Rangers over the years but at the end of the day we are all Americans. This whole thing was one of those atrocious things nobody ever wanted to see and now I had seen it twice.

The recovery operation was over, and Jake and I answered all the important emails and calls for a few days. For a lot of it we were just at a loss for words as to how to process or explain what had gone on. Open-source media like Fox, CNN, and others exploded with the news. For the most part the news was inaccurate, as first accounts always were. The biggest inaccuracy reported was that we were in a massive gunfight and that we needed to be rescued. In fact, there were two gunfights in six minutes or so and we were working a pretty decent target. The biggest irritation of the whole thing was the misrepresentation that we were being rescued when, in fact, the SEALs came in to start a new gunfight. Jake and I talked about it years down the road and sometimes we played devil's advocate. Should we have said, "Don't come down the valley," or were we right in saying, "Come in and do your own clearance"? What if they had come in the way we recommended them to come in; would it have worked out okay then? There was always a back and forth in our discussions.

Marcus Luttrell did the same thing reflecting on Operation *Red Wings* – if one decision hadn't changed, what would it have done for the entire operation? Marcus talked about the decision to let the locals go who had supposedly compromised them. They didn't. Back after *Red Wings*, we did talk about the circumstances. What would we have done if we had been compromised – the same thing or not? Most of our guys who were there during *Red Wings* probably would have tied up and held onto the individuals until we were ready to leave, and then let them go as the time came to exfil in order to avoid being further compromised. Practically, we would have released one and then run to exfil and let that detainee figure out what to do with the other one still bound. What one thing or decision or radio call would have changed the outcome of the day? It's a natural form of survivor's guilt, but it's also troublesome to dwell on what might have been once the decisions have been made.

I said something to the command sergeant major along the lines of wanting to get the guys back into a helicopter, or even to avenge. But avenge was not really the word I wanted to have used. He told me not to risk losing my credibility for a payback. But, in fact, that wasn't what I wanted to do. It wasn't about revenge. What I really wanted was to simply get the guys back on the helicopters out on ops because accidents happen, but it is also about the ability to have a say in the fight and not to worry too much about shoot-downs or crashes. I wanted to get the guys back after this target, apply pressure in the right way, and show relentless pursuit, to prove that the enemy didn't have the upper hand. The looks on their faces showed some strain when they finally got back into the helicopters, unlike previously when there was a calm confidence. The reality of life and war was showing on their faces. That was the basis for the emails and calls – about how long it would take to get the guys back out the door and on target, and that way things could still go our way during this deployment.

The first sergeant called to say the rest of the company was coming up to fill the void left by the dead SEAL team. We had to set up for the other two platoons and support element. An Army psychiatrist and a chaplain tried to pull the guys in and be available for anyone wishing to speak with them. I suggested everyone go to the fire pit, where the chaplain and shrink were, even if they had nothing to say. A lot of guys ended up talking to them. The two stayed at the camp for a few days and then rotated back, although they returned throughout our deployment just to check on us. It was good to see the guys get better, to lighten up and get a lift in spirits. There was a lot of paperwork and two days after the crash Jake was called into the Bagram JOC to talk through everything that had happened on the ground on the VTC (Video Tele Conferencing) with the big chief in charge of all SOF in Afghanistan. Although we had downloaded all the images from the operation and the crash site they had never been forwarded to the JOC and Jake was stuck in the position of trying to explain the whole chain of events while they questioned the integrity and accountability of our efforts to recover the bodies. In fact, Jake got hammered. The whole interrogation was for officers only and I got angry because my platoon leader was being unfairly criticized. I had led the crash recovery, while Jake ran the perimeter security and talked on the radio, and I wanted to know what the crap this was all about. It turned out that what had happened was that while we had included and counted spinal cords and skulls for our accountability report, Mortuary Affairs regulations only counted human remains when 51 percent of the body was present so there were discrepancies between the two figures. Higher up guys were making accusations and we were getting angrier by the day because we had never been told this.

Jake and I asked to attend the ramp ceremony to represent the platoon alongside the SEAL commander. We took a C-130 to Bagram. In the JOC people had cycled in and out over the years and I happened to know one of the officers from the regiment. He came over and shook our hands, telling us what a great job we did. I unleashed on him, telling him I was unhappy about the treatment of my platoon leader during the VTC, and that accountability of personnel was my job. He responded gruffly, "what are you on about Moore?" I said, "you questioned my accountability, you think I had sent you a false 100 percent accountability report." I vented my frustration and let it fly. I just didn't care anymore, I did not give a damn if I was going to get busted. I wasn't going to let my platoon leader take the crap for my job.

Jake and I left for the hanger and went through the rehearsal for the ceremony. I must have touched a nerve because some of the officers came to the hanger and apologized to Jake for the previous days' accusations. I got to vent and Jake got his apology.

We attended the ramp ceremony. Not everybody was identifiable from the crash. Afghans lay alongside Americans and an imam of the Afghan army gave a sermon for the eight members of the APU who had been killed. Everybody was there. Almost the entire base, over 1,500 people, was in attendance and it was not even mandatory.

For me, the unsung heroes were the riggers, who had built the pallets of resupplies for us. They scrounged and scrambled to get us everything. Usually they did not get a reward or even a thank you. Since they were from another battalion, I made an effort to call and send an appreciative email for their work in support.

The rest of our company showed up the next day. We had our own camp memorial service where the SEAL team commander was able to say some things about his guys. It was a good service for them.

The SEAL team that came in to backfill the fallen had to inventory the effects of the dead. I cannot imagine what it was like to close ranks when you lose 30. It was hard enough to close ranks with the loss of one – that void, the harsh knowledge that he is never coming home. The realization that packing up meant the end of everything – there would be no more calls, no more jokes, no more stupid training stuff to laugh at or get annoyed at.

●●●

But our company was here now and we had to figure out the game plan. How were we going to utilize the platoon still here and how were we going to fill the void of the deceased SEAL team while incorporating two more strike forces? Was there enough work to do, especially with a new SEAL team going to be standing up in the operational cycle once gear and effects had been packed? It turned out there were more than enough targets.

We wanted to prove to the people of the Tangi Valley that even though they had shot down a helicopter, the Americans were not afraid. We had a deliberate planning process to clear areas of interest, villages, and the compound where the shots had come from as well as the compounds that they had been watching after the crash. We observed the compound where the RPG fire had come from and watched the traffic in and out of the village area. If there was a lot of traffic back and forth between various compounds, that sparked interest. We wanted to clear our original objective again since we had abandoned it to move to the crash site. We thought about how we were going to clear the villages and the compounds, and the best ways to confirm and to deny intel. And ultimately, were they going to be dumb enough to fight us again the second time around?

We planned for a big operation. Company-sized operations were always fun. They were more of the traditional kind of Ranger operations. Ranger platoons had been handling platoon-sized objectives organized by company commanders and first sergeants. Bravo Company, however, had been able to fit in company-sized objectives in our previous three deployments. Operating at the company level was fun, and, if and when we got into firefights, you watched and observed your guys. It was an opportunity to see how other platoons performed.

We laid out the scheme of things and came up with a 24-hour mission on the ground, potentially leading up to 72 hours, depending on the enemy situation on the ground. If the fighting went well the first day, then we would stretch the operation. If no one showed up to fight, then we would reclear the original Objective *Lefty Grove* and move to exfil.

The planning took the focus of about a month, but we also had to deal with the destruction of the SEAL team, getting a new strike force up, and for us all to get back into the play. There were also lots of pieces that needed to be put in place for this large operation, considering what we usually did in Afghanistan. This included a lot of lift and other assets dedicated to this scale of operation. We moved chess pieces on the table.

On September 23, 2011, 1st Platoon, Bravo Company, 2nd Ranger Battalion was the lead on the ground for Operation *Red Dawn*. We landed on the HLZ where we had exfiled after the recovery mission of Extortion 1-7. The dust and the angle of the ridgeline forced the ramp to be laid downhill. It was a bad spot; everything got sucked into the aircraft. We slipped and slid out of the helo with the additional weight of rucksacks for our 72-hour packing list. I was the first one out, but I slipped and smashed my leg as first Doc and then five to six more Rangers landed on me and bruised my right leg. I thought I had broken it. If you break your shin you can still walk; you are just in extreme pain. During the next 24–30 hours of the operation it swelled up to the point that I was almost unable to pull up my pant leg.

We patrolled back down into the valley through a village in the Wardak Province. Second Platoon followed and passed through our lines after we had cleared the village. We pushed through the valley when my platoon crossed the bridge and we looked upstream to about 400 meters where the helo had crashed. We set up an ORP and dropped rucks in Ranger School style. During our movement down our assets ID'd four armed enemy fighters, maneuvering to an ambush position to sit, wait, and engage us. Instead they were engaged with aerial fire, killing two fighters as the other two wounded fled into an irrigation pump house on the side of the banks. We kept them in mind while setting up our pieces to clear the target building, the house from where the RPGs had been launched. We cleared the building and 2nd Platoon pushed through. The first night was almost a bust except for the two KIAs and the two wounded squirters.

We got ready to consolidate for the day, to a move to the planned "Remain Over Day" site, but before we left we had to go clear the two KIAs and the two fighters who had gone to ground in the pump house. I sent Brandon's 1st Squad to clear through the two KIAs, conduct an SSE, and take the required pictures. "Deal with it" were his brief instructions. The locations of both had been marked to expedite finding the location. Brandon's guys moved through the first objective, cleared it, conducted the SSE, and secured the remains. They pushed on to the second location to clear through the pump house. The team stacked at the door ready to enter when automatic weapons fire erupted through the front door. Senior Team Leader Tyler Holtz took two rounds into his collarbone above the plate, pretty much killing him instantly. Casey, a SAW gunner, was stacked as the No. 2 man directly behind Holtz, and he took two rounds below his chest plate into the hip bones.

Meanwhile some Rangers grabbed their rucks, ready to cycle into the order of movement. We did not anticipate a fight, because in the past it was usually the wounded who moved into these structures to hide and die. Once we heard the gunfight, we immediately stopped what we were doing. I grabbed Ben's 2nd Squad to reinforce Brandon in his gunfight and to recover Casey and Tyler. We got them out of the line of fire and the medics got up there along with our battalion surgeon who was also with us. I thought how awesome that was, having him here, as we pulled our guys away from the gunfight. It was also great to see young privates step up, doing what needed to be done without being told. A big tip of the hat to the team leaders whose teams did their jobs well. It showed the proficiency of their level of training. It was not every day we conducted drills on bunker complexes, or in this case, a small pump house, 2 meters high by 2 meters wide, which, in fact, was exactly like a bunker. One Ranger private, covered by snipers, maneuvered to the back of the building. He smashed a small window and tossed in two hand grenades. They exploded and a lull in fire happened. By now we had moved Casey and Tyler. The boys on overwatch secured the building. They took advantage of the lull and moved to the front door where they threw in two more grenades, then littered the interior with a bunch of SAW fire.

I loved Tyler – he was the prototypical Ranger team leader. He was a big boy, about 6' tall and probably 240 pounds without equipment – the proverbial barn door. He had been a high school football player and a gym rat who loved working out. He was unconscious and being worked on by our battalion surgeon while Casey was talking to the medics.

We coordinated a medevac and told the medics they had about 20 minutes to do their thing. I finally asked the surgeon, "Hey sir, what's the deal?" He told me Tyler had this injury and that while he was working on him. Casey was in bad shape and we needed to move to the HLZ. I needed to know what was up with Tyler. I could not cancel the medevac. The surgeon pronounced Tyler dead.

It took six guys to carry Tyler to the medevac instead of the four usually required. Casey required four and there was a security

OPERATION *RED DAWN*

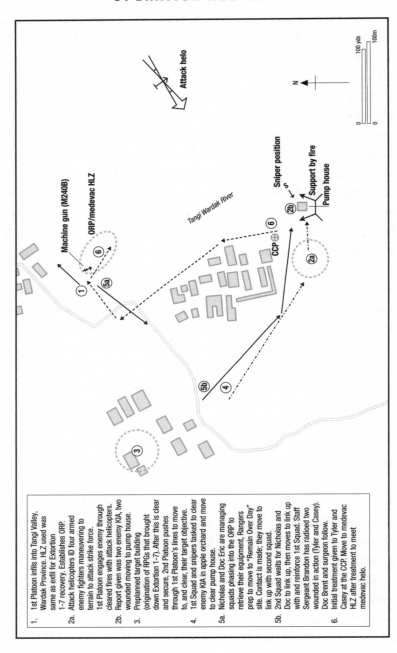

Attack helo

N

100 yds
100m

Machine gun (M240B)

ORP/medevac HLZ

Sniper position

Support by fire

Pump house

Tangi Wardak River

CCP

1. 1st Platoon infils into Tangi Valley, Wardak Province. HLZ used was same as exfil for Extortion 1-7 recovery. Establishes ORP.

2a. Attack helicopters ID four armed enemy fighters maneuvering to terrain to attack strike force. 1st Platoon engages enemy through cleared fires with attack helicopters.

2b. Report given was two enemy KIA, two wounded moving to pump house.

3. Preplanned target building (origination of RPGs that brought down Extortion 1-7). After this is clear and secure, 2nd Platoon pushes through 1st Platoon's lines to move to, and clear, their target objective.

4. 1st Squad and snipers tasked to clear enemy KIA in apple orchard and move to clear pump house.

5a. Nicholas and Doc Eric are managing squads phasing into the ORP to retrieve their equipment, Rangers prep to move to "Remain Over Day" site. Contact is made; they move to link up with second squad.

5b. 2nd Squad waits for Nicholas and Doc to link up, then moves to link up with and reinforce 1st Squad. Staff Sergeant Brandon has radioed two wounded in action (Tyler and Casey). Doc Brent and surgeon follow.

6. Initial treatment given to Tyler and Casey at the CCP. Move to medevac HLZ after treatment to meet medevac helo.

258

element. Half of the platoon was tasked with the medevac. The helo flew in, dropped straight down into it, made a 180-degree peddle turn, and slammed the bird into the dirt. We loaded them in and the aircraft took off.

An ultrasound was done on Tyler at the CSH – he did not have a heartbeat. The medics had done a great job on Casey who had two lacerated arteries in his abdomen. My medics had packed him with combat gauze and other stuff to clot the small arteries so he didn't bleed out. In fact, they did such a great job that the medical personnel at the CSH took pictures of the gauze when they opened up Casey in surgery. They subsequently used those images in their book on surgery to illustrate the perfect way to pack a wound. That was a big feather in the cap for the medics. They did an amazing job. Casey underwent surgery at the CSH on the FOB. He was then sent to Bagram for one or two more surgeries. Later he was transferred to Landstuhl, Germany, and finally to Fort Sam Houston where he stayed for a few months. Unfortunately, Casey's hip nerves controlling his leg had been cut by a bullet and he lost the ability to control his foot without a prosthetic holding device. Casey came back for accountability purposes and was medically boarded after about one year.

After we evacuated Tyler and Casey, I corralled the boys and told them to collect all the equipment and be ready to move 1km east to link up with rest of company for the Remain Over Day operation. It was a crappy walk. We were 0-2 in the valley now. We had lost people and our mood was bad. Tyler had been the team leader everyone dreamed of… He was a big guy with a big, booming voice. He had a commanding presence but was also friends with everyone. It just sucked.

We set up for a defensive position which, in this case, was a local compound. We set up a defense and stayed in the valley to show the locals that we were not afraid. We basically were asking them one question – "Are you going to come fight us?" We were hoping for it, but it didn't play out. We had lost two guys and the Task Force rule was that when you lost people you had to stand down. So 3rd Platoon cleared Objective *Lefty Grove* instead of us while my platoon was babysitting everyone's equipment.

We then moved the company element out of the valley by 3 klicks and called for an exfil to cycle the platoons out. Back at the base we dealt with the aftermath of taking casualties. We conducted a memorial service. I handled the paperwork and the equipment for both of my Rangers. Tyler had reenlisted the previous deployment at FOB Lagman. It was a tough pill to swallow. Tyler Holtz was going to be my next squad leader once the current one had gone off to Army Special Forces. It sucked and sucks to this day. Not a day goes by when I am not thinking about Casey and Tyler. Tyler was the first KIA in B Company since Panama. In ten years of GWOT he was the first loss for the company.

The memorial ceremony for Tyler saw the battalion commander and battalion sergeant major attend from Kandahar. They wanted first-hand accounts. It was like déjà vu. The chaplain and the shrink returned for more dead and to talk to our own guys again. Again, I did not make it mandatory to talk with the chaplain and the shrink but suggested at least going there. I said this was becoming a bad habit in a joking way. The same platoon had to deal with the same issues. The loss of life took its toll on them. We stood down for a few days, collected ourselves, and I talked to them not as platoon sergeant but as a friend and Ranger. We talked, hung out, and I watched them. I knew their personalities and wanted to make sure nobody was hiding anything. My running joke with the psychiatrist and the chaplain was that they were getting to know everyone by first name. The chaplain and I were trying to lighten the mood, and he said, "I might just move my equipment down here and stay with you guys."

"Not funny sir."

We were just kidding, of course – light-hearted moments helped and if the chaplain tried to be serious I don't think it would have helped my guys. By keeping the mood light, it helped our guys deal with the serious nature of their experiences.

I told my Rangers that they had had more experience in this one month than most people had in their careers. There was no shame to talk to the chaplain and the shrink. I told them to ask around – the battalion had only lost ten in ten years – so they had seen a lot of dead comrades in a very short space of time.

The battalion sergeant major spent a few days with us. He also career counseled me to see if I wanted to stay in longer and continue as a platoon sergeant. I responded with, "if you let me." In the regiment you might get three deployments as a platoon sergeant and maybe they would ask you for one more. He said they had plans for me and wanted me to do one further deployment but they wanted to know my future plans – in particular, if I planned to go to Army Special Forces Selection. I said no, I loved being a Ranger and would love to be a first sergeant. He said that was not his call although he could certainly recommend me. "I'll take the recommendation," I replied. I wanted to stay in the regiment. The battalion sergeant major said he would speak to the regimental sergeant major about shortlisting me for company first sergeant. That was really great. The pyramid at the top is very small at a battalion. There were 12 rifle platoon sergeant slots but only four first sergeant positions. Just being considered was a huge compliment.

• • •

Operation *Red Dawn* was over. Tyler's memorial service at the FOB was on September 25/26, 2011. I hobbled around with a bad limp and finally went to get X-rays. Fortunately, it was just a bad bone bruise, requiring me to sit still for a little while. No combat ops for a week was the order. That was a horrible feeling. My weapons squad leader now had to be acting platoon sergeant as well as lead his own squad. I lost the platoon for a week, during which they ran two operations. One resulted in another gunfight with barricaded shooters inside the target building. Mike, the weapons squad leader, caught a round to his left side underneath his body armor. The round went in and out. My dog handler Dave was shot through his forearm. Both were medevac'd. I was not on the ground and it was the worst-case scenario. Now we had casualties, and although the first sergeant had tagged along to even the playing field for leadership, he was not the platoon sergeant and could not run the platoon as well as I could have. I should say, it's not that he couldn't, but he had his own style, which wasn't mine. Our platoon style didn't match that of the first sergeant – he was more of a micro-manager. Each platoon has a personality and it is a collection of how well the leadership in the platoon meshes together, and we were a tight fit. I hobbled to the CSH to see the guys before they had surgery. Dave stayed in-country while Mike was medevac'd to Germany because of the lower abdomen injury where major organs were. Mike was still there when I also ended up in Germany. We'll get to that.

The platoon then stood down for a couple of days while waiting for me to get better, and the other two platoons in the company had priority. Third Platoon chased an IED facilitator and they got into a gunfight where they lost a squad leader, a team leader, and a SAW gunner, all from the same squad, all wounded in action. It was a hotspot for gunfights. Historically, if you looked at casualty figures they were always hot in the Logar and Wardak provinces.

I was finally cleared by Doc but my leg was still sore as hell. We had taken the brunt of getting it handed to us for two months. We had experienced more gunfights than pretty much the rest of the battalion put together. We were undermanned before the deployment and now had more losses to contend with: a squad leader, team leader, and our K-9 handler shot. I borrowed another K-9 handler from 2nd Platoon. "Can this get any better?" I asked myself sarcastically. Yes, it could.

October 7/8, 2011, saw us track a target for a few days to gather more intel and to see if it met the threshold for us to strike. It did and we planned and briefed Objective *Dakota River*. It was another night combat operation for us. We moved to the aircraft, loaded on, and flew out. On this op we also picked up the BSO's representative who was a first sergeant. Since my platoon was only at 90 percent strength, my first sergeant tagged along as well. We off-set the target and walked about 4 klicks to the target village. It was Afghanistan-black; there were no lights or streetlights commonly found in the Iraqi cities we had previously operated in. It was our favorite time to conduct our mission. If someone saw us they would have seen only our green eyes glowing from the NODs we all wore.

The problem on this tasking was that we only had a 25 percent chance of hitting the correct compound because four of the buildings shared adjoining walls. It was a cluster and impossible to know which building was the one to hit. We simply had to guess which one to begin with. Wouldn't you know it, it turned out we had picked the wrong one. We proceeded with a Call Out after we had set the pieces in place – isolation, security, and assault elements. The only thing at the site was a couple of women and children – all the men were gone. It was odd but nothing we had not encountered previously. The women told us that the men were most likely in Pakistan for supplies or selling their livestock.

We got ready to reset all the pieces to start clearance on the second compound. The snipers remained on the first compound's roof over-watching our movements, while my platoon leader Jake and his radio farm were in the courtyard. We moved back down the line and I grabbed Specialist Ricardo Cerros, Jr., who was part of 3rd Squad's assault force at the corner of the compound. He was going to come along with his squad shortly anyway, so I decided to take him as I moved to the new location. I told Shawn, his squad leader, that I had Cerros in tow to check the door. His squad did follow us fairly quickly in any case.

Our snipers, with one Afghan assault force member, saw all the doorways and illuminated one with an infrared laser for me to move to. This was going to be our next entry point. The doorway was on the left-hand side in a narrow, long alley. It was about 30 meters long by 2 meters wide. I was at the gate. Shawn was to my left, followed by Doc Brent and the rest of 3rd Squad. Directly behind me was Garret, a team leader from 3rd Squad. To my right was Cerros. The APU was behind us, across the alley at an intersection. We had all the pieces set and began the second Call Out when we noticed the gate into the courtyard was unlocked. Shawn slowly pushed it open and we had rifles pointed inside, ready to go in. Shawn gave last-minute guidance to one of his team leaders. As Shawn gave guidance, he pulled out of the doorway just enough to allow the gate to slowly swing shut. The left side swung toward my gun, I was a left-handed shooter, and my weapon almost got stuck. It's the little things that get you, or sometimes it's just bad luck. I knew better, but stupidly, or maybe instinctually, I used my right foot to push the gate back open... I remember a few things very clearly:

The three-round burst fired from an AK inside the compound slams hard into me – punches me back, spins me around, thumps me off balance like a marionette manipulated by invisible strings. My helmet's night vision device is knocked out, its comforting green hue extinguished. I shouldn't have stretched my leg across the gate opening the way I just did. My bell is rung and everything moves in slow motion.

Beside me, Shawn unloads his M4 through the gateway, hammering doors and windows of the target building – brass flips slowly and lazily through the moonlit night while bullets scream angrily downrange toward the compound. Close-quarters battle all around. I hear my guys running to the sound of the guns.

My leg feels like it's been hit with a sledgehammer. My head is a mess. My wife is gonna kill me.

Training kicks in: apply a tourniquet. I fumble for it in my calf pocket, slide it over my right leg as high as possible, and crank down hard. It hurts like hell; I grit my teeth and I am angry. I don't know if seconds or minutes have passed but small-arms fire continues to batter the alley and the compound. I think Doc Brent is around. Is he working on me? Garret seems nearby, Cerros crouched by my feet.

I make out Shawn's muffled warning of "grenade." I know there isn't a whole heck of a lot I can do but roll away from it to my left – hope that the explosion will hit my butt, hope for the best. The alleyway erupts; shrapnel promises more pain and death. Moans puncture the night, moans from my guys, my assault squad, my brothers…

What had happened was that a 7.62mm round had slammed into my right thigh, which spun me around and knocked me off balance outside of the gate. I had landed back outside. The second round hit under the armpit of my right shoulder and the bullet rode up through my shoulder, through the front arm to the biceps and out. The third and final round hit my helmet in the right temple area. It split the Kevlar lining, stayed just inside the helmet, and angled right by around an inch and traveled out, shattering my NODs mount. It knocked the right-eye NOD to the left, shifting it by 4 inches. My lights were going out – the tunnel got real narrow. My bell was rung. Stupidly I had caught my balance, while standing on my right leg. I thought, *Oh no, is my femur coming through or what – do I have a bone broken? No, oh, okay, leg is not broken.* This all played out in my mind within split seconds. I was completely disoriented. I only knew my leg was hit because it hurt so bad as if a sledgehammer had hit it. And my helmet. I didn't even know I was hit elsewhere. I slid down the wall, thinking, *Now what?* I had completed thousands of live-fire objectives with casualty play. But it still took a second to remember to put on a tourniquet when you have been shot yourself and I knew it was going to hurt a lot. I reached for my calf pocket on my combat pants and pulled the tourniquet out. I carried two – one in my bleeder kit that

OBJECTIVE *DAKOTA RIVER*

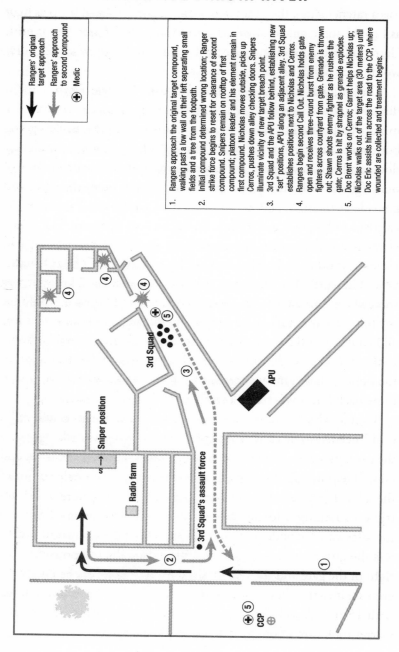

Rangers' original target approach

Rangers' approach to second compound

Medic

1. Rangers approach the original target compound, walking past a low wall on their left separating small fields and a tree from the footpath.

2. Initial compound determined wrong location; Ranger strike force begins to reset for clearance of second compound; platoon leader and his element remain in first compound. Nicholas moves outside, picks up Cerros, pushes down alley checking doors. Snipers illuminate vicinity of new target breach point.

3. 3rd Squad and the APU follow behind, establishing new "set" positions. APU along an adjacent alley, 3rd Squad establishes positions next to Nicholas and Cerros.

4. Rangers begin second Call Out. Nicholas holds gate open and receives three-round burst from enemy fighters across courtyard from gate. Grenade is thrown out; Shawn shoots enemy fighter as he rushes the gate; Cerros is hit by shrapnel as grenade explodes.

5. Doc Brent works on Cerros; Garret helps Nicholas up; Nicholas walks out of the target area (30 meters) until Doc Eric assists him across the road to the CCP, where wounded are collected and treatment begins.

3rd Squad

APU

Sniper position

Radio farm

3rd Squad's assault force

CCP

was a ratchet strap, the other in my calf pocket. I placed it up as high as I could and cranked down on it to make a tourniquet. Yes, it hurt. Garret offered a hand and asked if I was alright. I threw some choice words back out of anger.

The original contact was thought to have come from a room directly across from the gate. Maybe 10–15 seconds or maybe a minute had passed by now. I heard a two-way gunfight, bullets going both ways, and Shawn unloaded through the doorway, hammering doors and windows. Fire was incoming from several locations; one of our Afghans with our snipers got hit, when the enemy threw a hand grenade at them. Spencer, a junior sniper, got shrapnel through the cartilage of his nose at the bone. So far, we had two hurt. The sniper element was firing from the rooftop of the first compound we had cleared. Another hand grenade flew out into the alley. I heard Shawn yell, "Grenade!" But there was not a lot I could do. I knew it was somewhere, somewhere near me. I rolled left and hoped it would hit my butt or something else. I just hoped for the best because that was all I could do at the moment. The grenade detonated. I took shrapnel to the butt and thighs but I never felt it because of the trauma from the bullet. I heard moans coming from the assault squad. My vision came back but it was fuzzy. I saw Cerros on his back moaning.

Garret, who was now kneeling over me, asked me if I could walk, or if I needed to be carried. At the same time Doc was asking where the casualties were. I told Doc to help Cerros. I looked at Garret and said, "Help me up, I can walk." I remembered being helped out of the alley. I took a couple of steps, wanting to make sure I did not trip on anything. I looked around and saw a dead enemy fighter in the alleyway. I wondered where he had come from. Turned out he was the guy who had engaged us from inside the compound to the right of the gate and then had rushed to the gate where he threw the grenade into the alley. Shawn had laid into him and stitched him up with 15 rounds as he came rushing at the assault force. Shawn and Garret took care of business as the gunfight raged.

I could not remember anything much, but the reality was, which I found out after the deployment, that all of this had transpired in just five or so minutes. My mind was dazed. That was the reality of the pain and being knocked silly.

I made my way to our other medic, Doc Eric, who was about 25–30 meters away, almost at the end of the alleyway. My leg was numb and I asked Doc to help me walk the rest of the alleyway and across the road through a small hole in a wall where we had positioned the CCP. It was just outside of the target building. Doc took a look and said my tourniquet was not the best to stem the blood flow. I was still bleeding. He pulled out a ratchet strap tourniquet. It was so painful I cursed and cussed at Doc. But he stopped the blood flow. Cerros had been pulled out and set to the left side of the opening near me along with the Afghan guy from the sniper element. We had critical patient care. Everything came on line: critically injured were in one section, then urgent, and finally routine. Spencer fought on until we gained control. Finally, he came off the roof with his eyes watering. The gunfight raged on still.

At the CCP everybody was collected. Nobody knew I had been hit except for the guys in the firefight. I was still on the radio, directing traffic. I told the platoon leader I had got shot but nobody knew the severity of the injuries. The first sergeant came to the CCP. He thought I was still in the fight. He pointed at me and asked who I was. I gave him my call-sign and then it dawned on him – it was actually me. There was no senior non-commissioned officer in the gunfight, just the platoon leader. The first sergeant took off to help them. I had called in a team from isolation to provide security for the CCP when I was initially shot. My biggest concern and first clear thought was, *My wife is gonna kill me. Damn, how am I going to explain this to her?* I still directed the fight and brought in a squad for security and stretchers. I did not really panic until the guys cut off my armor and took away my radios. *Crap, what am I going to do now?* They checked out my injuries while I was pleading with them not to take my radios. "I am still doing my job; leave me alone." Then I started to panic. *Holy crap, this is not good.* They also did not give me a status on the other casualties because I was a casualty myself. I think I heard that Cerros needed to get going on the medevac for surgery and the injured Afghan soldier was probably not going to make it; that it was a priority to get Cerros and then me onto the helicopter. I was placed on a stretcher and strapped down. Doc Eric came over and stuck a Fentanyl light narcotic lollipop in my mouth to help calm me down. It did not help the pain in my leg though.

The HLZ medevac was about 800 meters from our location. At the last minute the docs changed priority of the casualties to me and Spencer. I knew it was bad for Cerros because he was going out with the Afghan who was expected to die on the second aircraft.

The birds came in fast, trying to be cool I thought, and the Black Hawk almost inadvertently landed on us, but it flared out at the last second and came back in but this time a bit further away.

At the CSH HLZ we were offloaded and taken to a triage tent. Here they made sure we did not have any weapons or ammo on us to prevent any accidental discharges or explosions. I still had my pistol on my left hip. Platoon Sergeant Kellet and the platoon leader had come to collect our equipment from the aircraft. They missed my pistol, but I rolled over and he retrieved it. I must confess I was not the greatest patient. Fortunately, Spencer looked okay and they told him to just sit on the table and wait with his head down. They focused their attention on me. I asked about Cerros and said they were not doing anything with me until they told me what was wrong with him. I was a grouchy, irritated Ranger platoon sergeant who didn't take no for an answer, and again asked what the hell was wrong with Cerros. But, in fact, it wasn't until I was stateside and able to read the complete after-action report that I actually found out what had happened to him.

Once I was out of surgery Kellet handed over a sat phone. But I had bad reception because the antenna pointed toward the ground, not up. I managed a brief static-filled conversation with my wife. She barely heard me. I was strapped down and could not sit up. I handed the phone back to my buddy and told him to tell her what had been going on. I was irritated I couldn't get it to work and just did not think about lifting the antenna skyward. A nurse showed up and said I needed to get moved to the HLZ. I passed out and remember waking up for a few minutes later, with Spencer on the bird to Bagram. Spencer's nose required a specialty surgeon to evaluate it, to ensure there was no underlying issue or complication. Spencer would stay at Bagram for a couple of days and then return to the platoon.

I had come out of surgery at the CSH on the FOB, then took a 30-minute ride to Bagram where I had another surgery – all of this within the three hours since I had left the battlefield. Once out of surgery I received a visit from Gabe, the logistics E-7 non-commissioned officer, whom I had known my entire career. He had been the Bravo Company supply sergeant when I showed up as a new private first class. He asked if I was okay. "I'm in hospital, so not really, but yes." He asked if I wanted to keep my helmet; otherwise they were going to keep it in the battalion display case. But I definitely wanted to keep it. I had not seen it after I had been shot. "You doing alright, need anything?" My only complaint was that I didn't have any Copenhagen. Gabe assured me he would get me some dip.

While at Bagram a buddy of mine, Platoon Sergeant Pat from another company, was ready to go home for the birth of his son. He had watched and heard my battle roster number called while he was in the big JOC. Pat showed up in the hospital as I came into the Bagram CSH from the helipad with tears in his eyes. He said, "Dude don't scare us like that. Do you know how many people are freaked out in the JOC?" I had no idea what he was talking about until he explained that everyone was upset that a 12-year guy, a staple, had got shot. I had been around for so long and was familiar to so many officers who rotated in and out.

More people filtered in from the big JOC and it turned into a family reunion. Guys basically ran across the street to see how I was doing. I asked them about Cerros and pushed for an answer. But they skirted the issue. Eventually one of them said the colonel of the regiment would be over soon and that he would tell me. But he was on the radio since Rangers were still in action on the objective. I sat there fighting the narcotics and the meds for another three hours.

Meanwhile, all hell had broken loose on the objective. The QRF comprised of 2nd Platoon had trailed the medevacs in and landed in support of 1st Platoon. Our company commander took control as ground force commander and cleared half the village. He tried to get locals to go inside the target building and tell the fighters to lay down their weapons. They declined to do so because they were not part of the village. The commander requested ordnance but was denied due to "collateral damage" rules, even though it was confirmed that the outlying buildings were clear. Instead four Hellfire missiles from Apaches, which were in orbit supporting the mission, destroyed the living quarter structures of the interior. The Rangers conducted a BDA afterwards and then moved to exfil.

I also subsequently found out that we had plenty of guys wounded. In fact, 13 additional Purple Hearts were awarded; 11 were from shrapnel of hand grenades thrown into the alley. Shawn and Garret also got shot. Shawn had the bottom of the triceps of his right arm shot, and Garret was hit on top of his hip flexor. Luckily, the round passed through without issue. Garret stayed in-country on light duty for a couple of weeks until the stitches came out and he had no infection. Garret had been tagged with the same bullet that had gone through my leg. He had stood behind me with his gun over my shoulder when I was shot. I initially thought that it had been Cerros. Garret and I talked about the events a year later and confirmed that the round which had hit him was indeed from my leg.

In combat it usually is after the adrenaline wears off that you find out you have been wounded. A lot of the guys had shrapnel subsequently removed by Doc. The op took a long time to conclude and it was hours past sun-up when they finally called for exfil. The conventional guys did not fly in due to restrictions from their chain of command, but SOAR aircraft had come in support from their FOB and were on stand-by. They flew in and took out the two platoons. This was awesome because our guys did not have to Remain Over Day on the objective.

The colonel of the regiment, who was also in charge of all Special Operations, finally came over. He tried to be funny but he was not really a funny individual.

"Don't know why I'm giving you a Purple Heart; you probably have six of them."

"No, this is the first one, Sir."

"Oh," he said, as he pinned it on me and then left. He never brought up what happened to Cerros.

I spent a week at Bagram and then was medevac'd to Germany. Guys kept cycling over to keep me company and we talked until my flight to Landstuhl.

• • •

Operations had a liaison officer at the hospital in Landstuhl simply to track Special Ops wounded. Gus had been a medic at battalion but was now the liaison officer for a couple of years to take a break from our grinding operational tempo. I sort of knew but Gus saw the reports and finally told me what happened to Cerros. Ranger Specialist Cerros had received shrapnel inside his chest cavity which lacerated some major arteries. Although the medics did a fantastic job he did not survive the surgery; in fact, he really should have died before arriving at the CSH. The aorta junction had been badly injured, and he lost so much blood volume in his body that they just could not get to him in time. It was a big downer. In fact, it sucked. Ricardo Cerros Jr. was 24 years old and from Salinas, California.

I tried to figure out what my new scenario was going to be. How long would I stay in Germany before going to the U.S.? Were they going to place me at Walter Reed or San Antonio? I was not the greatest patient to have. To be honest, I was kind of a dick. I kept insisting that I wanted to go to Madigan Army Medical Center at my home base of Fort Lewis. A couple of days after my surgery, the surgeon talked to me about my leg. He said it had been a miracle that the bullet that went through my leg did not split the artery or nerve. It was nearly parallel, leaving just enough room for one 7.62 round to fit in perfectly. There was almost no damage to the nerve. The bullet had essentially passed through, missing the artery and the nerve by the thickness of a thumbnail. I was awestruck and thanked him for the update. He also said, to my relief, that I was to go to Madigan.

A day or two later one of the old battalion surgeons came in and said that he had heard there was a cantankerous Ranger sergeant causing all kinds of problems. He had come over to make sure I was being compliant. There were always former guys everywhere. We talked about my injuries, the shot through my arm, near the brachial artery. The round had missed the artery and nerves too, just like in my leg. The bullet popped out in my biceps. It was amazing because the docs felt that I should have had more extensive damage. It did not feel like it, but, of course, it was good news. A few days later I was shipped back to the U.S.

At the stopover in Bethesda, Maryland, there was an annex wing, the triage hub, where guys were managed and sent to various locations. Another Ranger buddy, Erich, a liaison officer at the hub, greeted me when I offloaded from the plane. Erich enjoyed making fun of me. "Oh how the table has turned," he said gleefully. Erich had been shot in 2008 in Iraq on the outside of his knee in that green-on-blue incident with the Iraqi police. It was funny – I had carried him into the CSH three years earlier, and now this. We got to hang out for the night. I asked what the order of travel was going to be. "Washington first" was the answer. I was pumped – I did not have to fly all over the country.

In Washington I was met by the rear detachment commander and my former weapons squad leader, Brian, who had been a great friend for over ten years. Brian said, "Don't do that again; it scared everybody. Don't get shot again."

"Yeah, that's funny Brian."

The Air Force allowed the rear detachment to carry me off the C-17 into the awaiting ambulance. Brian rode with me.

I had had three surgeries so far. When I was still at Landstuhl, I managed to call back to the platoon but Jake was off to chow so I spoke with Specialist Dan who put me in touch with the first sergeant. He still had my helmet. He said I absolutely had no idea how lucky I was. Nobody really knew anything until they did an inventory of my gear and they were doing the paperwork for the investigation. The first sergeant held onto my helmet for the rest of the deployment. It was on his desk and he did not allow anyone to touch it. It now sits in a glass display box in my house.

CHAPTER FOURTEEN

FROM TRIGGER PULLER TO PENCIL PUSHER

Afghanistan, 2012–2013

I spent eight days at Madigan in a single room. There were four more surgeries while there, and four more afterwards for a total of 12.

My arm was successfully stitched up in Germany but it was the leg which kept getting me back into surgery – to change the wound vacuum, clean it out, and make sure there was no infection. Pain management for the nerves was tough. It was hard to get it under control. They tried a femoral nerve-block. This was placed in my hip flexor, at the top of the nerve, and it numbed the entire leg. For the first time in ten days I had no pain for a couple of hours. Doing physical therapy was hard and I couldn't feel my leg. It was being dragged around and my rehab was supposed to be done by simply walking. "Seriously?" I asked, but I appeased my physical therapist by walking to the door and that was that. The nerve block gave me muscle cramps all the way into my back and so forcefully that it arched me off the bed. They tried to figure out to how to remove it given the contortion of the muscle spasms. At the end of the day an anesthesiologist was needed, and then they pulled out the wire. Had I known what to do I would have pulled it out myself. We basically ran the gamut of medication combinations, and then the nerve block, only to resort back to what I was on when I originally arrived at Madigan. It wasn't the greatest hospital experience, though I can't fault the doctors and surgeons. Being in hospital is never great.

My brother had left the Ranger Regiment and was with the 2nd Infantry Division Stryker Brigade when he visited me in the hospital. From around 2008 onwards, platoon sergeants had to attend the Ranger Assessment and Selection Program. RASP had two components. RASP I was for E-5s and below, whereas new incoming E-6s and up and all officers attended RASP II. We lost a lot of experienced non-commissioned officers to this policy, including my twin brother. RASP was good for new officers who had been in the regular army for four years before joining the regiment. Privates and officers were young; senior non-commissioned officers were older, shot, or beaten down and could do the job but simply could not pass all the physical requirements condensed into one week. Senior platoon sergeants with 15–16 years in service took a lot of beating and most would not become first sergeants. They usually rode out their careers as staff, although they were still very capable of doing their previous jobs.

After I had been shot and to keep the platoon operational, a promotable squad leader was named platoon sergeant to finish out the deployment. I could not have picked a better replacement, as Joe fit the mold perfectly and he only had to move from 2nd over to 1st Platoon.

I was told of the manning change and wondered what this meant for me. I remained on the books assigned to B Company through Christmas and New Year to help with the company change of command, with a new commander coming in and the inventories it required. Before Christmas I was told I would be moving to the S-2 shop, as the non-commissioned officer in charge, and that this position would allow me to focus on "me" and getting right. Great in theory.

I thought back about my time as a platoon sergeant. We usually lost about a few enlistees; some left the Army, while others decided to go to college or join the Reserve Officer Training Corps. The ones who stayed were experienced combat veterans who led with confidence and intelligence that was based on their own experiences with the kind of leaders they had worked alongside during active duty. Part of being a platoon sergeant was to counsel your men, as every couple of years there was a big drop in retention. When I reached that rank I never kicked anyone to the curb but made them rethink things and properly plan their futures upon leaving the Army. That way they would not flounder but had some plan regarding what to do post-military. Never did I tell anyone they could not reenlist, especially the guys I liked and wanted to be in combat with. Those men I counseled about the leadership roles they could fill. Some Rangers did not want to fill those positions and were content in their roles but that inevitably meant a limited run. In my years there were only three to four Rangers to whom I, and the platoon leader, said they might be better off elsewhere but we always wanted them to have a plan for whichever career path they chose. The overall quality of guys and training was always to such a high standard and we always had some very exceptional Rangers.

The day I decided not to stay at Madigan anymore was when two fellow Rangers, Sergeant First Class Kristoffer Domeij and Private First Class Christopher Horns, were killed by an IED in

Afghanistan in October 2011. I received 30 days' convalescent leave with more surgeries throughout November.

The battalion was about a week from coming home. I was placed on light duty and rehab. During this time I received a very nice note from the commander of the SEAL team killed in Extortion 1-7 thanking us for the job we had done recovering his men and wishing me "Godspeed" in my recovery. He signed off with, "Long live the Brotherhood."

I monitored the chalks to meet my guys when they came back at the runway but I didn't make it because the arrival times shifted to earlier. They had been sped up in Germany. I had hoped to walk onto the aircraft to greet them, to show everyone I was going to be alright. I was at home waiting but nobody called to notify me of their new arrival time. I had to go to the barracks to meet them, which was irritating.

I thought I could still do my job, but physical limitations told me differently, although I had officially finished rehab in the battalion fitness center. The rehab staff included an Army officer and two civilians with professional sports experience. They turned a guy around pretty quickly, just like a professional athlete, in two weeks. I regained mobility and flexibility back into my appendages and joints but it was torture. I returned to duty in February 2012 but only because I willed myself to do it, not because I was physically ready. I couldn't stand the thought of being broken any longer, so I ate the pain and declared myself good to go. I had the battalion surgeon sign me off. I knew I could not run pain free and things got progressively worse.

I was cleared to jump again and exited the aircraft a couple of times before I volunteered for jump master duties, which counted to stay qualified and was easier on the body. During the GWOT you needed four jumps per fiscal year to stay on jump status. We had a proficiency jump coming back off the deployment to get everyone on the same sheet of music. We conducted two jumps during fixed-wing training exercises and airfield seizures. There were a couple more for others who came back. We had a lot of qualified jump masters but not with a lot of experience. There may have only been a handful of master-rated jump masters in the battalion. The first sergeants and even the sergeant major acted as "super safeties," making sure everyone was good to go – in other words, that everything went smoothly and you were doing the job you were supposed to do. If you jump long enough you will see injuries and casualties. All the while I was in the S-2 shop running security checks and handling the physical security for the battalion. New battalion facilities were being constructed and revamped so we had a lot of security issues to meet for the new SOPs for our facilities. There was a lot of keyboard time. We revamped our SOPs through May 2012.

We were six weeks away from another deployment to Afghanistan and a platoon sergeant from A Company was relieved of his duty. I went to HHC to take over the role of the sniper platoon sergeant, who in turn was the new platoon sergeant in A Company – all of this with an upcoming Afghanistan deployment in 2012.

The way I found out about the opportunity itself was telling. Rangers got ready with packets and other paperwork. I was in the hall talking to a buddy of mine, Staff Sergeant Brian, when the sergeant major hollered at me to come to his office. *What did I do now? I have been in the hall for three minutes*, I thought to myself. Even though I had 12 years in the battalion, I still looked at my uniform like a private trying to figure what was wrong with it. Instead, the sergeant major asked me if I was physically able to deploy. Instantly I gave the Ranger answer of "yes," instead of the mature, responsible, answer of "no." That was how I found out about the job. Since snipers were tasked out to the companies for training and during the deployments, it was not going to be a lot of work. I was told that it would basically be a liaison officer job for accountability. I had to figure out what to do as a liaison officer, but the sergeant major assured me that he would find someone to show me. I was happy to deploy again, although not in a combat capacity. I was not physically ready, but it was important for me, mentally, to have another deployment after getting shot. I wanted to go out on my terms – to finish things out.

As a sniper platoon sergeant, once the battalion goes into final evaluations to "certify" prior to the deployment, all specialty platoons such as snipers and mortars become attached to their rifle platoons. So, for me, as the new, never-been-a-sniper guy, it gave me the chance to read some manuals, ask questions, and learn a skill that I knew absolutely nothing about. And, believe me, there is so much more to precision marksmanship than looking through a scope. The deployment would see me work with every type of sniper rifle we employed, so I could learn the finer points and the capabilities of the .50cal Barrett, the .300 Winchester Magnum and the .308 Winchester. I got to shoot almost every day, in a new style, so not only was it new and different, but distance is king! I learned about reading the wind, more accurate range estimations, and ballistic properties, as well as bullet drop. When questions arose I just asked the experienced section leaders and they explained the theories and the calculations.

● ● ●

But the reality was that not much happened in Afghanistan once we were deployed. Instead, I sat for 18 hours a day in a chair as a liaison officer. I tried to get added to the manifest as an add-on, but, not being on the same FOB as the platoons, it never worked out to get me on a mission. But I really wanted one more mission, even if it meant sitting in a blocking position pulling security.

Back at the FOB my leg became infected and I flew to Kandahar to see if I had a blood clot. It turned out to be cellulitis and I was given antibiotics. I stayed there for three days under observation. Two weeks later we handed the FOB over and headed home.

This was my last deployment as a Ranger and I had been hiding my issues. I just wasn't ready to be done. After the deployment I had an MRI, and although I had no bullets in my leg, there was still plenty of shrapnel in it. It was not a great idea to do an MRI with metal in your leg but it was not deemed dangerous to do the procedure. Stupid Ranger. I felt things move around in my leg, and I had a lot of problems after the procedure. I had started to walk with a limp but I managed to jog a little. In fact, running may have caused cellulitis. Back after the deployments, I fought my way through the training cycle.

I got busted during the battalion physical training event, an 8-km non-standard run overland. It included orienteering to a particular point and then we had to conduct a goofy task of carrying 5-gallon jugs, the Skedco or something like that. I ended up at the end of another company. The company commander and the first sergeant saw me falling back and back and back and being miserable. The first sergeant asked me what was going on and I explained it to him. He said to take it easy.

Later I took the snipers off post for some long gun training. On our post we could only fire .308s due to range restrictions. But the Department of Energy had a range where we could shoot long range. We shot for four days when the first sergeant and company commander saw me hobbling around. They called me on it. "When you get back you need to go see somebody; we know you have problems. You gotta get it fixed." I did, and the neurologist said, "Do you want to walk when you are 40? Keep doing what you are doing and you probably won't be walking. You might want to call it quits."

The Medical Board process began. The battalion was not happy to hear I was to be med-boarded since I was in place to be a future first sergeant in a rifle company. But I knew there was no way for me to pass a 3-km run, an 8-km run and a 19-km march in RASP II. I was not happy about it either. The neurologist finally opened my eyes – quality of life as I got older or being a first sergeant. I was medically retired in November 2013. And that was it.

There was the possibility of a civilian contracting job at the battalion or the Army but I also suffered from short-term memory issues because of the gunshot injury to my head and the resulting traumatic brain injury. I was starting to forget a few things. All of these problems were overlooked because I had been there for so long, the battalion leadership had plans for me even though I wasn't as good as I had been before.

I received a folded flag and my discharge certificate, and I finally left 2nd Battalion, 75th Ranger Regiment, in reverse order of how I had arrived. One day you show up and you are there; this time it was one day I was there, and then I was simply gone – the exact way in which I wanted to go. There was no retirement ceremony. I was glad; I dreaded the thought of one.

• • •

It was amazing to see the evolution of the regiment during my tenure as an Army Ranger. It evolved from a large-size, "destroy everything" perception, to a precision, small unit surgical strike capability unit. When the GWOT began, we joked that the regiment had a stigma – that it was like a fire extinguisher, kept behind a locked glass door, with the words "Break only in the event of all-out war" on the front. But through great leadership at both the officer and non-commissioned officer levels, and the trust shared between both, the regiment transformed itself from a large-scale Special Operations support unit to a stand-alone Special Operations strike force that most of the other units see as their equal. What was once seen as the regiment's greatest weakness, its privates, is now what I would consider one of its greatest strengths. It keeps everyone focused on always relearning the basics, not getting tied into trying to develop some new technique. It is a regimental hallmark. There is nothing wrong with being the master of the basics because everything else required, be that a new TTP or operational system, is founded on the basics and all the new stuff is employed through a simple series of rehearsals. It can then be employed with accuracy and not violate any principles or place Rangers at undue risk.

Starting every training cycle with a revisit to the beginning affords all leaders the opportunity to correct bad habits, and yes, we do get some over time, and perhaps find a new, more simple approach to a technique we already use. During this time, it never seemed like a big deal. We were just adapting to our ever-changing deployment environments and perfecting our craft. But once I began thinking about it and remembering events, I realize how much and how drastic it has in fact changed. Not only the use of our vehicles from open air HUMVEEs to Strykers and everything in between, but weapons, optics, personal kit, tactics, combat enablers, and so many other things too numerous to mention.

We do not like the idea of being the center of attention. It's not in our nature as Rangers. We epitomize the idea of the Quiet Professionals. We let our professionalism talk for us. It is in that mindset that I vacillated back and forth about writing this book, but through the encouragement of my wife, I decided that writing it would not be disloyal to my friends but instead shine a little light onto them and what they have accomplished over the years.

Moreover, I am happy that my moral compass was not busted during combat. I say this, because I have heard it explained in two ways. First the Army or the military does not make a person "good" or "bad." It enhances those characteristics we already have inside ourselves, the morals that were given to us when we were young. If your parents raised you properly, the military life, and even the hardest of combat situations, only helps define and shape your already established moral core. The second description I can offer is inside everyone there are two dogs, one "good" and one "bad," and depending on which dog you choose to feed it will define you as a good or bad person. I credit my parents and grandparents with instilling these values in me and for always holding me accountable. People and family members ask me if I would do it all over again. "Yes" is always my answer, and I also tell them I wouldn't change the outcome either. I would also say that the reason I'm not as messed up as some is that my wife never let me bear the burden of my experiences alone. She, at times, forced me to open up and share. Guys don't do the job because they are warmongers – it's about camaraderie and friendships formed. That's what keeps us doing this. I can't even really explain it. I do not miss the formations, the deployments, the Army politics – but I miss the guys. I miss being a leader of men even during bad times. I miss being a Ranger leader. It was an honor and a privilege to have stood for so long among these giants.

A SHORT HISTORY
OF RANGERS

The 75th Ranger Regiment draws its history and lineage from a number of famous fighting units throughout America's military history. In colonial times the most famous of all ranging units was that of Robert Rogers (1731–95) and his Rangers. Their mission was to harry and harass the enemy. Reconnaissance, ambushes, raids, and prisoner snatches were the main tactics of the colonial Rangers and these direct-action missions have changed very little over the centuries.

During the American Civil War (1861–65) hundreds of various units on either side claimed the title Ranger or Partisan.

But Rangers were then absent from the Army until World War II (involved from 1941 to 1945). It was in Carrickfergus, Northern Ireland, that Americans volunteered for the 1st Ranger Battalion under the command of West Pointer Major William Orlando Darby (1911–45). This battalion was the spearhead for the first American assaults into Europe and North Africa. The 3rd and 4th Ranger Battalions were founded in North Africa and participated in the assaults into Sicily and mainland Italy. The 2nd and 5th Ranger Battalions participated in the invasion of France during D-Day. In the Pacific theater of war, the 6th Ranger Battalion famously executed a POW raid, freeing 500 Allied soldiers. The Merrill's

Marauders, led by General Frank Dow Merrill (1903–55), officially called the 5307th Composite Unit (provisional), conducted deep penetration patrols in the China–Burma–India theater. All Ranger battalions were deactivated after the war.

During the Korean War (1950–53) Ranger units were raised again but this time they were airborne qualified. The 2nd Airborne-Ranger Company was the first and only all-black Ranger unit. All Ranger companies were disbanded in 1951.

Returning to their original roots of ranging in the Rogers tradition, the Vietnam War (1955–75) saw 13 long-range patrol and ranging units fight in the conflict. These units traditionally operated in four- to six-man teams deep behind enemy lines. Four Medals of Honor were awarded, three of them posthumously (*). Gary Lee Littrell, Sergeant First Class, Advisory Team 21, 11 Corps Advisory Group, 23rd Battalion, 2nd Ranger Group, Republic of Vietnam Army. Robert D. Law*, Specialist Fourth Class, Company I (Ranger), 75th Infantry, 1st Infantry Division. Robert J. Pruden*, Staff Sergeant, G Company, 75th Infantry, Americal Division. Laszlo Rabel*, Staff Sergeant, Team Delta, 74th Infantry Detachment (Long Range Patrol), 173rd Airborne Brigade. The Vietnam-era Ranger companies were all deactivated by August 15, 1972.

In 1974 the U.S. Army created the 1st and 2nd Battalions, 75th Infantry (Airborne) with the stated purpose to be the best light infantry unit in the world. By 1986, the 75th Ranger Regiment boasted three battalions and a headquarters unit.

The Global War on Terrorism (2001 ongoing) led to the addition of two new companies for each battalion, raising each battalion to one headquarters company and five rifle companies. Each Ranger Rifle Battalion was authorized approximately 800 personnel, who were assigned to one of four rifle companies, a support company, and a headquarters company. The regiment transformed itself from elite light infantry to executing exclusively Special Operations missions akin to those of Army Special Forces and the SEALs. One

Medal of Honor was awarded to Leroy Arthur Petry, Staff Sergeant, D Company, 2nd Battalion, 75th Ranger Regiment.

The 75th Regimental Special Troops Battalion (RSTB) was officially activated on October 16, 2007, responsible for reconnaissance, intelligence, and communication among other duties.

In 2017, the 75th Ranger Regiment added the 5th Ranger Battalion, expected to be fully staffed by 2019. The new battalion, called the Ranger Military Intelligence Battalion, will be located at Fort Benning, Georgia, alongside the Regimental Headquarters, the 3rd Ranger Battalion, and the Ranger Special Troops Battalion.

GLOSSARY

APU	Afghan Partnering Unit
ASS	Assault, Security, and Support
BDA	Bomb Damage Assessment
BDU	Battle Dress Uniform
Bi-Lats excercise	bi-lateral exercise
BSO	Battlespace Owner
CCP	Casualty Collection Point
CDS	Combat Delivery System
COP	Combat Outpost
CP	Command Post
CQB	Close-Quarters Battle
CSAR	Combat Search and Rescue
CSH	Combat Surgical Hospital
DAR	Downed Aircraft Recovery
DZ	Drop Zone
EOD	Explosive Ordnance Disposal
exfil	exfiltration
FARP	Forward, Arming, and Refueling Point
FLIR	Forward Looking Infrared
FOB	Forward Operating Base
GAF	Ground Assault Force
GMV	Gun-Mounted Vehicle
GWOT	Global War on Terrorism

HE	High-Explosive
helo	helicopter
HHC	Headquarters and Headquarters Company
HLZ	Helicopter Landing Zone
HUMVEE	High Mobility Multipurpose Wheeled Vehicle
HVT	High-Value Target
IED	Improvised Explosive Device
infil	infiltration
intel	intelligence
ISR	Intelligence, Surveillance, and Reconnaissance
JDAM	Joint Direct Attack Munition
JOC	Joint Operations Center
KIA	killed in action
klicks	kilometers
LCE	Load Carrying Equipment
MAM	Military-Aged Male
medevac	medical evacuation
MICH	Modular Integrated Communications Helmet
MOLLE	Modular Lightweight Load Carrying Equipment
MOPP suits	Mission Oriented Protective Posture suits
MOUT	Military Operations in Urban Terrain, usually pronounced "mount"
MRAP	Mine-Resistant Ambush Protected vehicle
MRE	Meal, Ready to Eat
NOD	Night Optical Device
ODA	Operational Detachment Alpha of the

	Special Forces, the Green Berets
ORP	Objective Rally Point
PC	patrol caps
PMCS	Preventative Maintenance Check and Services
POW	prisoner of war
PX	Post Exchange
QRF	Quick Reaction Force
RASP	Ranger Assessment and Selection Program
RIP	Ranger Indoctrination Program
RPG	Rocket-Propelled Grenade
RSOV	Ranger Special Operations Vehicle, based on the Land Rover Defender
SAW	Squad Automatic Weapon
SEAL	Sea, Air and Land Team of the U.S. Navy
SERE School	Survival, Evasion, Resistance, and Escape School
SF	Special Forces
SOAR	Special Operations Aviation Regiment
SOF	Special Operations Forces
SOP	Standard Operating Procedure
SSE	Sensitive Site Exploitation
SWAT	Special Weapons and Tactics
Tabs	Ranger School graduates
TI	Targeted Individual
TOC	Tactical Operations Center
TST	Time-Sensitive Target
TTPs	Tactics, Techniques, and Procedures
VDO	Vehicle Drop-Off area
VTC	Video Tele Conferencing
WMD	Weapons of Mass Destruction

FALLEN C
RANGERS KI

GRENADA
(listed alphabetically)
Randy E. Cline
Phillip S. Grenier
Kevin J. Lannon
Markin R. Maynard
Mark A. Rademacher
Russell L. Robinson
Stephen E. Slater
Mark O. Yamane

REPUBLIC OF PANAMA
Larry Barnard
Roy Brown, Jr.
Philip Lear
James W. Markwell
John Mark Price

SOMALIA
James M. Cavaco
James C. Joyce
Richard W. Kowalewski
Dominick M. Pilla
Lorenzo M. Ruiz
James E. Smith

GLOBAL WAR ON TERRORISM
(listed chronologically)
Kristofor T. Stonesfier
John J. Edmunds
Matthew A. Commons
Bradley S. Crose
Marc A. Anderson
Russell B. Rippetoe
Ryan P. Long
Nino D. Livaudais
Andrew F. Chris
Timothy M. Conneway
Jay A. Blessing
Patrick D. Tillman
Nathan E. Stahl
William M. Amundson
Michael C. O'Neill
Damian J. Garza
John M. Henderson, Jr
Timothy M. Shea
Dillon M. Jutras
Ricardo Barraza
Dale Brehm
James J. Regan
Kristofer D. S. Thomas

OMRADES
D IN ACTION

Ryan C. Garbs
Jason M. Kessler
George V. Libby
Benjamin C. Dillon
Steven C. Ganczewski
David L. McDowell
Christopher Gathercole
Thomas F. Duncan
William Rudd
Anthony Davis
Ryan Casey McGhee
Benjamin S. Kopp
Jason Dahlke
Eric Hario
Roberto Sanchez
Joel D. Clarkson
Michael D. Jankiewicz
James R. Patton
Jason A. Santora
Ronald A. Kubik
Kyle A. Comfort
Jonathan Kellylee Peney
Joseph Dimock
Anibal Santiago
Justin Bradley Allen

Bradley David Rappuhn
Andrew Cote Nicol
Martin Lugo
Christopher Wright
Lance Vogeler
Kevin M. Pape
Jeremy Andrew Katzenberger
Alessandro Leonard Plutino
Tyler Nicholas Holtz
Ricardo Cerros Jr.
Kristoffer Bryan Domeij
Christopher Alexander Horns
Tanner Stone Higgins
Thomas R. Macpherson
Patrick Hawkins
Cody J. Patterson
Joshua P. Rodgers
Cameron H. Thomas
Etienne J. Murphy
Christopher A. Celiz

INDEX

POSTSCRIPT

Men and women enlisting in the U.S. military today do so
knowing that the United States is a nation at war and that U.S.
veterans are at greater risk for unemployment, homelessness and
suicide than non-veterans. GallantFew is a non-profit, founded by
veterans for veterans, that aims to prevent veteran isolation by
connecting new veterans with hometown veteran mentors, thereby
facilitating a peaceful, successful transition from military service to
a civilian life filled with hope and purpose.

They do this by creating and supporting a nationwide network
of successfully transitioned veterans that engage locally with new
veterans with the same military background now going through
transition and by motivating communities all over the nation to
take responsibility for veterans returning; welcoming, connecting,
and including. This is all done in an effort to prevent veteran
unemployment, homelessness and suicide.

If you are a veteran and want to join the network, or just to
find out more information, then details can be found here:
www.gallantfew.org.

Revolutionary Veteran Support Network®